PROTESTANT NONCONFORMISTS
AND THE WEST MIDLANDS OF ENGLAND

STUDIES IN PROTESTANT NONCONFORMITY
EDITED BY ALAN P. F. SELL

PROTESTANT NONCONFORMISTS AND THE WEST MIDLANDS OF ENGLAND

Papers Presented at the First Conference of
The Association of Denominational Historical
Societies and Cognate Libraries

Edited by Alan P. F. Sell

KEELEUNIVERSITY**PRESS**

First published in 1996 by
Keele University Press
Keele, Staffordshire

© respective contributors, 1996

Typeset by Carnegie Publishing Ltd
18 Maynard St, Preston
Printed by Hartnolls
Bodmin, Cornwall, England

ISBN 1 85331 173 1

Contents

General Editor's Preface

The volumes in this series will comprise critical evaluations of the Protestant Nonconformist heritage of England and Wales, with special reference to the historical development of the several groups and their contribution to modern Christian thought.

The series will include conference papers of The Association of Denominational Historical Societies and Cognate Libraries, a body established in 1993 to foster co-operative research in the field; and a sub-series entitled Protestant Nonconformist Texts. In the latter, significant texts from the several traditions will be edited and introduced.

Alan P. F. Sell

Contributors

Alan Argent is minister of Trinity, Brixton, St Helier, Morden, and Dundonald, Wimbledon, Congregational Churches, and editor of *The Congregational History Circle Magazine*.

J. H. Y. Briggs is Head of the Department of History, University of Keele, and editor of *The Baptist Quarterly*.

Margaret E. Gaynor is Keeper of the Records, Warwickshire Monthly Meeting of the Religious Society of Friends.

E. Dorothy Graham is General Secretary of the Wesley Historical Society, and Connexional Archives Liaison Officer of the Methodist Church.

E. Eifion Powell is Principal of The Welsh Independents' College, Aberystwyth, and editor of *Y Cofiadur*.

David M. Thompson is a Fellow of Fitzwilliam College, Cambridge, and University Lecturer in Modern Church History.

David L. Wykes is Research Lecturer in the Department of History, University of Leicester.

Preface

In September 1989 Randolph Vigne of the Huguenot Society and I were among those attending a conference at Torre Pellice to mark the tercentenary of the Waldensians' 'Glorious Return'. During the course of the proceedings we had a vision of an organization which would foster good relations between the several denominational and related historical societies and libraries at home, and which would encourage co-operative ventures as appropriate – all of this as a dissuasive against that 'tunnel vision' which can afflict denominational history.

The several societies and libraries were invited to send representatives to preliminary meetings which were held at Dr Williams's Library, London, in November 1991 and October 1992. The response was favourable, and on 28 October 1993 the Association was formally constituted, a Constitution was unanimously adopted, and officers and a committee were appointed. The objectives of the Association, as specified in the Constitution, are:

(a) To facilitate the exchange of information among members by means of a newsletter and occasional conferences.

(b) To encourage research into the several traditions, with special reference to projects which relate to more than one tradition.

(c) To perform such other tasks as may from time to time be determined by the majority vote of the members.

It is not the intention of the Association to compete with its members, but rather to undertake tasks which complement their work, and to do this without multiplying meetings needlessly. The pattern at present is that an Annual General Meeting is held at which business is transacted and a paper is read. A programme of publication has been authorized, which will include four volumes of Protestant Nonconformist Texts and the papers of the Association's occasional conferences. The publications will appear within the series of Studies in Protestant Nonconformity of Keele University Press.

'Protestant Nonconformists and the West Midlands of England' was the theme of the Association's first occasional conference, held at

Westhill College, Birmingham, 28–30 July 1995. The theme and venue were chosen because it was felt that since the majority of the member societies and libraries had interests in the West Midlands, an attempt to take soundings of the traditions' diverse contributions to the region would be worthwhile. Member societies were invited to nominate conference speakers, and I should like to thank the society secretaries for their good offices in this matter. With this volume the conference papers are offered to a wider audience.

Margaret E. Gayner (Friends' Historical Society) offers an account of Quaker organization in the eighteenth century which makes plain the objectives and challenges of good order, and is enlivened by illustrations drawn from the history of her own family. Organization with a view to world mission is the theme of Alan Argent (Congregational History Circle), whose paper marks the bicentenary of the founding of the London Missionary Society (1775), and recalls the stimulus provided by George Burder and the Warwickshire Independents to the Society's birth, and their contribution to its early years.

In his paper David L. Wykes (Unitarian Historical Society) concentrates upon the victims of the 1791 Priestley Riots in Birmingham, whose theological convictions, so different from those which inspired the Warwickshire Independents, engendered violent opposition, not least because they were deemed to threaten that religious consensus on which national security was thought to depend. J. H. Y. Briggs (Baptist Historical Society) takes up the Baptist story in Birmingham from 1791, noting that, theological differences notwithstanding, Baptists and Unitarians were united in advocating socio-political reform, and indicating the breadth of view combined with zeal for church planting which characterized so many Birmingham Baptists of the nineteenth century.

With his paper David M. Thompson (United Reformed Church History Society) marks the centenary of R. W. Dale's death. He shows not only that for Birmingham's leading nineteenth-century Nonconformist divine civic affairs and national politics were complementary concerns, but that both were viewed by Dale in the light of a combination of incarnational and ecclesiological principles.

W. Eifion Powell (Welsh Independents' Historical Society) recalls the arrival of the Welsh Nonconformist denominations in the English West Midlands, noting that while their primary objective was to minister to those who had come to the industrial areas in search of work and a new life, their influence extended beyond the walls of their chapels.

Finally, E. Dorothy Graham (Wesley Historical Society) offers the first full account of a Primitive Methodist venture, Bourne College, Birmingham. She locates the college's origins in the context of Primitive

Methodist educational concerns at large, discusses its life and work, and suggests reasons for its demise.

Taken individually, the several papers contribute to our knowledge of the topics discussed, and I reiterate my thanks to all the contributors. Taken together, the studies reveal attitudes and concerns which transcend denominational boundaries. We are reminded of the quest for corporate identity which was pursued in different ways by the Quakers no less than by the Welsh Nonconformists. The deep friendships between some of the denominationally distinct pioneers of modern world mission are striking. The importance of socio-political witness is a recurring theme, and the great exponent of the 'civic gospel' was inspired in that direction by the erstwhile Baptist, George Dawson. Birmingham Quakers became prominent practitioners of what Dale called 'the sacredness of secular business'. The passion for education which inspired the Primitive Methodists to establish Bourne College burned no less brightly in the Congregational founders of Spring Hill College.

A number of the papers suggest that at their best the members of the traditions here discussed understood that while those truly concerned with the gospel cannot but have local and regional anchorage, they may not justifiably be parochial in outlook.

Alan P. F. Sell
Aberystwyth

CHAPTER 1

Eighteenth-century Quakerism: The Move towards a Stable and Organized Society

Margaret E. Gayner

My first question is where to begin? You cannot discuss the developments in the eighteenth century without clarifying the state of the Society of Friends (Quakers) in 1700, and how that comes about. Should I go back to the time when George Fox started on his serious travels to seek answers to his questions on God, Christianity and the church in general? Or to his birth in 1624? Or even further back to Henry VIII, to remind ourselves of what happened in the country over the next century? I opt for the birth of Fox.

George Fox was born in 1624 in the small village of Fenny Drayton on the Warwickshire–Leicestershire border. His family would seem to have been fairly comfortably off and respected in the village. His father was a weaver and a churchwarden. Fox's was a basically stable background. Whether George ever actually attended school is uncertain, but he could certainly read and write and knew his Bible. Later he was to speak with authority. He was apprenticed to a shoemaker who also kept sheep and cattle, but questions and doubts were increasingly worrying him, and he could not accept what he saw as the hypocrisy of the clergy. George was about nineteen when he left home for good, to seek answers at a time which more or less coincided with the Civil War. He eventually made his way towards the north-west of England, where he found not only individuals but also like-minded groups already organized under varying names, some straight from existing churches, meeting together. George Fox's own answer came from insights within himself, the first being 'there is one, even Christ Jesus that can speak to thy condition'. Added to this was the realization that God is there, available to all who seek him, without the need for intervening clergy, and that there is that of God within everyone. So worship can take place anywhere, alone or in a group; it consists in

1

waiting upon the Lord. Groups were gradually linked together into a communicating network. By about 1650 George Fox and his first helpers had spread the message round Great Britain and also to Europe and America.

The real need for this network became clear to George Fox as he saw and shared the suffering of so many under the Clarendon Code. Quakers and other Nonconformists were caught in Acts which, among other things, necessitated attendance at the parish church, and forbade building meeting houses and living within five miles of a corporate town. Birmingham was not a corporate town, probably because it was too small at the time to be of significance; hence the strong Nonconformist element which has always been there. This was a time of great suffering: men were generally fined first, and then because they would not take the oath, sent to prison. The women suffered too, and there are numerous tales of interrupted meetings where the children were left to fend for themselves. In my own family in 1681 John Gayner and his wife and his brother Richard and his wife were fined, and John went to prison for eight months.

Nevertheless, Quakers continued to try to live as they saw fit – Living in the Light – positively spreading the word, seeking the will of God, and following the leading of the Spirit. The Act of Toleration which was passed in 1689 eased things somewhat. In particular it made legal the Quaker form of marriage in the context of a Meeting for Worship, and gave no reason for declaring that those that had already so taken place were invalid. The earliest recorded marriages date from about 1650 in most areas. In 1653 Fox gave a paper of advice, suggesting that there should be at least twelve faithful witnesses to Quaker marriages. I have the marriage certificate of John Gayner and Alice Williams who were married in 1678 in Olveston Meeting House near Thornbury in Gloucestershire. There are indeed twenty witnesses. What may surprise us is that all but three of them could sign their names. One of the three is John's father William. He was a blacksmith and used a horseshoe as his mark.

I

Let us now move into the eighteenth century. The national structure of meetings is in place. Individual worshipping groups hold a monthly business meeting, a preparatory meeting for the important group of meetings forming the Monthly Meeting – usually three to five. Several Monthly Meetings make up Quarterly Meetings, normally on a county basis. The latter appoint representatives to the Yearly Meeting when held. Yearly Meeting's function was advisory for the most part. It consisted of 'men of most weight' brought together for conference and friendship, and for the rekindling of vision. From 1727 onwards it could be attended by any Friends, not just ministers.

Who were these early Quakers? An analysis of Banbury Monthly Meeting given by Jack Wood in his book, *Some Rural Quakers*, suggests that in the 1690s, out of 55 Friends, nineteen were in farming, ten were blacksmiths, coopers, etc., ten were in the cloth/clothing group, and the rest were evenly divided in small numbers between the other practical jobs, law and teaching. Over the next fifty years, out of 133, 47 were in farming, eighteen were shoemakers and fifteen were in clothing. Between 1750 and 1799 numbers fell again to 65, with shop-keepers rising to ten, though farming was still just on top with eleven. This is a small town and rural area and the decline in numbers may have come about more gradually than in some towns.[1]

We have now reached the generation who were grandchildren of the original Friends, born in the last decades of the seventeenth century when life had become easier and the direct fire of George Fox had gone. Both numbers and standards were falling. One who saw the dangers was Samuel Bownas, born in 1696. In an extract published in the new edition of *Quaker Faith and Practice* he quotes the words of Anne Wilson:

thou comest to meeting as thou went from it, and goes from it as thou came to it but are no better for thy coming; what wilt thou do in the end?

He goes on:

This was so pat to my then condition that like Saul I was smitten to the ground as it might be said, but turning my thoughts inwards, in secret I cried, 'Lord what shall I do to help it?' And a voice as it were spoke in my heart, saying 'Look unto me, and I will help thee.'

I saw by experience wherein my shortness had been in being contented and easy with a form of truth and religion, which I had only by education, being brought up in plainness of both habit and speech; but all this though very good in its place, did not make me a true Christian; I was but a traditional Quaker, and that by education only and not from the Scriptures because they were a book sealed to me. And I now saw plainly that education though never so carefully administered would not do the work . . . there was no other way but this, viz. by the Spirit of Christ alone, to attain true faith, which works by love and gives victory over our infirmities and evil deeds, working such a change in us that we can in truth from experience say we are born from above.[2]

Samuel Bownas later became a travelling minister. As far as plainness
in dress and general life-style is concerned, we find two pieces of advice
from the 1690s. The first comes from Yearly Meeting:

> It is our tender and Christian Advice that Friends take care to keep
> the truth and plainness in language, habit, deportment and behaviour;
> that the simplicity of truth in these things may not wear out nor be
> lost in our days, nor in our posterity's, and to avoid pride and
> immodesty in apparel and all vain and superfluous fashions of the
> world. [3]

The second is a quotation from Margaret Fox, George's wife: 'It's a
dangerous thing to lead young Friends much into the observation of
outward things which may easily be done. For they can soon get into
an outward garb, to be all alike outwardly. But this will not make them
into true Christians: it's the spirit that gives life.' [4]

Friends were anxious to halt the decline and also to keep to the strict
beliefs and behaviour that George Fox had 'preached' (I use that word
intentionally). There should be no slipping of standards, no accepting
as Friends those who could not wholly follow the advices.

The area needing the greatest care and receiving the greatest
attention was that of marriages. The choice of suitable partners
among Friends was becoming smaller and (added to that) many single
people were disqualified by virtue of blood relation. Already in 1675
Yearly Meeting had passed a minute denouncing marriage between first cousins, and in 1709 it warned against that between second
cousins.

A minute was also received ensuring that a marriage proceeded
according to right ordering.

> It is our judgment that for better satisfaction to all parties, and that
> there may be due time for enquiry of clearness of the persons
> concerned, it is convenient that marriages be at least twice pro-
> pounded to the Meetings that are to take care therein (both to the
> men's and women's Meetings where both are established) before they
> are accomplished. And when things are cleared, that the marriage
> be accomplished in a grave and public assembly of Friends and
> relations.

It was such an enquiry that, in 1772, reported that Jane Sturge was
of sober conversation and clear from any marriage engagement, but
that John Gayner acknowledged that he had several times frequented
plays and associated himself with some of the actors; however, he did
not intend to do so again. In view of this and their very young years,

Monthly Meeting could not permit them to proceed and desired them to wait patiently until Friends could concur.

Unfortunately, the measures taken with regard to marriage had the predictable result of reducing numbers further. Was this really not foreseen? Friends married by a priest, and to those 'not of our persuasion', were visited and usually disowned. This, too, happened in my family. In 1718 Richard Gayner and Sarah Champneys were, for some reason I have not discovered, married in St Augustine's church in Bristol. They were duly visited and disowned. A Yearly Meeting minute on the procedure ends 'but if the Christian Care of Friends do not prevail to bring them to a true sense of their error then the Monthly Meeting is hereby directed to give forth a Testimony against such for the clearing of Truth and Friends.'

Richard and Sarah wrote a letter of apology five years later and were readmitted. What puzzled me was how their two children, born in the meantime, could be listed as members. However, I should have known that Friends would have a reasoned way through. Disownment meant: i) that you could not attend business meetings; ii) that you could not contribute to funds (both of which would be popular today!); and iii) that you could not yourself receive financial help. You could not be prevented from attending Meeting for Worship as this was (and still is) open to any who liked to come in. So I imagine that Richard and Sarah continued to go, with their children, to Frenchay meeting every Sunday.

There were, of course, other reasons for disownment. John Punshon notes the estimate that there were three disownments for every two convincements.[5] Monthly Meeting Minute Books (those of Warwickshire North start in the 1690s) make interesting reading, for Friends did not moderate their language. Reasons include the bland 'disorderly practices', but also scandalous behaviour and fornication, joining the Militia, marrying a member of another church, profanity and assault. Increasingly as the century wore on, as more Friends were in business and probably wealthier, mismanagement of business affairs and bankruptcy were reasons for disownment. An examination of the Warwickshire North Minute Books from 1778–89 alone reveals all of these examples of unacceptable behaviour.

If a Quaker was disowned, one would imagine that their name was on a list of members from which it could be removed. However, this was not the case until 1737. There was no official list of members. Disownment existed to clear truth, not to humiliate the offender.

Once a list of members of a Monthly Meeting had been established, there arose the problem, which still exists today, of keeping it up to date. In the first place this had much to do with the responsibility for the poor under the laws of Settlement. I have noted a minute sent by Warwickshire North Monthly Meeting to Worcester in 1746 declaring that 'Mary Hewson, widow, is fallen into necessitous circumstances. She is an object of charity ... and she belongs to *your* meeting.' This sounds harsh perhaps but each Monthly Meeting had its own responsibilities, and collections for charity do frequently appear in the minutes. I note that in that same year, 1746, a collection had been made for victims of the Rebellion in the North. Friends moved around surprisingly often, both travelling to visit relations, or as ministers, and they might also move permanently. I have long been puzzled as to how John Gayner, blacksmith, mentioned earlier, met his second wife, a widow in Bow. He is not named as a representative to Yearly Meeting, and I cannot think that his job took him to London, so perhaps she had relatives in Gloucestershire.

In 1737 all Friends were deemed members of the Quarterly Meeting where they were living on 1 July. A move might even be to somewhere abroad. In 1684 George Pearce went to America with his wife Anne (Gayner) and three children. Even then he took with him letters of transfer from Frenchay Monthly Meeting, and Thornbury Meeting, which were read in the Monthly Meeting at Philadelphia and accepted.

In 1747 Warwickshire North Monthly Meeting wrote the following letter in answer to a question from Pennsylvania:

> Dear Friends, we have received a ... from a letter which came from our Friend Joseph England of a certificate upon act. Of the said Joseph Rotherham would be agreeable. If anything we can say will give any satisfaction to Friends shall readily comply tho' tis now upwards of 20 years since his removal which makes this seem the less necessary. Albeit these may certifie you that he was educated amongst Friends and was a sobre young man in his Life and Conversation and free from any Engagement upon account of marriage so far as we know, we believe he did not then attend meetings so closely as he might have done being engaged in apprenticeship and afterwards to work with Persons of different Persuasions upon act of his occupation which was that of millright. So with desires for his welfare and prosperity in the Truth we recommend him to your notice.[6]

They did try!

II

So far I have dealt with the problems of the eighteenth century which, though being universal throughout the Society of Friends, most obviously affected local Friends and their Meetings. I now need to look at the situation from the top downwards, so to speak.

In 1660 a representative meeting of men Friends out of many counties had been held at Skipton, concerning the affairs of the church. This was one of several such gatherings. A few years later George Fox developed a strong corporate sense of consciousness by establishing the system of Monthly and Quarterly Meetings. 'The least member in the Church hath an office, and is serviceable; and all the members have need one of another',[7] he said. An epistle from a Yearly Meeting in London in 1668 about the period called Christmas states: 'we did conclude among ourselves to settle a meeting, to see one another's faces and open our hearts to one another in the Truth of God once a year as formerly used to be.' The intention of Yearly Meeting was to bring together from all parts of the country the men of most weight in the movement for conference and fellowship and the rekindling of vision, as a true way of development of a corporate life which should carry the Society forward in one common service.

But what of the women? Fox believed that women have an integral place in the church. So there began the creation of a structure of women's meetings parallel with the men's, with considerable pastoral responsibility. Some Meeting Houses had wooden removable screens so that the women's room could become part of the main room. There were, however, for a long time various parts of the organization from which women were excluded, including the men's business sessions where, if women were present, they were not allowed to speak.

One of the reasons why George Fox saw the urgent necessity of setting up a complete countrywide organization was to enable Friends to see a total picture of their sufferings. In 1682 the following three questions were asked by Yearly Meeting, and representatives of Quarterly Meetings were to answer them orally:

1. What Friends in the Ministry in their respective Counties departed this life since last Yearly Meeting?

2. What Friends imprisoned for their Testimony have died in prison since last Yearly Meeting?

3. How the Truth has prospered amongst them since the last Yearly Meeting, and how Friends are in Peace and Unity?

In 1700 there was added an advice relating to their godly care for the good education of their children in the way of truth, and how plainness of habit and speech was to be practised. Answers were now to be given in writing. This was the beginning of a list of Advices and Queries continuously added to and adapted right up to the latest version approved and printed in 1995 after much heart-searching and discussion.

In 1735 an actual request had come from Yorkshire for an abstract of guidance; this led three years later to the important publication of

Christian and Brotherly Advices. Friends were increasingly ceasing to believe that all the nation would realise the truth that they had been preaching, and this is an attempt to preserve a precious remnant. Friends tended to become more introspective, looking inwardly to see what was wrong with their own Society. In 1742 a particularly large number of additions were made. These included the following Queries:

1. How many Meeting Houses built, and what Meetings new settled?

2. How many public Friends died and when?

3. What is the state of your Meeting? Is there any growth in Truth? And doth any Convincement appear since last year? And is Love and Unity preserved amongst you?

4. Is your Care, by Example and Precept, to Train up children in all Godly Conversation, and in the frequent reading of the Holy Scriptures as also in Plainness of Speech, Behaviour and Apparel?

5. Do you bear a faithful and Christian testimony against the Receiving or Paying Tithes? and against Bearing of Arms? and do you admonish such as are unfaithful therein?

6. Do you stand clear in our Testimony against defrauding the King of his Customs, Duties or Excise, or in Dealing in Goods Suspected to be run?

7. How are the Poor among you provided for? and what care is taken of the education of their offspring?

8. Do you keep a record in your Quarterly and Monthly Meetings, of the Prosecutions and Sufferings of your respective members? and have you a Record for your Meeting houses, Burial grounds etc.? [8]

III

Knowledgeable Friends at least will have expected to find here one particular word in connection with the eighteenth century, and I have not used it. Under my title it is only here perhaps that I should refer to what was a developing direction in the Society of Friends, and not a, so-to-speak, man-made structure. I refer of course to what has become known as the period of Quietism, and I intend to deal with it by quoting directly from Elfrida Vipont's *The Story of Quakerism*. Referring to the accumulation of wealth she writes:

Not only did Friends tend to be successful in their business undertakings, but their religious principles enjoined thrift, economy and simplicity in their private lives. For those who held faithfully to their Quaker testimonies, extravagant expenditure on dress, furniture and style of living was prohibited; moreover, the puritanical influence surviving from the days of their forbears debarred them from any indulgence in music, drama and the dance. To some, this tendency to accumulate wealth brought lessons in wise stewardship and social service; for others, the urge to lay up treasure on earth became strong.

Another result was a tendency which was to strengthen as time went on, for Friends to draw slightly apart from one another. Some were impelled by their wider interests to launch out into the world; others felt that in order to maintain the testimonies of the Society in all their strength and purity, sacrifices must be made, of which a withdrawal from the world was one. The Society of Friends became more and more a closed community, where innovations were looked on with suspicion. Itinerant ministers still travelled widely over the British Isles, on the Continent and in America, encouraging meetings and keeping the Society alive and its organisation working through their devoted efforts, but their message tended to lack the joyous missionary zeal of the early days. They were addressing their efforts to a 'peculiar people' rather than to a Universal Church. The Quietist influence in the Society was pre-eminently responsible for the almost imperceptible but steady change which came about during the eighteenth century. It was not an influence to be deplored, for Quietism as practised by the Quakers flowered in some of the most beautiful lives of service and self-sacrifice that the Society has ever known, but it is not the whole of Quakerism.

Increasingly the Light Within became regarded as something entirely separate from natural man, a gift of God working salvation in the human heart without the aid of human intellect or human powers. Man of himself could do nothing and less than nothing; his task was to wait, to obliterate self, and to let the divine power work through him. This openness of the spirit to the Divine influence could of itself bring nothing but good. Unfortunately it was accompanied by such a mistrust of the intellectual faculties that it was felt that only a blank mind could receive the impress of God's will. Friends felt that the right preparation of heart and mind for Meeting for Worship lay in banishing all thoughts, memories and ideas, and thus waiting passively for the divine message. Week after week no message would come. Friends accepted the discipline of the silence, and as they opened their hearts to its purifying influence, many were helped and strengthened; other less sensitive souls found nothing to satisfy their hunger save physical rest which often solaced itself with sleep, so that the minute books of the period are full of references to the tendency amongst Friends to fall asleep in meeting. Visiting ministers often went through periods of profound spiritual torment in their efforts to fulfil their service. They would visit meetings or attend public meetings, only to find that no message came to them, and their eager listeners, often strangers in search of spiritual help, would go away disappointed. Attributing their apparent failures to their own human frailty, these Friends went through agonies of self-abasement; only the most heroic, saintly souls could win through to such an awareness of God that nothing could hinder their ministry.

Through such rare spirits, the divine message flowed unhampered; through such a completeness of self-giving Friends were to learn at last that all the powers and gifts and talents of mankind can be used and sanctified by God. The lesson had to be learnt, and the Quietist period was a necessary stage in the learning of it.[9]

I am left with my second omission: particular reference to the West Midlands. By the nature of my subject, most of what I have said and detailed has applied to the country as a whole, and very little else appears in the local Minute Books. In any case, where is or was the West Midlands? Quaker divisions have basically followed the old county boundaries. Rutland has had little to do with the Birmingham area, Leicestershire is not the West Midlands, and Staffordshire looks the other way. In earlier times Stow on the Wold, Shipston on Stour, Brailes and Broad Campden were all associated with Warwickshire South or Middle Monthly Meetings. In the early years of the eighteenth century meetings tended to appear and disappear in this area. Apart from Birmingham itself, which is not officially a part of the West Midlands, there were meetings at Coventry, Warwick, Stratford on Avon, and Stourbridge; some of these still exist, although those at Henley on Avon, Atherstone, Bromsgrove, Baddesby and Wigginshill do not.

Minute books for Warwickshire North Monthly Meeting contain little that is unusual. Marriage applications and disownments appear regularly. I note that in 1790 John Heydon (whose name occurs in my own 'wider' family):

having been visited by appointment of our last Monthly Meeting for assaulting and consciously wounding his master by stabbing him with a penknife and afterwards purloining a part of his master's property, from which charges he could not exculpate himself and therefore for the clearing of our Society from this scandal of such conduct, we do testify against and disown him.

In eighth month 1748 there is a minute which says that Friends are desired 'to inspect the title of their several Meeting Houses and burying grounds and bring an account in whose possession they be, likewise whether there be occasion to make any addition to Trustees', to the next Monthly Meeting. In tenth month 'we find there is occasion to renew the Trust in relation to Wigginshill M. H.', and Jon Freeth and Nathaniel Whitehead are to enquire in whose possession the title of Henly M. H. is. In 1748, in eleventh month, the deeds are to be transcribed into one book, and Henry Bradford is to get it done. Four years later Birmingham and Badgley are requested to hand over their deeds. In 1754, after another two years, Birmingham is again asked. No great hurry here. Friends like to take time to get things right. It took thirty years before the wording of an acceptable form of affirmation went through.

Finally I must refer to the campaign which began in the 1780s to abolish the slave trade, an issue in which Birmingham had much interest, economic as well as moral. Birmingham, the city of a thousand trades with its manufacture of everything from 'toys' which were given in 'payment' for slaves, to the guns and chains used in their restraint, saw the slave trade as an issue which tended to unite not only all radicals, but also evangelical Tories, a high point of collaboration. Thomas Clarke, the leader with William Wilberforce of the Abolitionists, came to Birmingham in 1787, and apparently contacted the Quaker community, mentioning John Sampson and Charles Lloyd. This leads us into the nineteenth century, when names such as Cadbury, Albright, Wilson, Barrow, Gillett, Gibbins and Southall became nationally recognized in the business world.

Notes

1. Jack V. Wood, *Some Rural Quakers* (York: 1991), pp. 142–4.
2. Samuel Bownas, quoted in *Quaker Faith and Practice* (The Yearly Meeting of the Society of Friends, London: 1995), 19. 60.
3. Minutes of Yearly Meeting, 1690.
4. Margaret Fox, quoted in *Quaker Faith and Practice*, 20. 30.
5. John Punshon, *Portrait in Grey. A Short History of the Quakers* (London: 1984), p. 135.
6. Minutes of Warwickshire Monthly Meeting North, 8 February 1747.
7. Samuel Tuke, *Selections from the Epistles of George Fox* (1698) (London: 2nd edn, 1848), p. 127.
8. From *Friends' Queries and General Advices*, The Library, Friends House, London.
9. Elfrida Vipont, *The Story of Quakerism* (London: 2nd edn, 1960), pp. 149–50.

CHAPTER 2

The Founding of the
London Missionary Society
and the West Midlands

Alan Argent

At the close of the eighteenth century the self-confidence of the evangelical revival revealed itself in a concern for foreign missions which led to the founding of the Baptist, the London, and the Church Missionary Societies. Developments in North America, the teaching of Philip Doddridge, and the example of the Moravians all proved influential. However these societies were not born to universal acclaim. The founders of the LMS endured suspicion and ridicule before their ambition was realized, and have been severely criticized in this century also. The story of the Great Awakening and the writings of Jonathan Edwards, especially his *An Humble Attempt to Promote Explicit Agreement and Visible Union of God's People in Extraordinary Prayer for the Revival of Religion and the Advancement of Christ's Kingdom on Earth* (Boston, 1747), led many to concerted prayer for missionary work and religious revival. Edwards spent six years as a missionary among the native Americans and also wrote *The Life and Diary of the Rev. David Brainerd* (1749) who had devoted himself to the Indians of Delaware and New Jersey.

In 1737 Philip Doddridge, minister of Castle Hill church, Northampton, read Edwards's account of the initial stages of the Great Awakening in New England, *Faithful Narrative of the Surprising Word of God ... in Northampton in New England* (1737), in an edition prepared by Isaac Watts and John Guyse, and in 1749 he read the *Life* of Brainerd. Both works stimulated his interest in missions. Doddridge also corresponded with Count Nicholas von Zinzendorf about Moravian missionary work and met him at St Alban's in 1741. Influenced by Zinzendorf, the Moravians during the 1730s had sent missionaries to Greenland, the West Indies, Ceylon, Lapland, North America, Surinam and South Africa, having despatched 68 in all by 1740.[1]

In June 1741 Doddridge presented, to the Independent ministers of Suffolk and Norfolk, ten pointers to a more profound spiritual life in

13

their churches and, in August, he presented the same proposals to the Northamptonshire ministers. In 1742 the proposals were published in the preface to a sermon (preached at Kettering) and, among his emphases, he stressed the value of prayer, envisaging quarterly prayer meetings as an initial, but essential, preliminary to an active missionary movement. In the published version Doddridge added an eleventh point.

> Whether something might not be done ... towards assisting in the propagation of Christianity abroad, and spreading it in some of the darker parts of our own land? In pursuance of which it is further proposed, that we endeavour to engage as many pious people of our respective congregations as we can, to enter themselves into a society, in which the members may engage themselves to some peculiar cares, assemblies, and contributions, with a regard to this great end.

A footnote set out the rules of the missionary society which he hoped to establish in his own church. In time Doddridge became more critical of the Moravians, and his missionary plans, although sounding 'a prophetic call', proved premature.[2]

Forty years after Doddridge's death the missionary movement began in earnest. Indeed, the Baptist Missionary Society was formed in Northamptonshire, Doddridge's own county, and its initial organization for recruiting financial and prayerful support clearly resembled the pattern he had suggested in 1741. The influences which moved Doddridge (the Moravians, Edwards's works and the missions to the native Americans) also moved the young Baptist pioneer, William Carey. Although no record survives to show that Carey had read Doddridge's Kettering sermon and its postscript, published in 1742, Ernest Payne concluded that 'it is surely no coincidence that it was in Northamptonshire ... that the first of the modern missionary societies had its birth' and it was in the neighbouring Midland counties 'where Doddridge's personal influence and that of his students were strongest, that missionary enthusiasm most quickly spread'.

Payne posed the question whether Doddridge's interest in missionary matters was 'somewhat too romantic'. Certainly, romanticism was at work in the hearts of the promoters of the missionary societies.[3] Just as Rousseau imagined the South Sea islanders to be noble and free in their savage state and primitive innocence, so the Christian evangelicals understood the same natives, 'poor benighted creatures', to be at the mercy of their crude desires and heathen lusts and, therefore, in need of saving. Indeed, Tahiti in particular had a fascination for the eighteenth-century mind, which saw it as the equivalent of Utopia or the garden of Eden. One of the founders of the LMS wrote of Tahiti thus: 'if any thing could realize the fable of the Hesperides, it seems to be this favoured spot'. The successive publications of Captain James Cook's volumes of *Voyages* in the 1770s and 1780s, as well as those of other naval explorers, stimulated the imagination, leading Carey and other evangelicals to dream of carrying the gospel to exotic, faraway peoples.[4]

The emergence of the two separate missionary societies (the BMS and LMS), with different names and distinctive traditions of service, does not immediately suggest close early links but the reality is more complex. Both sets of promoters and founders shared the same vision and the same inspiration, and some, at least, came from the same geographical area. Yet the concentration of management in the BMS (or more properly the Particular Baptist Society for the Propagation of the Gospel to the Heathen) remained firmly but narrowly fixed in Northamptonshire while, from the outset, the LMS (originally simply, if arrogantly, the Missionary Society – it only acquired the name London in 1818 to remove confusion) stressed that its base lay in the metropolis and included a board of directors in 1795 numbering twenty ministers and fourteen laymen and drawn, not only from London, but from all the regions of Britain. By 1798 the number of LMS directors had grown to a total of 112 (42 in London, 43 in the country, fifteen in Scotland, four in Ireland and eight 'Foreign Directors').

The social pretension which clung to the LMS's annual gatherings was a 'dangerous concession to worldliness' to many BMS supporters. The BMS was marked by 'unobtrusive modesty' while the LMS held public meetings, presided over 'by wealthy notables … full of speechifying'. Even allowing for these apparent contrasts, the two societies were linked by their spiritual ideals, by personal friendships, by sources of prayerful and financial support, and by their origins.[5] This paper will examine the parts played by Baptists and Independents, in particular, in the West Midlands, especially Warwickshire, in the churches' growing awareness of the need for Christian witness overseas, leading to the founding of the LMS.

I

In June 1784 the Northampton association, linking some twenty Baptist churches stretching from Hertfordshire to Lincolnshire, met in Nottingham. Moved by John Sutcliff of Olney, the ministers present agreed to hold regular prayer meetings, on the first Monday of every month, for the revival and spread of the Christian faith. Andrew Fuller of Kettering, who had preached to the gathering, printed his sermon, adding some notes, to encourage and assist prayer for the 'revival and extent of real religion'. He suggested that the 'present religious state of the world' should be considered. Sutcliff urged that the 'whole interest of the Redeemer be affectionately remembered, and the spread of the gospel to the most distant parts of the habitable globe be the object of your most fervent requests'.[6] These calls to prayer were quickly taken up in other counties.

In 1786 the Warwickshire association of Baptist ministers recommended that prayer meetings should be held on the first Monday of the month and from these Baptist churches the movement spread to nearby fellowships of Independents. In June 1786 the association of Baptists meeting at Northampton noted with pleasure that 'several churches not in the association, and some of other denominations' had joined in prayer meetings on the first Monday in every month.[7] By then some Independents in Leicestershire were meeting regularly for such prayers. The BMS, founded in October 1792, emerged from the spread of these Monday evening prayer meetings. Significantly, among those churches giving early support to the BMS were several in Warwickshire and the Midlands where the prayer call had been heard.[8]

The Warwickshire Independents, who adopted the plan of monthly Monday evening prayers, were themselves led to consider the spread of the gospel and this proved to be one vital force in the formation of the LMS. The LMS directors, within months of its founding in 1795, also called for the holding of a missionary prayer meeting on the first Monday of every month, and soon four such regular meetings were held in London alone. George Burder (1752–1832), minister of West Orchard chapel, Coventry 1783–1803, came into contact with the prayer movement there and James Moody (1756–1806), minister of Cow Lane chapel, Warwick 1781–1806, was also influenced by it. Burder and Carey knew each other well in these years, while Moody was a friend of John Ryland (1753–1825), the Baptist scholar and also a founder of the BMS, who was minister of College Lane chapel, Northampton and who in 1793 moved to Broadmead, Bristol. Ryland had close family ties with Warwick and was also well acquainted with George Burder whom he described in 1791 as 'so wise and good a man'.[9]

In addition Samuel Pearce, minister of Cannon Street Baptist church, Birmingham 1790–99, who supported the BMS from its beginning and had hoped to be a missionary, had strong friendships with Independent ministers in the Midlands. In May 1794 Pearce reported to Carey in India that 'our Mission Society has been the means of provoking other Christians to love and good works'. The Independents of Warwickshire had formed an association for the propagation of the gospel there, and if possible among the 'Heathen' too. He stated that he had preached for them two weeks earlier from Galatians 5:13 – 'By love serve one another.' Pearce hoped it might be a means of 'uniting us more firmly in the common cause'. To that end he delighted to report the formation of the Worcestershire association in December 1793, with seven churches served by five Independent and two Baptist ministers. Pearce showed great interest in the founding of the LMS, and attended its first general meeting. He told Carey in 1796 that the LMS publicly recognized 'that our zeal kindled theirs: we lighted our torch at yours; and that it was God who first touched your heart with fire from his holy altar'. Pearce also seriously considered preaching a fund-raising sermon to boost LMS finances.[10]

Within a few months of the founding of the BMS George Burder was involved in the formation of the Warwickshire association of ministers for the spread of the gospel at home and abroad. On 27 June 1793 (the same month in which Carey and his companion, John Thomas, sailed for India) a meeting was held in James Moody's house at Warwick where the question under discussion was, 'What is the duty of Christians with regard to the spread of the Gospel?' The ministers present resolved to promote the knowledge of the gospel 'both at home and abroad' and passed a series of resolutions.

1. It appears to us, that it is the duty of all Christians to employ every means in their power, to spread the knowledge of the Gospel, both at home and abroad.

2. As ministers of Christ, solemnly engaged by our office to exert ourselves for the glory of God, and the spiritual good of men, we unite in a determination to promote this great design in our respective connexions.

3. That we will immediately recommend to our friends the formation of a fund for the above purpose, and report progress at the next meeting.

4. That the first Monday of every month, at seven o'clock in the evening be a season fixed on for united prayer to God for the success of every attempt, by all denominations of Christians, for the spread of the Gospel.

5. That the Rev Dr Williams be desired to prepare a circular letter, on the subject of spreading the gospel by the next meeting.

6. That the next meeting be held at Nuneaton, on Tuesday, August 6, 1793.

In his absence the choice of Edward Williams (1750–1813), the minister of Carr's Lane meeting house, Birmingham 1792–95, to act as scribe reveals his high reputation among his fellow ministers and also his known sympathy for the missionary cause. This meeting at Moody's house appears to have been 'the first business-like approach' towards the founding of an ordered society among the Independents. These Warwickshire ministers were not looking to London for leadership but acted on their own 'convictions of immediate duty', achieving 'considerable success both in their own and other counties'. Their letter became a powerful tool in the development of the opinion that the time was ripe for missionary action.[11] Following the Baptist pattern they too set aside the first Monday in each month for prayer and their desire for the success of all attempts to spread the gospel reveals no narrow approach. A collection, held in Moody's house, then produced five guineas.[12]

Six weeks later Burder was one of the preachers at the ordination service of Daniel Fleming at Nuneaton where he spoke on *Diligence in the Christian Ministry*. He stated that it was the duty of Christians at large 'to do something more ... for the spread of the Gospel in foreign countries'. Burder added a footnote to the sermon in print, in which he related the recent Baptist missionary ventures. 'Two missionaries have been actually sent into Bengal. The Independent ministers of Warwickshire have also consulted together, with an earnest desire to promote a similar work.' The Warwickshire initiative was prompted directly by the Baptist mission to India. Dr Williams's letter was presented to the meeting of ministers, following Fleming's ordination, and it was decided that the letter should be circulated, not only within the county, but to all the associations of Independent ministers throughout the country. Those interested were urged to contact Burder or Williams.[13]

William Carey had first hoped that overseas missionary work might be undertaken on a broad evangelical basis but reluctantly decided that 'the present divided state of Christendom' had made it 'more likely for good to be done by each denomination engaging separately in the work'. Burder agreed with this view. The prayer movement of the Baptists produced significant effects on the Independent churches, especially in Warwickshire, where 'closer fellowship, deeper spiritual life and a wider vision' followed and, as Samuel Pearce noted, Carey's account of the state of the world moved them to thoughts of missionary work.[14]

Williams's circular owed much to Carey's earlier pamphlet and it recommended to the county associations of Independent ministers:

i. That annual county associations should be held and annual circular letters published for the guidance of the churches.
ii. That a prayer meeting should be held on the first Monday in every month to pray for the revival and success of religion.
iii. That funds should be raised for the work of propagating the gospel both at home and abroad.
iv. That circulating charity schools should be established in each county for the purpose of teaching the principles of religion.

v. That a supernumerary minister should be appointed in each county to superintend the schools and undertake itinerant preaching.
vi.   That the importance of sending missionaries among the heathens should be generally realized.

The recommendations are clearly not confined to missionary matters but reflect widespread evangelical concerns. The advocacy of schools was dear to both Burder and Williams.[15]

In the 'impassioned and earnest' postscript to the Independent Associations of Ministers in all the counties of England and Wales (which may have been written by Burder) the writer pleaded:

Has not the poor heathen world waited long enough? If not, how many centuries longer must the ignorant and uncivilized wait? Were one man of God truly qualified for the work, sent from each county in the kingdom, what great things might we not expect? Or even were some of the larger and more opulent counties to do this, while the smaller ones joined together to send one between two or three? The Lord pardon our too long continued indifference towards an object of such magnitude and moment ... The nature of the pastoral office requires that ministers should embrace every opportunity to promote the growth of the gospel tree, that it may not only take deep root, but also extend its branches, that its fragrance and fruit may be communicated to all the world ... It deserves the closest enquiry, whether the want of a powerful and lively acquaintance in our own souls with Jesus Christ and the benefits of his gospel, be not at the bottom of all indifference about the salvation of others; whether those blessed characters who were so greatly honoured in propagating truth in their several situations differed from us in anything so much as the strong conviction and awakening appre-hension they had of spiritual things.

The postscript accepts that missionary work may be expensive:

On the subject of giving, the following guidance is offered: if it be asked, why application should not be made to all denominations without distinction? We reply; that our design is not to reject any contributions that may occasionally be made, but rather would be thankful for the least; and in some cases it may be prudent to solicit them; but we wish the churches in our immediate connexion, to act without the least dependence on supplies of so precarious a nature. Though a union of different denominations, in promoting any chari-table end, appears in some respects desirable, yet it must be granted by all who consider attentively human nature that an effect greatly superior may be expected from each denomination exerting itself separately ... And when this mode of procedure originates not in a bigoted partiality but in the purest benevolence; when one denomination rejoices in the success of another, while the same object is in view, it gives exercise to many Christian virtues at once.[16]

The Warwickshire ministers would have known the prominent people to whom to address this challenging letter. It was read all over the country during 1793 and elicited positive responses from other counties. The singular importance of the Warwickshire circular letter is that it was the first attempt to place before the Congregational churches the necessity of foreign missions. It emulated the Baptists but its appeal to the denominational spirit is not undertaken out of narrow prejudice. Rather the postscript's intent in this regard is practical. Precarious, unsolicited contributions from churches of other allegiances would be welcome but careful budgeting would be needed also. A reliable source of income from like-minded churches would give confidence to treasurers and administrators enabling plans for foreign missions to proceed. To the Warwickshire ministers, at this stage, financial need would practically necessitate societies with a denominational base, like the BMS. The postscript expressed concerns which George Burder consistently addressed – the need for adequate funds for such an ambitious undertaking.[17]

At the meeting of the Warwickshire association of ministers, held at Coventry in January 1794, a committee of three was appointed to carry out the association's resolutions. The three were Williams, Moody and Burder, clearly the leading figures in the association and all intimately bound up with its concern for missionary work.[18]

II

George Burder had been converted by the sermons of William Romaine and George Whitefield and, encouraged by Fletcher of Madeley, began preaching himself in June 1776. Although he lacked formal theological training, he became minister of the Congregational church at Lancaster in October 1778, while remaining active as an itinerant preacher. Invited to become minister of West Orchard chapel, Coventry in 1781, he did not move there until November 1783. In June 1785 he began Sunday schools at Coventry in co-operation with Christians of other denominations. Burder was the chief mover in the founding of the Religious Tract Society in 1799 and in 1803 he left Coventry to become unpaid secretary of the LMS and editor of the *Evangelical Magazine*, both in succession to John Eyre. He was also minister of Fetter Lane

Congregational church in London until his death. He was a prolific author, writing several volumes of his popular *Village Sermons* which were translated into many languages. However, above all, his love for the LMS dominated. Burder's son wrote:

> I well remember, young as I then was, the deep interest my Father expressed in the formation and in the prospects of the Missionary Society. It was the very subject on which he always delighted to converse, when in the bosom of his family. It had taken possession of his heart. He viewed every engagement on earth as inferior in importance to that of aiming at the conversion of the world, and the universal extension of the kingdom of Christ.[19]

Burder's ministry at Coventry was characterized by his delight in the gospel and his desire to convey 'the knowledge and saving influence of it' to all within reach. Burder preached the gospel because 'his constant aim was to do good; to gain, not the applause, but the souls of men'. Such an attitude leads easily to the advocacy of foreign missions.[20]

Whilst at Coventry Burder provided meeting places for worship and evangelism on the outskirts of the city where he preached regularly. He and James Moody of Warwick were indefatigable in evangelistic work in the towns and villages of the county and the 'amiable and ardent' Moody became Burder's most intimate friend in Warwickshire. The two men were both Londoners by birth and, like Burder, Moody had often heard the sermons of William Romaine and was converted at Spa Fields chapel. After training for the ministry at Hoxton Independent academy, Moody moved to Warwick where the congregation grew markedly, necessitating enlargements to the chapel. He was involved in most schemes of evangelistic activity in his day, enduring 'abuse and tumultuous violence' in his efforts to bring the gospel to neighbouring towns. When he accepted the charge at Warwick in 1781 the church had only eighteen or twenty members and the congregation of less than fifty could not maintain him financially, so that, in 1782, an appeal was made to friends outside the church. In 1798 the chapel was enlarged and, during his twenty-five years' ministry, he accepted perhaps 150 church members, multiplying his congregation to nine or ten times the original number. On his death in 1806, the sculptor John Bacon (1777–1859) presented a tablet to the church in his memory. Moody was remembered for his ceaseless labours 'in the sacred cause of religious truth, as it appeared to his own honest conviction'.[21]

Edward Williams was born near Denbigh and, as a youth, was influenced by the evangelical revival. He became a member of the Independent church at Denbigh and in 1771 he began his studies at the Dissenting academy at Abergavenny. He was minister at Ross 1775–77 and at Oswestry 1777–91, where he also took charge of the academy there (on its removal in 1782 from Abergavenny). In 1792 Williams became a co-editor of the *Evangelical Magazine* and also began his ministry at Carr's Lane, Birmingham. In September 1795, after three and a half years, he moved to be the principal of Rotherham academy where he remained until his death in 1813.

Williams was an influential advocate of moderate Calvinism, a theological approach which argued that the atonement was universal. According to Williams, man has, as his due, certain gifts from God, including the freedom to exercise a moral choice and the 'moral means' to make it. The gospel is included in the moral means and, therefore, those who have not heard the gospel have been deprived of their due as accountable moral agents. Thus 'man's state of accountability' creates the need to proclaim Christ's gospel to all people and indifference to the propagation of the gospel to non-believers was, to Williams, 'a great sin'.

Some grasp of his academic interests is vital for an understanding of Williams, but he also had qualities of pastoral warmth and imagination, revealed in his concern for missionary work and his support of schools in many Welsh counties. At Birmingham Williams suffered the death of one daughter and of his invalid wife whose death, aged 37, in 1795 left him to care for the surviving four of their nine children. Williams was an admirer both of Jonathan Edwards and Philip Doddridge (whose works he edited in 1802), not least for their stress on the importance of the churches' missionary work, and he shared with Burder a concern for missions which 'amounted almost to a passion'.[22]

In 1783 George Burder had asked the advice of Matthew Wilks, the minister of Moorfields Tabernacle, concerning the pastorate at Coventry. Wilks replied that West Orchard's congregation was increasing in regular hearers and in members and they should become 'under a godly minister to be a very large interest; for the city is large, populous and very ignorant; and yet there is a great spirit for hearing'. Wilks's positive attitude towards West Orchard chapel contrasts with his view of Coventry itself.

Edward Williams took an even more dismal view of Birmingham on his arrival there in 1792.

Because of the dark and malignant spirit of prejudice, bigotry, and riot, which often discloses itself in the church-and-king party; and because of the determined hostility, even among a party of Dissenters, to the doctrines of grace, this town is too much like a synagogue of Satan.

Williams felt that church discipline at Carr's Lane was 'at a low ebb' and was confident that God would enable him to put up 'a firm defence of the truth' in the town.[23]

Birmingham had been the scene of a 'great riot' of the 'High-church mob' in July 1791, resulting in the burning of the Unitarian Joseph Priestley's meeting house, and also of the private mansions and large houses of wealthy Dissenters, as Burder observed. The West Midlands was not always fertile ground for the evangelicals at this time. Burder noted:

> the terror spread through the country, and base people threatened our meetings at Coventry: a mob waited every night at ten o'clock to hear the news from Birmingham, and seemed only to want a leader to begin the work of destruction among us; indeed, it was suspected that some bad men of Coventry were the principal incendiaries at Birmingham. I was under some apprehensions, as it was rumoured that Dr Priestley, who had fled from Birmingham, had taken shelter in my house. We had our plate and writings packed up, to be ready for departure on the first alarm. But some soldiers arrived, and no attempt was made. Blessed be God!

Burder was convinced that these riots were planned and were designed to intimidate the Dissenters. The violent opposition which he and his fellows met suggests they had enough to occupy themselves at home, without having to worry about converting the heathen overseas. That they did so worry and were so active and successful in advocating this cause testifies to the strength and sincerity of their evangelical concern. They were not just starry-eyed idealists with their heads full of dreams.[24]

The founding of the BMS, and the influences which brought it into being, were factors affecting the climate of opinion in the churches, especially the Dissenting churches, in the 1790s. Burder, Moody and Williams were moving spirits at the beginning of the Warwickshire association and used the tried and tested methods of the Northamptonshire Baptists to promote its concern for mission. The circular letters, the monthly prayers, the encouragement of other ministers, and contact with other counties were all proven means which Burder learned at Coventry from his Baptist friends. His admiration for the BMS, and particularly for Carey, led him often to praise Carey's pioneering evangelism and to recommend his treatise *An Enquiry into the Obligations of Christians to Use Means for the Conversion of the Heathens* (Leicester, 1792).

The Warwickshire ministers' circular letter of 1793 led to the adoption of the missionary prayer meeting on the first Monday in each

month by most Independent churches in England and Wales. The idea
derived immediately from the Baptists yet behind them lay the recommendations of Doddridge and Edwards. However the Moravians too
must take some credit, for Zinzendorf introduced a monthly Congregation 'Prayer Day' at Herrnhut in 1728 and then announced his plans
for evangelism overseas. The following day 26 of the brethren
covenanted together to pray for the world mission of the church,
holding themselves ready to respond if called. The close relationship
between the praying congregations and the blessing of God upon the
outgoing missionaries set a pattern for the early promoters of the BMS
to follow.[25]

One early historian of the LMS stated that 'it is questionable whether
any minister out of London took a more lively interest in the formation
of the London Missionary Society' than George Burder. Such praise
implies that other factors were more telling, that these were rooted in
London and that, laudable as the contributions of Burder and his
Warwickshire colleagues were, they simply could not have had more
than a marginal influence, albeit a lively one, on the society's formation.

III

In his printed Nuneaton sermon, Burder had commended Carey's
Enquiry and also Melvill Horne's *Letters on Mission; Addressed to the
Protestant Ministers of the British Churches* (Bristol, 1794) which Horne
had written after serving as chaplain to the Sierra Leone colony, placed
there by the Clapham Sect. Again in 1795 Burder praised these two
works in his printed address, included that year in the official account
of the inaugural meetings of the LMS.[26]

John Eyre (1754–1803), an itinerant preacher in his youth, was
educated at Trevecca college, and later at Emmanuel, Cambridge,
before becoming an Anglican clergyman. He was minister of Ram's
chapel in Homerton (named after its founder) from 1785 until his
death, and founded, and was the principal editor of the *Evangelical
Magazine* which first appeared in July 1793. This journal became the
'channel of the new missionary enthusiasm', serving as a 'clearing house'
of information. In May 1794 Eyre met at least three of the Scots
ministers present in London at the Dissenters' library in Red Cross
Street. These three – Alexander Waugh (1754–1827), minister of
Wells Street church, John Love (1756–1825), minister of the Scots
church, Artillery Street, Bishopsgate, and James Steven (1761–1824) of
Crown Court chapel, Covent Garden – joined Eyre in a spirited
discussion of Horne's book *Letters on Mission*. Horne's condemnation
of the churches' indifference to overseas missions excited them, as did

his view that a missionary should be 'far removed from narrow bigotry, and possess a spirit truly catholic'.

> It is not Calvinism, it is not Arminianism, but Christianity that he is to teach. It is not the hierarchy of the Church of England; it is not the principles of the Protestant Dissenters, that he has in view to propagate. His object is to serve the Church Universal.

Therefore Horne concluded: 'Let Liberal Churchmen and conscientious Dissenters, pious Calvinists and pious Arminians embrace with fraternal arms' and this, of course, was the approach eventually adopted by the LMS.[27]

John Eyre, stimulated by this discussion, went straight to the house of his friend, Matthew Wilks, who was initially critical of Horne's sincerity as he had not made any evangelical inroads in Africa. Horne had confessed he had done 'nothing in Africa, as a Missionary', apart from preach one sermon through an interpreter. He was 'sorry'. Wilks joined Eyre and the Scots ministers at their next meeting. From these informal beginnings, regularly fortnightly meetings for scripture reading, discussion and prayer came to be held at the Castle and Falcon, Aldersgate Street, involving an ever larger group of enthusiasts for mission.[28]

In July 1794 John Ryland of Bristol, having received the first letter sent by William Carey from India, shared its contents with H. O. Wills, a manager of the Bristol Tabernacle, David Bogue (1750–1825), since 1777 minister of the Independent church at Gosport, John Hey, minister of Castle Green Congregational church, Bristol, and James Steven. Bogue's immediate response was to exclaim, 'Why can't we have a Missionary Society too?' Bogue was from Berwickshire and had trained at Edinburgh for the ministry. After serving several pastorates, he moved to Gosport where in 1780 he opened an academy to train men for the Congregational ministry.[29]

Bogue felt called to write a paper for the *Evangelical Magazine*, published in September that year, entitled *To the Evangelical Dissenters who practise Infant Baptism*. It is an appeal to evangelize the heathen overseas and is addressed neither to Baptists nor Anglicans but rather to paedobaptists and Nonconformists, that is the Independents and the Calvinistic Methodists – 'all other bodies of professing Christians … are doing something for the conversion of the Heathen … We alone are idle.' He found encouragement from the efforts of others as all who had engaged in missionary work had met with success. It would be necessary 'to found a Seminary for training-up persons for the work'. Funds would be contributed by 'annual subscribers' in every congregation. In pursuit of these 'delightful prospects', Bogue called upon the ministers of London to propose a plan to this end. He concluded: 'nothing is wanting but for some persons to stand forward, and to begin' and signed his address, 'An Evangelical Dissenter'.[30]

Bogue's ambitious vision is of a society altogether grander than that of the Baptists. He could not imagine failure in the mission field and, realizing finance and leadership would be needed, he appealed to London. Thus admiration of Baptist initiative did not lead to Bogue's advocating the emulation of their methods. He felt the Independents could make significant improvements to the Baptist system and did not share the Northamptonshire Baptists' reservation about London. His letter was a 'summons to action', the 'immediate stimulus to definite commitment which made the London Missionary Society a fact'.[31]

David Bogue had travelled extensively in Europe and in 1792 had preached on behalf of the Scottish SPCK in London. This sermon had caused some alarm as he had praised the revolutionaries in France for overthrowing 'the tyranny of civil governments, that most formidable engine against the religion of Jesus Christ' (thus incurring the suspicion of sedition) and also had appealed for more Christian zeal both at home and abroad. He exclaimed:

How pleasing it would be to hear of pious missionaries labouring among the natives of injured Africa, preaching the gospel among the newly-discovered islanders of the South Seas, and ... to the mild inhabitants of the Pelew Islands.

Thus Bogue's published address of 1794 was not merely the spontaneous outpouring of a passionate soul, newly seized by Carey's missionary fervour, but was also the release of a profound reflection.

The London ministers meeting in the summer of 1794 at the Castle and Falcon eventually decided 'to give it publicity, and to write to certain leading men in the country, some at our meeting objected to Mr B[ogue] as an high and overbearing man, but that was over-ruled, and he was addressed'. Bogue's views were mostly of a decisive character. If he himself entertained neither suspicion nor hesitation about the London ministers, at least some there had reservations about him, perhaps because of his notorious 1792 sermon. The coming together of these vigorous and excited men shifted the focus of their mission concerns to London, rendering the emerging society London-based, as Bogue desired, although the London developments made it unthinkable that it would be restricted to Independents. The hopes and visions of the disparate London evangelicals, meeting and praying regularly, which included Anglicans, Calvinistic Methodists and Scots Presbyterians, had become intertwined, through the medium of the *Evangelical Magazine*, with those of Bogue, and the Warwickshire Independents.

This coming together could not be ignored. Perhaps James Steven, present with Bogue in Bristol at the reading of Carey's letter, spoke at the London meetings in his favour. Yet Bogue's address had touched a nerve among the Christian public and the London committee needed his co-operation to give their hopes a wide appeal. The missionary society was intended to be a 'people's undertaking from the start'.[32]

Bogue had received the Warwickshire circular letter before setting out on his summer preaching tour in 1794 and John Angell James, Bogue's pupil, later suggested that Edward Williams's circular of August 1793 had prompted Bogue to write his celebrated paper: 'In all probability Bogue had his mind directed to the subject by the resolutions and letter of the Warwickshire ministers.' Certainly, the Independent churches of Hampshire began to hold regular prayer meetings, influenced by both Bogue and the Warwickshire letter. John Campbell wrote that: 'It is clear that Dr Bogue and the men of Warwick contemplated a Congregational Society, but the brethren in London one of a more general, comprehensive and Christian character.'

The Warwickshire Independents were encouraged by Bogue's paper in the *Evangelical Magazine* and Williams was deputed to write in approval of Bogue's proposals. This letter, published in the *Evangelical Magazine* in December 1794, contained a strong recommendation 'that the Independents should unite in sending missionaries abroad' and that the Warwickshire association was ready 'to concur in such a measure'. Williams noted that his circular of August 1793 and its 'call' had been 'attended to in some neighbouring counties' and that some efforts have been made to spread the gospel both 'at home and abroad'. 'But as we are more and more convinced of the propriety and importance of such attempts, we ardently desire ... a more general concurrence.' These words do not necessarily suggest a readiness to combine with Christians of other denominations but rather imply a more general agreement among the Independent churches. The Warwickshire Independents were clearly very keen but they were still thinking of a missionary society for Independents, even though in supporting Bogue's appeal they differed from the Baptist approach which steered clear of London.[33]

The editor of the *Evangelical Magazine* inserted, after Williams's letter, a note that 'the formation of a Society, for sending missionaries abroad, is in contemplation – that two meetings have already been held by ministers in London of various denominations for that particular purpose'. Then he drew attention to the review of Horne's treatise published in the previous month. The vision had shifted subtly in favour of an interdenominational co-operative venture.[34]

In October 1794 the *Evangelical Magazine* published a review of a sermon by John Ryland, *The Certain Increase of the Glory and Kingdom of Jesus*, because its 'intrinsic merit' was worthy of 'public esteem'. The reviewer praised Ryland's plea for an enlarged vision of evangelism, noting his proud boast that Baptist churches had been planted in Africa and Jamaica and his hope that 'our missionaries have reached the East Indies, and are employed in rolling away the stone, that the sable stocks of Hindoos may drink of the water of life'. Thus Eyre used the Baptists' achievements to promote his own concern for missionary matters.[35]

A few months earlier, Eyre had asked Thomas Haweis, another evangelical Anglican, and formerly chaplain to Selina, Countess of Huntingdon, to assist in writing and editing for the *Evangelical Magazine*. In the summer of 1794, when Haweis was about to go to Brighton, Eyre begged him to take Horne's *Letters on Missions* to review for the magazine.[36] Haweis was 'tremendously stirred' by the book. He wrote:

> I read and my heart ... kindled afresh into a flame. I had met such bitter disappointments in my first efforts made some years before to send the Gospel to Otaheite ... that I began to despair of seeing this first desire of my soul ever accomplished.

This referred to Haweis's training, in 1789 and 1790, of two of Lady Huntingdon's Trevecca students for a mission to Tahiti. Haweis had felt challenged by the accounts of James Cook, Samuel Wallis and William Bligh of their voyages to the Pacific and, like Carey, was touched by the sting of Cook's prophecy that Tahiti would never be the subject of a Christian mission. This attempt failed in 1791, due to the unrealistic demand of the prospective missionaries to be ordained as clergymen of the Church of England before sailing. Eyre may have asked Haweis to review Horne's book because he knew of this frustration.[37]

Horne himself, in the preface to his book, wrote of his admiration of William Carey's *Enquiry* and recommended that his readers should peruse this work. He stated that Carey had 'given to his precepts the force of example, by actually embarking on a Mission to India'.[38] Haweis's review, published in the *Evangelical Magazine* in November 1794, proved 'one of the turning-points in the modern missionary awakening', according to his modern biographer. It ended with an unequivocal proposal for a broad-based missionary society.

> Could a new society be formed for promoting the Gospel ... without respect to different denominations of Christians ... and begin with one corps of missionaries to the heathen in the South Seas, would they pursue their object without being discouraged by disappointment ... till it should please God to open the way for success, no expense attending it deserves for a moment to come into consideration.

In conclusion Haweis made an anonymous offer of £500 as a first donation to equip the missionaries, on the condition that they evangelized the Pacific islands which had become 'familiar' to him, by much thinking and some expense. For him the proposed missionary society must be on a 'large scale'. Anything less would not produce lasting results. Thus the Baptist efforts and the original view of the Warwickshire Independents who sought to emulate them were brushed aside.[39] He appealed to the 'faithful brethren of all denominations ... to associate and form a society' because 'former experience had convinced' Haweis 'that only by a general union ... could a broad basis be laid for a mission'. The treatment he had received from the bishops taught him to expect nothing from them and to 'look to the zealous and spiritually minded ... only for cordial co-operation'.[40]

His hope for a co-operative venture of evangelical Christians accorded with the approach taken by Eyre and the London meeting but was at variance with Burder and the vision of the Warwickshire Independents. However, Burder was quick to acknowledge the importance of Horne's book. Haweis was disappointed that the Countess of Huntingdon's Connexion had become a Dissenting body, and in 1790 had warned her that the Connexion might form 'a branch of the Independent churches'. His turning away from the bishops and his alignment with Dissenters did not imply any wish to join the Independents.[41]

The missionary idea seized the imaginations and the consciences of evangelical Christians in the early 1790s. The initiative of the Warwickshire Independents was caught up, if not entirely overtaken, by the swelling chorus of London evangelicals – Anglicans, Scotsmen and Dissenters alike. The London meeting was keen to include the Warwickshire Independents in its plans and the *Evangelical Magazine*, the mouthpiece of the London meeting, gave them publicity too (although the June 1793 gathering at Warwick was reported only in December 1794). Nevertheless, the Warwickshire association's circular letter was written one year before Bogue's paper and Haweis's review and it too proved inspiring. Later in 1793 the ministers of Worcestershire associated for similar purposes to those of Warwickshire, recognizing 'the duty of aiding in furthering the same great object' of missionary work. George Osborn of Worcester preached to them on this theme.[42]

Similarly, the Independent ministers of north Staffordshire met in a newly formed association at Leek in 1794, stating, among their aims, that they wished to send 'a missionary abroad'. Their report that year was in large part 'the substance of one of William Carey's pamphlets, with a statistical account of the state of religion as it was then known in the world'. Again their concern reflects the influence of Edward

Williams's circular.[43] The Cambridgeshire ministers, both Baptists and Independents, opted for 'a plan similar to that of the ministers of Warwickshire' in December 1794. That same month the *Evangelical Magazine* noted that the Independent ministers of Suffolk had formed a county association. The editor suggested 'humbly' that they might adopt the plan and principles of the Warwickshire association.[44]

In June 1795 the Independent ministers of Kent resolved to set up monthly prayer meetings to spread God's truth 'particularly in foreign parts, where missionaries are intended to be sent'. Also in June 1795 the Western association, meeting at Plymouth, made a similar decision and stated its readiness to support the London committee in any plan to promote this cause. A meeting of ministers at Maidenhead at Easter 1795 had also adopted this policy. Thus the Warwickshire initiative, albeit modified by the involvement of the London evangelicals, continued to have effects in the counties, both in bringing ministers together in associations, and in directing their prayers towards foreign missions.[45]

IV

Bogue's address, which appeared in the *Evangelical Magazine* in September 1794, was reported in January 1795 as having 'awakened considerable attention'. By then Eyre, with his advocacy of a missionary society with a wide appeal, had rendered Bogue's desire for a society for Independents alone somewhat outdated. The report continued: 'That something may be done with effect, it is hoped that not only Evangelical Dissenters and Methodists will ... unite in instituting a Society for this express purpose, but that many members of the established Church of evangelical sentiments ... will also favour us with their kind co-operation'.

Such 'co-operation' would enable the enterprise to be carried off with 'effect' because separate, denominational action would lessen the impact of their missionary efforts. This address appears to accept that 'Evangelical Dissenters and Methodists' were in principle already committed but that evangelical Anglicans still needed persuading. Later the address makes mention of the prayerful example of 'our brethren in Warwickshire' whose conduct was 'worthy of general notice'. Nevertheless urgency was the order of the day, for 'every argument that recommends the object at all, tends also to stimulate to instant exertion'.[46] In February 1795 the *Evangelical Magazine* included an extract from a letter from the Warwickshire association, pressing for 'immediate steps' to propagate the gospel abroad. They were ready to send a delegate to a meeting whenever it should be held and believed a 'sufficient fund may be readily provided'.[47]

By November 1794, with Bogue's address and Haweis's review of Horne's letters both published, and religious opinion increasingly pre-occupied with the missionary cause, opposition to Bogue was cast aside and he joined the London ministers, meeting at Baker's Coffee House in the city. On 'the memorable 4th November 1794' Bogue attended this meeting. Others present were Eyre, Wilks, Steven, John Reynolds of Camomile Street Independent church, London, John Love (1756–1825), minister of the Scots' church, Bishopsgate, John Townsend, minister of Bermondsey Independent church, and Joseph Brooksbank, minister of the Independent church meeting at Haberdashers' Hall, London. The next day, 5 November, Bogue met many of the same ministers again with the object of forming 'a Society for the preaching of the Gospel among heathen nations. To qualify and appoint missionaries for that important end.' There was unanimous agreement.[48] The minutes for 17 February 1795 include the declaration that the signatories (34 in all) 'unite together' to plan 'an extensive and regularly organized Society to consist of Evangelical Ministers, & Lay Brethren of all denominations' to introduce the gospel to 'heathen and other unenlightened countries'.[49]

The third volume of the *Evangelical Magazine* declares in its preface that:

> the interest of religion in our own country may be said to be advancing ... Other counties following the example of their brethren in Warwickshire, begin to associate for the purpose of promoting the life of godliness in their own souls, and disseminating the knowledge of Christ ... Feeling for the millions of poor Heathens, perishing in their sins for lack of knowledge many wish to see a Society formed for sending Missionaries among them; and some steps are actually taking [place] to accomplish the laudable design.[50]

The Warwickshire ministers had set the pattern for other county associations to follow. They provided the example of missionary-minded evangelical Independents which the London ministers used to draw in the interest of other country churches, so that the demand for a missionary society became truly national.

In January 1795 the London committee sent out a circular letter in connection with the planned society. It outlined the progress made and announced the hope that a general meeting would be held early that summer. In April 1795 the Warwickshire Independents met at Stretton-under-Fosse to discuss the question, 'What can be done to encourage a foreign mission?' They expressed their frustration with the London committee's leadership of those attempting to found a missionary society – what is the cause of the apparent delay?, they demanded.

When was the general meeting? However, in a few days the Warwick-shire ministers had appointed three delegates to attend a meeting in London – George Burder, Robert Little and Sir Egerton Leigh.[51]

Sir Egerton Leigh, the 'preaching baronet', came from a family of Loyalists from the American colonies and settled at Little Harborough Hall, near Rugby, in Warwickshire about 1793. He set up an old farmhouse as a chapel where he preached, assisted at times by Moody, Burder and other ministers. Leigh preached in the neighbouring villages with some success although he met violent opposition also and was denounced in print by his brother, Sir Samuel Egerton Leigh, who insisted he abandon all hypocrisy and return to the Church of England. His brother claimed that Sir Egerton had obtained his estate only by marriage (referring to his recent union with a local heiress) and styled himself a 'Methodist Preacher'. Sir Samuel stated that Sir Egerton had 'not a true spark of Gratitude, Humanity, Charity, or any one Christian Virtue' while the *Evangelical Magazine* described him as a 'signal monu-ment of sovereign grace'. Another source states that 'he did not particularly excel' as a preacher and was 'by no means qualified' to be one. In May 1797 he was ordained in London 'to an itinerant ministry' with Rowland Hill, Wilks, Eyre and Burder all taking part in the service. In time Sir Egerton became a Baptist and founded Baptist churches in and around Rugby.[52]

Robert Little was serving Paradise Street Independent church, Birm-ingham 1791–97, when he became minister of Hanley Tabernacle, Staffordshire. At this time he appears to have been a 'strong earnest Evangelical' but in 1801 he left Hanley and was at Perth until 1806. He embraced first Sandemanian and then Socinian views and, after ministering at Little Cannon Street meeting house, Birmingham, he moved in 1817 to the Unitarian congregation at Gainsborough, Lin-colnshire. In 1819 he settled as Unitarian minister in Washington DC, where President Adams attended his church.[53]

George Burder kept in touch with London developments. In addition to its circular of January 1795 (itself widely distributed – Samuel Pearce sent a copy to Carey in India) the London meeting published an address written by George Burder. This was 'very widely circulated' and was judged to be 'an excellent performance'. Initially 300 copies were printed but one month later 15,000 were needed.[54] In his *An Address to the serious and zealous Professors of the Gospel, of every denomination, respecting an attempt to evangelize the Heathen*, Burder asked, 'Where are the heroes of the Church' who would willingly 'spend and be spent for Christ?' He pointed out that 'modern discoveries in geography', the voyages of Captain Cook and others 'have presented to us … a new world … of islands in the vast Pacific Ocean'. Missionary enterprises overseas, supported by the Danes, the Moravians, and the Scots 'have had some success' and the recent Baptist venture was said 'to wear a promising aspect'. Burder ended with a plea. 'Let us do something immediately. Life is short.' He proposed a general meeting in London at which 'a minister, or some other intelligent person, be deputed by the united congregations of each county' to attend, 'with some estimate of what each society may be ready to contribute annually'. In July 1795 Burder attended the London meeting for the first time.[55]

The *Evangelical Magazine* that month dispensed with its usual format and, instead of leading with a biography of spiritual interest, began with a letter headed *The Very Probable Success of a Proper Mission to the South Sea Islands*. The editor justified this decision by stating that 'this is a subject of the greatest magnitude, and occupies at present the attention of a considerable part of the religious world'. The author wrote:

> On frequent reflection ... of these islands, ever since their discovery, I have been strongly persuaded, that no other part of the heathen world affords so promising a field for a Christian mission ... No-where are the prospects of success more flattering, or the dangers and difficulties of the Missionaries less to be apprehended, except, as the worthy Admiral Bligh informed me, such as may arise from the fascination of beauty, and the seduction of appetite.

The writer expressed his admiration for the Moravians among 'the savage Eskimaux', and those 'pursuing the wandering tribes of American Indians ... I bow before such ardent zeal and feel the sharp rebuke of my own lukewarmness'. With regard to the Pacific islanders, he wrote: 'We have discovered them, and in a sort have brought them into existence ... We have contaminated them with our vices' yet have not informed them of the truths leading to salvation.

The letter was initialled T. H. (otherwise Thomas Haweis) and was an attempt by Haweis to persuade the promoters of the missionary society to evangelize Tahiti. The society did not then even exist (being founded formally in September 1795) but Haweis was keen to direct its policy. Haweis waxed lyrical in a 'descant of rapture' on Tahiti which, 'surrounded with a cluster of islands alike beautiful, rises as the Queen' and to him represented a realization of the classical fable of the Hesperides. Haweis then stands as a man of his time, entranced by Tahiti, with the image of its nymphs, golden apples and island gardens. Later he suggested to Burder that the mission to Tahiti, his own obsession, 'laid the broad basis of the Society'.[56]

The editor of the *Evangelical Magazine* noted, with this address, that the meeting 'for establishing this Society will be held in London, on the 22nd, 23rd, and 24th of September next'. The original plan had been to meet in late August at the Castle and Falcon but the date was changed. Six ministers were appointed to preach during the September inaugural meetings, with Burder, Bogue and Haweis among the first choices. The preparatory assembly, which met on the evening of 21 September, was chaired by Sir Egerton Leigh and letters of support were read out, including that of George Burder, on behalf of the Warwickshire association. Burder took to London a donation from his church in Coventry and, therefore, it is claimed that 'the first money ever contributed to the LMS was raised at a meeting held in the vestry of West Orchard chapel'. In addition Burder acted as secretary on 21 and 22 September and preached in Crown Court meeting house, Covent Garden, from Jonah 3:2, 'Arise, go unto Nineveh, that great city, and preach unto it the preaching that I bid thee.' The meeting house was so crowded that many doubted the wisdom of proceeding but as Burder began, 'the most serious and pleasing attention pervaded the whole congregation'. Among the first LMS directors were Burder, Leigh and Edward Williams, the only Welshman among them.[57]

George Burder was 'profoundly stirred' by the dramatic events of September 1795. He pondered on it immediately afterwards and also years later.

> It was a memorable season, to me the most memorable and interesting occasion of my life ... I remember that on the morning of my leaving London, the passengers getting out of the coach to relieve the horses, I walked up Highgate Hill; I stood and then took a parting view of the metropolis. I was deeply affected, and felt an earnest desire that my future life might, if preserved, be devoted to the aid of this work.[58]

Burder's realization of the importance of these inaugural meetings, both to him personally and to the churches' understanding of the gospel, shows the correspondence between the demands of a world-wide Christian vision and the warm evangelicalism of a sensitive and awakened soul. Here is no parochial evangelism, confined to the villages of Warwickshire or even England. Burder was simply overwhelmed.

The LMS directors had their differences of opinion. Thomas Haweis found David Bogue unyielding and prejudiced. Bogue was keen that the first missionaries should go to India but Haweis's proposal of the Pacific islands was unanimously passed although it was resolved that missions should be sent, as early as possible, 'to the coast of Africa, or to Tartary, by Astracan, or to Surat, on the Malabar coast, or to Bengal, or the Coromandel coast, or to the Island of Sumatra, or to the Pelew Islands'.[59]

In July 1800 Bogue agreed to train prospective missionaries at his Gosport academy. Haweis objected to sending educated men who aspired to be gentlemen but favoured sending artisans. He felt that Bogue would dissuade the candidates from serving in the South Seas, or from pioneering new territory, in favour of work in the colonies (each student chose his own place of service) and that the inter-denominational character of the LMS was threatened by grafting a missionary college onto an existing Dissenting academy, designed to train Congregational ministers. In later years Haweis complained to Burder that his protests had resulted in Bogue's pressing for his 'expulsion from the Society'. He saw Bogue as a tyrannical bishop. 'We refuse episcopal government and have adopted another Independent authority and set him at the head of it.'[60]

V

The Missionary Society took the name London in 1818 in part because its interdenominational aspirations had not been fully accepted. The evangelicals in the Church of England, led by the Clapham Sect and Charles Simeon, had founded the Church Missionary Society (the Society for Missions to Africa and the East) in 1799. Simeon had written: 'We cannot join the LMS; yet I bless God they stood forth. We must now stand forth ... directly not a moment to be lost.' Although they realized the breadth of vision of the LMS, Anglicans holding high offices felt unable to work within it, for episcopal government was a chief tenet of the CMS. Carey's view that Christians must engage separately in the mission field was borne out. In 1813 the first moves to found the Wesleyan Methodist Missionary Society were made and in 1824 the Committee for Foreign Missions of the General Assembly of the Church of Scotland was set up. Thus support from Scotland, from evangelical Anglicans, and others was diverted from the LMS, rendering it as a body closer to, and more reliant upon, the Independents, whose support remained secure.[61]

In January 1796 a committee of the three LMS directors – Burder, Leigh and Samuel Greatheed, minister of Newport Pagnell Independent church – met members of the Warwickshire association at Burder's chapel in Coventry to interview candidates for the proposed mission to Tahiti. Several were approved and recommended, among them two members of West Orchard chapel.[62] The first missionaries who travelled under the auspices of the Missionary Society were set apart in July 1796 when Edward Williams delivered the charge to them. He advised them to 'Enter therefore thy closet, or penetrate the woods of Otaheite, to converse with Jesus ... and then warmed with this holy fire go and warm others by social intercourse'.[63] He also stated that they should read the life and journal of David Brainerd, written 'by another who had drank deep of the same spirit, Mr Jonathan Edwards'.[64]

In 1789 a cheap edition of Edwards's *Humble Attempt* was published in England by John Sutcliff, the Baptist minister of Olney. This not only inspired the Northamptonshire Baptists but also Burder and the Warwickshire Independents. In 1814 Burder published an abridgement of Edwards's book entitled *United Prayer for the Spread of the Gospel Earnestly Recommended*, and in it he observed that regular and expectant prayer meetings were held as far afield as North America, Holland, Switzerland and Germany. He also published and edited Doddridge's Kettering sermon of 1741, noting its importance for the missionary movement.[65]

The importance of prayer was recognized by contemporaries. George Gill, minister of Market Harborough Independent church, where Philip Doddridge had served in the 1720s, wrote in February 1796 in enthusiastic support of the Missionary Society.

> ... it is now more than eleven years since a monthly meeting was established in this place, and which has been regularly attended to pray for a more general spread of the Gospel, and that the Lord would visit the heathen world with this invaluable blessing. I cannot but think that the formation of this Society is in part an answer to our prayers ...

Such a monthly prayer meeting was clearly an Independent response to the Baptist prayer call of 1784 and in Doddridge's former church too![66]

On 28 September 1795 John Eyre, George Burder and John Love (secretary of the provisional committee which launched the society) were appointed 'to draw up a Narrative' of the events which led to the society's formation. They designated the meeting of 4 November 1794 in London as 'the first concerted meeting'. Before this were 'various private conversations' held among 'a small, but glowing and harmonious, circle of ministers of various connections and denominations'. These resulted from Bogue's appeal of September 1794. They focused attention on Bogue, therefore, as the leading influence on events prior to the society's founding. However, they themselves, all three, were 'in the picture before Bogue' and arguably 'Burder's influence ... was at least as great, if not greater, than Bogue's though his personality did not lend itself to the role in which they set Bogue'. At his funeral in 1825 Bogue was referred to as 'the father of the Missionary Society' and some have seen Bogue as exercising 'a stronger directing influence' than any other founder. Burder and the Warwickshire ministers have been accorded a more modest place. Certainly 'persons and events were interwoven, one influencing another, as the leading figures were drawn into ever closer contact'. Yet other personalities than Bogue and other currents of influence were clearly at work.[67] Some historians have placed alongside Bogue as 'outstanding' both John Eyre and Thomas Haweis. Yet Ernest Payne saw the 'enthusiasm of Haweis', the 'fire' of Bogue, the London preparations, and the 'earnestness of Burder' as essential factors in the society's founding.[68]

The London group of LMS founders has been described as consisting of at least two parties – one loosely described as Methodist (including the Countess of Huntingdon's Connexion men, evangelical Anglicans and some Independents) and the second party consisting of Presbyterians, mainly Scotsmen ministering to London churches. John Eyre saw himself and Thomas Haweis as identifying with the Methodists. When contemplating resigning as secretary of the Missionary Society Eyre wrote to Haweis, concerning his successor. 'But who shall succeed me? It must not be one of the Party which have given us so much trouble.' However Eyre considered George Burder to be free of partisan affiliation. Burder was thus broadly acceptable and became secretary of the LMS in 1803, remaining in that position until 1827.[69]

The importance of Burder and alongside him, of Moody, Williams and the Warwickshire association is therefore easy to undervalue. Although they were first in the field, both as an organized body (following the Baptists), and as visionaries calling for prayer and action, their appeal was primarily denominational. As Burder recognized, they could not be accorded too great a prominence if the society was to gain widespread support on a broad evangelical base. Yet the Warwickshire ministers provided a model of enthusiasm and financial commitment which was crucial in rendering the Missionary Society national, rather than merely metropolitan in appeal and support. If the missionary societies were born out of 'a people's movement founded in prayer upon the personal experience of the saving power of Christ and a conviction that the proclamation of this to the whole world was an imperative necessity', then the people nationally must be involved rather than a select band of London ministers. The Warwickshire Independents brought the LMS closer to the people.[70]

Notes

1. A. J. Lewis, *Zinzendorf the Ecumenical Pioneer* (London: 1962), pp. 78–97; M. Deacon, *Philip Doddridge of Northampton* (Northampton: 1980), pp. 133, 145; R. H. Martin, *Evangelicals United* (London: 1983), p. 23.
2. E. A. Payne, 'Doddridge and the missionary enterprise', in G. F. Nuttall (ed.), *Philip Doddridge 1702–51* (London: 1951), pp. 79–101; P. Doddridge, *The Evil and Danger of Neglecting the Souls of Men* (London: 1742), pp. vii–ix.

3. Payne, 'Missionary enterprise', pp. 79, 100; *Before the Start* (London: 1942), pp. 5–6. In 1795 Samuel Pearce sent some sermons of Doddridge to Carey in India for Felix Carey, his son: S. Pearce, *Missionary Correspondence* (London: 1814), p. 40.

4. James Cook (see *DNB*) left records of his three principal voyages in *An Account of a Voyage round the World 1768–71* (London: 1773), *A Voyage towards the South Pole 1772–3* (London: 1777), *A Voyage to the Pacific Ocean 1776–80* (London: 1784); B. Willey, *The Eighteenth Century Background* (London: 1950), p. 14; Thomas Haweis writing in the *Evangelical Magazine* III (London: 1795), p. 264.

5. B. Stanley, *The History of the Baptist Missionary Society 1792–1992* (London: 1992), pp. 27–8. No more than three-fifths of the LMS directors were to live in or near London.

6. E. A. Payne, *The Prayer Call of 1784* (London: 1941), pp. 1–2; T. S. H. Elwyn, *The Northamptonshire Baptist Association* (London: 1964), pp. 16–18; J. C. Marshman, *The Story of Carey, Marshman, and Ward* (London: 1864), pp. 7, 10; Martin, *Evangelicals United*, p. 40.

7. *A Circular Letter from the Baptist Ministers and Messengers Assembled at Northampton* (London: 1786), p. 8.

8. Payne, *Prayer Call*, p. 6; J. Ryland, *The Life and Death of the Revd Andrew Fuller* (London: 1816), p. 153; I. Fletcher, 'The fundamental principle of the London Missionary Society, Part II', *The Transactions of the Congregational Historical Society* XIX (1963), p. 198.

9. R. Lovett, *The History of the London Missionary Society 1795–1895* (London: 1899), I, p. 12; H. F. Burder, *Memoir of the Rev George Burder* (London: 1833), p. 151; Payne, *Prayer Call*, p. 12; *Before the Start*, p. 9; Elwyn, *Northamptonshire Baptist Association*, pp. 30–1; A. H. Driver, *The London Missionary Society and the West Midlands* (London: 1945), p. 8.

10. Pearce, *Missionary Correspondence*, pp. 3, 4, 51–2; Driver, *London Missionary Society*; Martin, *Evangelicals United*, p. 59. On 30 October 1793 a small meeting house was opened for worship in Tamworth on the borders of Staffordshire and Warwickshire. Three sermons were preached – by Pearce of Birmingham, Burder of Coventry, and Hopper of Nottingham: *Evangelical Magazine* I (London: 1793), p. 252.

11. *Evangelical Magazine* II (London: 1794), p. 509; Lovett, *London Missionary Society*, pp. 171–2; Burder, *Memoir*, p. 157; W. T. Owen, *Edward Williams* (Cardiff: 1963), p. 58; J. Campbell, *Maritime Discovery and Christian Missions* (London: 1840), pp. 171–2.

12. J. Sibree and M. Caston, *Independency in Warwickshire* (London: 1855), p. 93; Lovett, *London Missionary Society*, pp. 12–13; *Evangelical Magazine* II (London: 1794), pp. 509–11.

13. Pearce, *Missionary Correspondence*, p. 4; Payne, *Before the Start*, p. 9; *Three Discourses delivered at the Ordination of Rev. Daniel Fleming* (Coventry: 1793).

14. W. Carey, *An Enquiry into the Obligations of Christians to use means for the Conversion of the Heathens* (Leicester: 1792), p. 84; Martin, *Evangelicals United*, p. 41; Payne, *Before the Start*, p. 11.

15. Owen, *Edward Williams*, p. 59.

16. Fletcher, 'Fundamental principle', part III, p. 224.
17. Owen, *Edward Williams*, p. 59; E. Davies (ed.), *The Works of the Rev. Edward Williams, DD* (London: 1862), IV, pp. 427–30; Driver, *London Missionary Society*, p. 9.
18. Burder, *Memoir*, p. 158.
19. *DNB*; Burder, *Memoir*, p. 170.
20. Burder, *Memoir*, pp. 223–4.
21. Sibree and Caston, *Independency*, pp. 91–2, 94, 134–41; Burder, *Memoir*, p. 210; H. McLachlan, *English Education under the Test Acts* (Manchester: 1931), p. 236; *Pious Remains of the Rev. James Moody* (London: 1809), pp. 9–11, 30; W. Field, *An Historical and Descriptive Account of Warwick* (London: 1815); 'Notes for a history of Brook St Congregational Church, Warwick', Warwick Record Office.
22. *DNB*; *Dictionary of Welsh Biography*; Owen, *Edward Williams*, pp. 56, 64, 67; A. H. Driver, *Carr's Lane 1748–1948* (London: 1948), pp. 31–3.
23. Sibree and Caston, *Independency*, p. 89; Driver, *London Missionary Society*, pp. 6–7; Owen, *Edward Williams*, p. 67.
24. Burder, *Memoir*, pp. 148–9.
25. Owen, *Edward Williams*, p. 60; Lewis, *Zinzendorf*, p. 78.
26. J. Morison, *The Fathers and Founders of the London Missionary Society* (London: 1864), II, p. 80; *Three Discourses*, p. 16; Lovett, *London Missionary Society*, pp. 21–2.
27. Martin, *Evangelicals United*, pp. 41–2; Fletcher, 'Fundamental principle', part III, p. 225; C. Northcott, *Glorious Company* (London: 1945), pp. 17–18. Eyre founded a school at Hackney which was attended by Burder's sons, John and Henry: Burder, *Memoir*, p. 170. Among the 24 original 'contributors' to the work of the *Evangelical Magazine* in 1793 were David Bogue, George Burder, John Eyre, Andrew Fuller, John Hey, John Ryland, Edward Williams, and Matthew Wilks: *Evangelical Magazine* I (London: 1793), flyleaf.
28. M. Horne, *Letters on Missions* (Bristol: 1794), p. vi.
29. *DNB*.
30. Lovett, *London Missionary Society*, pp. 6–10; Fletcher, 'Fundamental principle', p. 225; *Evangelical Magazine* II (London: 1794), pp. 378–80.
31. Stanley, *Baptist Missionary Society*, p. 27; Fletcher, 'Fundamental principle', p. 222; N. Goodall, *A History of the London Missionary Society 1895–1945* (London: 1954), p. 3. The Palau Islands are in the western Pacific, south-west of the Caroline Islands – under US sovereignty.
32. Fletcher, 'Fundamental principle', p. 225; Northcott, *Glorious Company*, p. 23; J. Bennett, *Memoirs of David Bogue* (London: 1827), pp. 36–146; Payne, *Before the Start*, p. 12; Morison, *Founders and Fathers*, I, p. 494; Goodall, *London Missionary Society*, p. 4.
33. Campbell, *Maritime Discovery*, pp. 172–3; Burder, *Memoir*, pp. 158–9; Payne, *Before the Start*, p. 11; *Evangelical Magazine* II (London: 1794), pp. 510–11; J. A. James, *Protestant Nonconformity* (London: 1849), p. 121.
34. *Evangelical Magazine* II (London: 1794), pp. 510–11.
35. *Evangelical Magazine* II (London: 1794), pp. 437–8.
36. Fletcher, 'Fundamental principle', p. 226.

37. A. S. Wood, *Thomas Haweis 1734–1820* (London: 1957), pp. 170–2, 177–8; G. Redford and J. A. James (eds), *The Autobiography of William Jay* (London: 1854), p. 476. Samuel Wallis (1728–95) first brought European attention to the Society Islands, including Tahiti. Bligh (1754–1817) made his epic voyage after the mutiny on the *Bounty*: *DNB*.

38. Horne, *Letters on Missions*, p. xii.

39. *Evangelical Magazine* II (London: 1794), p. 476; Campbell, *Maritime Discovery*, pp. 170–1; Redford and James, *William Jay*, pp. 476–7.

40. Wood, *Thomas Haweis*, pp. 191–2; *Evangelical Magazine* II (London: 1794), pp. 476–8.

41. E. Welch, *Spiritual Pilgrim: A Reassessment of the Life of the Countess of Huntingdon* (Cardiff: 1995), p. 207.

42. W. Urwick, *Nonconformity in Worcester* (London: 1897), pp. 113–14.

43. A. G. Matthews, *The Congregational Churches of Staffordshire* (London: 1924), pp. 171–2.

44. *Evangelical Magazine* II (London: 1794), p. 513.

45. Campbell, *Maritime Discovery*, pp. 179–80, 188–9.

46. *Evangelical Magazine* III (London: 1795), pp. 11–15.

47. *Evangelical Magazine* III (London: 1795), p. 73.

48. *Sermons Preached in London at the Formation of the Missionary Society* (London: 1795), p. vi.

49. LMS Board of Directors' Minute Book, 1795–98 – 17 February 1795, held at the School of Oriental and African Studies, London.

50. *Evangelical Magazine* III (London: 1795), p. iii.

51. Burder, *Memoir*, pp. 158–60; J. Waddington, *Congregational History* (London: 1878), IV, pp. 63–4; Lovett, *London Missionary Society*, pp. 17, 24–6.

52. Morison, *Founders and Fathers*, II, pp. 556–7; Sibree and Caston, *Independency*, pp. 393–8; *Letter from Sir Samuel Egerton Leigh, Knight Addressed to his Brother, Sir Egerton Leigh, Bart* (London: 1795), pp. iii, v; L. G. Champion, 'The preaching baronet', *The Baptist Quarterly* X.8 (October 1941), pp. 429–33.

53. W. D. McNaughton, *The Scottish Congregational Ministry 1794–1993* (Glasgow: 1994), p. 83; *The Victoria County History of Warwickshire*, VII, p. 45.

54. Pearce, *Missionary Correspondence*, p. 44; LMS Directors' Minute Book, 1795–98, pp. 2, 8; *Evangelical Magazine* III (London: 1795), pp. 160–3.

55. *Sermons Preached in London*, p. xiv.

56. *Evangelical Magazine* III (London: 1795), pp. 261–70; Wood, *Thomas Haweis*, pp. 197, 247–8; Campbell, *Maritime Discovery*, p. 201.

57. *DNB*; *Evangelical Magazine* III (London: 1795), pp. 261, 334, 421; Lovett, *London Missionary Society*, p. 30; *Reports of the Missionary Society 1795–1814* (London: 1814), I, p. 26.

58. Burder, *Memoir*, p. 169; Payne, *Before the Start*, p. 10.

59. Waddington, *Congregational History*, pp. 65, 78; *Reports of the Missionary Society*, p. 20.

60. Wood, *Thomas Haweis*, pp. 237–8.

61. Northcott, *Glorious Company*, p. 169; E. A. Payne, *The Church Awakes* (London: 1942), pp. 33, 34, 36–7.

62. Sibree and Caston, *Independency*, pp. 93–4; *Reports of Missionary Society*, I, p. 33.
63. Owen, *Edward Williams*, pp. 61–2.
64. E. Williams, *A Sermon and Charge* (London: 1796), p. 45; Owen, *Edward Williams*, p. 57.
65. G. Burder, *United Prayer for the Spread of the Gospel* (London: 1814); Payne, *Prayer Call*, pp. 11–12; Doddridge, *Evil and Danger* (London: 1819), pp. x, xi.
66. Fletcher, 'Fundamental principle', part II, p. 198; *Evangelical Magazine* IV (London: 1796), pp. 72–3.
67. *Sermons Preached in London at the formation of the Missionary Society*, p. vi; LMS Directors' Minute Book, p. 35; Fletcher, 'Fundamental principle', part III, pp. 222–3; Goodall, *London Missionary Society*, p. 4; J. Bennett, *The Translation of Elijah* (London: 1825), p. 3.
68. Wood, *Thomas Haweis*, pp. 194–5; Payne, *Before the Start*, pp. 11–12.
69. Fletcher, 'Fundamental principle', part II, pp. 192–3.
70. Northcott, *Glorious Company*, p. 14.

CHAPTER 3

'A finished monster of the true Birmingham breed': Birmingham, Unitarians and the 1791 Priestley Riots[1]

David L. Wykes

The 1791 Priestley Riots are perhaps the best known and certainly the most dramatic event in Birmingham's religious history. They are also one of the most formative events in the history of modern Unitarianism. Much has been written about the riots, and the observation of the bicentenary in 1991 provided further evidence of this continuing interest. The Priestley Riots have been a particular focus of attention amongst historians because of the level of interest which has developed during the past three decades concerning the subject of eighteenth-century crowds, rioting and other forms of popular activity.[2] This interest has, however, concentrated primarily on the behaviour, motives and composition of the crowd. Far less attention has been paid to the victims or to the longer-term consequences of the rioting,[3] though Professor Money's detailed study of eighteenth-century Birmingham was concerned with the question of the longer-term impact of the riots on the town. Dr Rose in the main study of the riots also sought to identify the victims, but this was largely in the context of trying to determine why they were the object of the mob's fury.[4] Despite the work of both these historians, little attention has been paid to the victims or to the lasting consequences of the disturbances, in particular their religious significance. Most accounts of the riots have been concerned with the rioting itself, and when the victims have been discussed the focus has been Joseph Priestley. Priestley was very far from being the only victim, nor was the impact of the riots confined to Birmingham or to the four days of rioting in July 1791. It is not only clear that the outrages at Birmingham encouraged 'Church and King' disturbances in other towns, and that at the time there were very real fears that the riots would spread, but that after Priestley had been forced to leave the town and the riots had ended, Dissenters in and around Birmingham remained

43

extremely apprehensive about the outbreak of fresh disturbances and were to continue to experience serious harassment and intimidation.[5]

I

The broad outline of the riots is well known. A dinner held at the Birmingham Hotel on 14 July by supporters of the French Revolution to commemorate the second anniversary of the fall of the Bastille was the incident that touched off the riots. Shortly before the dinner was held a seditious hand-bill was circulated in the town which served to heighten tension and led to fears of trouble. Probably at this point Priestley decided not to attend the dinner, which passed off without serious incident, though a noisy crowd greeted those who did attend with abuse, both on their arrival and when they departed. After the dinner had ended, at about 5 p.m., a mob gathered and around 9 p.m. attacked the hotel, breaking the windows and later looting the premises. They then attacked the New Meeting, where Priestley was minister, and set it on fire before marching to the Old Meeting. There they demolished the pulpit and pews before burning them in the street. The rioters moved on to Priestley's house at Fairhill in Sparkbrook, which they ransacked and then burnt, destroying Priestley's laboratory, library and manuscripts. Priestley escaped with his wife just before the mob arrived. The next day the rioters attacked John Ryland's mansion at Easy Hill, William Hutton's house and shop in the High Street, and John Taylor's house, Bordesley Hall. By the evening of the 16th, more houses had been ransacked and destroyed, including the house of William Russell, chairman of the New Meeting congregation, who was Priestley's friend and leading supporter. William Hutton's country house at Washwood Heath was also destroyed. On the evening of the 17th the first soldiers arrived and the rioters rapidly dispersed.[6]

During the four days of rioting about twenty buildings were seriously damaged or destroyed in the town, including both Old and New Meetings and the Unitarian chapel and parsonage at Kingswood. In addition, a Baptist chapel at King's Heath was ransacked. The victims were Unitarians, or those thought to be sympathetic to Unitarianism and Priestley. Recent studies of popular disturbances have emphasized social and economic factors when interpreting crowd behaviour, and have identified mobs as behaving in a rational, disciplined way, with specific targets and often having a high degree of organization. This approach was adopted by Rose in his study of the Priestley Riots, and, while recognizing that most of the victims were leading Unitarians, he emphasized instead their wealth and economic position, seeing the riots as 'an explosion of latent class hatred'. In part this may have reflected his interest in the origins of the working class.[7] Dr Ditchfield, however, has convincingly argued in a review of the current literature for the importance of religion as an explanation for the riots. He points to a series of studies by Professor Money, who, while finding evidence for contemporary difficulties in the Birmingham buckle and button trade, stressed the growing sectarian conflict between High Churchmen and radical Dissenters, as well as Priestley's own part in provoking that conflict. Dr Ditchfield also points to the broader developments in recent historical interpretation which stress the centrality of religious issues. In particular he cites the work of Colin Haydon, who reasserts anti-Catholicism, rather than Rudé's alternative of latent class hatred, as the prime motivation of the 1780 Gordon Riots. The established church, with the state's encouragement, had preached against Popery and anti-Trinitarianism for over a century; it is therefore not surprising to find the mob's concern with the defence of doctrinal orthodoxy, particularly on the question of the Trinity.[8]

The tendency of historians to describe the Old and New Meetings as Unitarian in this period can lead to confusion. During the eighteenth century many of the leading Presbyterian congregations in England were profoundly influenced by the intellectual developments of the period and by the doctrinal divisions which emerged within Dissent, especially over the Trinity. English Presbyterians came to modify traditional Calvinist doctrine by appealing to reason in matters of controversy. The appeal to reason and personal conscience inevitably led Presbyterians to tolerate a wide divergence in belief. It is not, however, easy to identify the doctrinal changes taking place, especially within individual congregations. In concentrating on the evidence for the opinions of the minister, there is a danger of assuming that such opinions were also shared by all the congregation. The evidence from local studies suggests that this was not the case, and that during the eighteenth century a diversity of theological opinions was to be found in most Presbyterian congregations.[9] During the first decades of the nineteenth century the rational Dissent of late eighteenth-century Presbyterianism came to be replaced by a more open declaration of Unitarian principles. Nonetheless, congregations which had adopted Unitarian sentiments before the nineteenth century continued to describe themselves as Presbyterian, in part because of a traditional aversion to sectarian labels, but also because until the Trinity Act was passed in 1813 Unitarians were specifically excluded from the limited benefits of the 1689 Toleration Act. An exception was the chapel opened in 1774 by Priestley's friend, the Revd Theophilus Lindsey, in Essex Street, London, as the first avowedly Unitarian chapel in the country. Interestingly, the chapel was originally registered under the Toleration Act for the religious worship of Protestant Dissenters.

The efforts to modify Calvinist orthodoxy were perceived by many as an attack upon fundamental Christian truths, in particular the Trinity, and as a result any departure from orthodoxy came to be equated with Socinianism, the abusive term generally used to describe Unitarianism in the eighteenth century. Rational Dissenters were therefore isolated from the rest of Dissent. In turn, following the French Revolution the state came to see the challenge to doctrinal orthodoxy and the demands for reform as subversive. Although most of the leading Presbyterian congregations had adopted rational religious beliefs by the end of the eighteenth century, the number where Unitarian opinions predominated was small. Historians, like contemporaries, have been too ready to describe any heterodox beliefs held by Presbyterians as Unitarian. Opponents of Dissent were even more indiscriminate. The Rector of Oldswinford, Robert Foley, in his *Defence of the Church of England*, claimed that Dissenters 'almost universally reject the Divinity of Christ'. Thomas Best, the Independent minister of Cradley, rejected the accusation, and continued:

> In Birmingham, where the proportion of their number to the rest of the Dissenters is greater than in any other Town in the Kingdom, it appears from Dr Priestley's account of the matter, that those called Orthodox are nearly three to one: And throughout England and Wales, they have been supposed to be as two, if not three to one, to the Socinians and Arians inclusive.[10]

Most contemporaries appear to have described the principal victims of the Priestley Riots as Presbyterians, or simply as Dissenters, but it is clear that Priestley's friends and the members of the Old and New Meetings were the focus of the riots because they were believed by the mob to be Unitarians and therefore a threat to both Church and State.

II

The full destructive force of the riots was directed against Priestley and his fellow Unitarians, and the extent of the mob's rage against them is clear. Samuel Garbett, one of the best-informed witnesses, with friends amongst both the victims and the magistrates, found 'the manner in which Resentment has been shewn to [the] Presbyterians', though falling short of murder, 'is astonishing'.[11] Priestley scarcely had time to escape before the mob arrived, and there is little doubt that, had he remained, he would have lost his life. After the destruction of their property, the other victims also fled from Birmingham, seeking refuge in neighbouring towns and villages, though not without difficulty because of the widespread intimidation.

Some of the Fugitives were under the necessity of wandering in the Night: to allow them Carriages was dangerous, & those of the Church of England, who benevolently received Presbyterian Females & Children into their Houses, were threatened with violence.[12]

In addition, many members of the Old and New Meeting congregations, fearing they too were likely to attract the attentions of the mob, also withdrew from the town, after taking what steps they could to safeguard their property. [13] At the end of the four days of disturbances, the whole town and much of the surrounding countryside had suffered intimidation from the mob. According to Samuel Garbett, in addition to the damage and destruction which the principal victims suffered, 'many other Houses have been injured', and many more in the town had their cellars emptied. Furthermore, 'Money was required I believe from Thousands'. Garbett himself had been subject to 'the violent Wrappings' on his door by 'many different Parties who came requiring Money'. These he had 'peremptorily refused', having, he believed, no reason to fear the mob. Nonetheless, 'I buried my Books of Accounts and Files of Letters, as seeing the Bounds of Law broke and that the worst might be expected from the Passions of some and Intoxication of others.' [14] Joseph Jukes, who had attended the dinner, 'Being informed my house was in the list of those intended to be Destroyed', enlisted the help of his friends, who 'recommended the speedy removal of all my furniture which was instantly adopted by means of Mr Wm Simpsons Cart and Mr Isaac Hortons waggon'. Having persuaded him to withdraw, his friends successfully preserved the house from destruction by the mob in his absence, though it cost Jukes the contents of his cellar and the 11 guineas he had left as bribes.[15] George Humphreys, another of the victims who had attended the dinner, was less fortunate. On the 15th, the day after the destruction of Priestley's house which was nearby, several parties of rioters threatened Humphreys and demanded money and liquor, 'which was given them in the hopes of preventing them from doing mischief'. Seven guineas and much drink was distributed. But the following morning a large mob assembled in front of the house, and:

with horrid Imprecations demanded more Liquor and money calling out Church & King and swearing they would pull the House down. Money & Liquor was given them & every persuasion & Temptation offered them to desist that could be thought of, [but all efforts proving in vain] ... Between the hours of 10 & 12 they began to put their Threats into Execution by breaking the Windows and in a very short time they forced their way into the House and demolished & destroyed all the Furniture that was in it partly in the House and Partly

by throwing it out of the Windows and knocking and breaking it to
pieces upon the Pleasure Ground before the House.

Fortunately, the rioters were unable to obtain any fire to burn the
house or the furniture. [16]

There is evidence at the outbreak of the rioting that the mob had
clearly identified its targets: the two Unitarian meeting houses and
Priestley's house at Fair Hill. There is also evidence for the complicity
of the local magistrates in the disturbances. Certainly they appear to
have made little effort to prevent the destruction of the two Unitarian
chapels and Priestley's house. [17] The situation becomes less clear as the
disturbances developed and the attacks became more generalized.
Priestley and his fellow sufferers, however, became convinced that they
were the victims of a conspiracy, that their houses had been carefully
marked for destruction, and that the local magistrates had connived at
the actions of the mob. As the rioting spread, the magistrates made a
belated attempt to stop the disturbances, but by that time their efforts
were ineffectual.[18] The actions of the 'Church and King' mob clearly
attracted others from outside the town, whose motivation was more
obviously personal gain than the defence of the church. As a result,
the character of the riots changed as the disturbances spread into the
surrounding countryside. Bands of rioters moved out of Birmingham
in pursuit of further targets, and were joined by rioters from the
neighbouring villages, while in turn 'Colliers, Lime men and other
disorderly persons about Dudley, Sedgley, Tipton, Bilston, Darleston,
Wolverhampton & Wednesbury' visited Birmingham attracted by
the disturbances still continuing in the town. [19] Garbett told his
patron, the Marquis of Lansdowne, that:

> the Terrour that is spread thro' the country by Depredations for 10
> Miles from Birmingham by the South West to Bromsgrove & from
> thence towards Dudley, & the mischief done is prodigiously more
> than will ever appear in Print.[20]

The disorders and general lawlessness at this late stage became an
excuse for other groups to extort drink and money from townspeople,
irrespective of whether they were Unitarians or not, though the 'Church
and King' element still clearly persisted. Jukes, on his return to the
town after the disturbances had ended, saw:

> the words CHURCH and KING on every house as likewise on most of
> the doors – I also learned that no person had been permitted to pass
> in safety unless he wore a blew ribbon on his hat or Coate and cried
> Church and king for ever – Damn the prisbyterians.

Colonel De Lancey, who commanded the troops sent to restore order, was also struck by the outward professions of loyalty, for there was 'not a house even for miles round the town on which there was not written in very conspicuous characters "Church & King for ever"'.[21] Furthermore, although the whole town suffered from this lawless behaviour, the principal victims who had their property ransacked and destroyed were, with the exception of William Hutton, all Unitarians.[22] Garbett was convinced that the magistrates' neglect in defending the Unitarians and their property would have serious repercussions for the future law and order in the town. 'And tho' all is now quiet, a Consideration of the future is still a frightfull Circumstance.' For the same reason he was greatly concerned by the failure of the authorities to pursue and punish the rioters after the disturbances had ended. In the week following the riots he told Lansdowne of 'the very mortifying Lukewarmness of the Magistrates not to say discouragement to such Measures as would be likely to bring Offenders & Pilferers to Justice'. He was quite clear as to the consequences of this failure for Unitarians: 'From what I see He must be a Bold Presbyterian who will have a House in the Country near this Town'.[23]

III

Unitarians continued to suffer serious intimidation after the riots had ended. As a result of the intensity of the attacks upon Unitarians and their property, the Priestley Riots undoubtedly gave great encouragement to 'Church and King' feeling in the town, and, it is clear, also in many other parts of the country.[24] But the riots were also to transform Priestley into a demonological figure, and nowhere more vehemently than in Birmingham. Although Priestley had hopes of returning to preach to his former congregation, he quickly realized that he would never be able to live in the town again. He was to find that the party spirit in Birmingham prevented him from making even a brief appearance. He had thought of returning to preach on the last Sunday in July, only two-and-a-half weeks after the riots. The visit was postponed because of the Assizes, when a number of rioters were to be tried. It was feared that an appearance by Priestley would only inflame the situation. A further attempt early the next month was also put off for similar reasons, as affidavits were being sworn against some of the magistrates. Priestley and his friends at this time concluded that, far from dying down, the party spirit in the town seemed actually to be increasing. Samuel Garbett told Priestley's old patron, the Marquis of Lansdowne, that 'the Rage against him personaly is more extravagant than anybody can believe who doth not see it'.[25] In addition to the earlier attempts, a visit planned by Priestley for mid-August also had to be abandoned, for in the words of his friend, the Revd Theophilus Lindsey, minister of Essex Street chapel:

> The state of things at B——m is really frightful. Dr P. cannot come there with safety of a long time, if ever. Had he ventured to come and preach, there was a scheme formed to have defeated him, and to have attacked and overpowered the soldiers, had he been protected by them.[26]

An attempt a month later, during the second week in September, to pay a passing visit to see his friends in Birmingham while on his way to stay with his daughter at Dudley, also foundered because of the continued threats to his safety and to the peace and well-being of the Dissenters in the town:

> he had received letters from one of his friends, that encouraged him to come to Birmingham, just to show himself for one day, and go and to see his daughter ... But the next day a letter came from his son William representing the state of the town in a more unfavourable view.[27]

Even his congregation at New Meeting, though anxious for him to resume his ministry after so long a delay, concluded reluctantly that it would 'be better for him not to come at all, "Lest the savages should be let loose upon him" ... the intolerant spirit grows worse and worse'. The sermon that Priestley had intended to deliver himself 'upon the ruins of his late meeting-house' was eventually given on his behalf by John Coates, one of the two ministers of Old Meeting. Priestley was never to return to Birmingham.[28]

If the intense hostility towards Priestley made it impossible for him even to visit Birmingham, then, as he himself acknowledged, the town was a most uncomfortable place for the other victims and for Unitarians in general. William Russell, who had returned to Birmingham a week after the disturbances, was so convinced that more rioting was inevitable that 'He is getting arms into his own house, and means openly to train his servants to the use of them, and to advise all his friends to do the same. He never goes abroad without a brace of charged pistols.' A month after the riots had ended, a family of Unitarians from Manchester visiting the town found 'even now, the words Church & King are printed in capital letters with chalk on most houses under the windows of the second floors',[29] while Lindsey told a friend that:

> The Birmingham Newspapers are full of the most inflammatory things, and handbills of the same kind are in continual circulation.

There are two printed answers to Dr Priestley's letter, one a pamphlet, full of the most virulent invectives.

But even more disturbing was the evidence for the hostility towards Unitarians from those in authority. Priestley, also writing at this time, told his brother-in-law that 'the Magistrates, who deserved the severest punishment, have had the thanks of a town meeting, and presents voted them'. Particular anger was felt at the reported reception given to the under-sheriff, John Brooks, who, despite the affidavits sent up to the Treasury Solicitor establishing his part in the riots, not only escaped punishment but returned to Birmingham in triumph, having had, it was believed, 'a most gracious reception both from Mr Pitt and Mr Dundas'.[30] According to the future law reformer Samuel Romilly, who had attended the trials of the rioters at the Warwick Assizes:

> The rage which prevails in Warwickshire against the Dissenters is not to be conceived by any one who has not been there. There is no story so incredible, no calumny so gross, as does not meet with implicit credit, and the most speedy propagation among the friends of Church and King; and the complete refutation of one calumny, instead of begetting distrust of the truth of another, only procures it a more easy reception In a word, the spirit that prevails against Dissenters now in Warwickshire, and, I believe, in some of the adjoining counties, is not unlike that which raged against the Catholics in the time of the famous Popish plot.[31]

Further difficulties were created for the Unitarians in Birmingham by the decision of 'the Church people in general ... to have no dealings with the Dissenters'. Unitarians in Stourbridge, and almost certainly in other towns, faced similar boycotts as a result of the increase in 'Church and King' feeling aroused by the Priestley Riots.[32]

Not surprisingly, there were reports concerning the Unitarians in Birmingham that 'a spirit of great timidity had seized many, so as to make them reluctant to avow their principles'. The two leading victims of the riots, John Taylor and John Ryland, were so fearful of fresh disturbances that they were anxious, almost at any cost, to avoid giving occasion for further offence. Since they were leading townsmen, as well as the greatest sufferers from the riots, their opposition to any move which might prevent popular feeling from subsiding created considerable difficulties for those Dissenters who wanted to see the authors of the disturbances, and in particular the magistrates, punished. Taylor and Ryland were almost alone in declining to sign the address sent by the members of New Meeting on 5 September requesting Priestley to return as minister. It seems likely that they were also the two members who called upon the chapel warden to insist that the letters exchanged with Priestley in early August 'should not be printed as ordered'.[33] Priestley himself, when preparing his *Appeal to the Public*, found that his determination to expose the part played by the magistrates and the clergy in the riots was clearly not welcomed by some of his supporters in Birmingham. He admitted to his brother-in-law that 'several of my friends in Birmingham wish to have it either suppressed or much softened', though his friends in London 'approve of it as it now is'. 'In my own opinion, if I write at all, it ought not to be with less spirit than I have usually shewn; and there are as bold, and as offensive things in several of my former publications as in this.' Nonetheless, 'if cancelling a few leaves will satisfy my friends, I shall have no objections to do it'. A year later, in October 1792, Priestley was still referring to 'the Quietists', those Birmingham Unitarians who disliked the aggressive stance that he and certain of his supporters had adopted.[34] The concerns expressed by Unitarians still living in Birmingham were not unfounded. Priestley's attack on the charity feoffees at Stourbridge in the second part of his *Appeal to the Public*, published in 1792, was to exacerbate the ill-feeling which already existed in that town between High Churchmen and Dissenters.[35] But attempts to temporize proved even more disastrous. The victims, having engaged the best counsel to pursue their claims for compensation at the Worcester Assizes, were persuaded to give him up, because, they were told, their use of leading counsel:

> would hurt their cause & blow up the flames which all wise & moderate men would chuse to avoid ... [and because they] dreaded another attack – they resigned Plomer, their best advocate at Worcester, to their antagonists, [and Plomer] now from resentment became their most bitter enemy & disputed the value of almost every individual article.[36]

IV

The trials of the rioters at the Worcester and Warwick Assizes gave Priestley and his supporters further evidence of the level of hostility towards them, and of the general unwillingness of their fellow townsmen to see the individuals responsible for the outrages punished. Only a handful of the rioters were indicted and the juries seemed determined not to convict.[37] Lindsey told Samuel Shore that at the Worcester Assizes in mid-August:

> of four rioters, three of the most notorious are acquitted, contrary to the opinion of the judge, and all the council that attended; and only

one condemned, and he so insignificant, that Mr Russell said he should recommend him to mercy. This being the case at Worcester, one may guess what will be done at Warwick, where prejudices run so much higher.[38]

Lindsey's fears were to be confirmed. At the Warwick Assizes held at the end of the month, twelve prisoners were indicted, of whom eight were acquitted, including Robert Whitehead, 'which rather surprised some people'.[39] John Stokes, accused of demolishing the Old Meeting, was also acquitted despite the production of the original registration certificate of 1689. The confusion over street names was used as an excuse to dismiss the case, for it was claimed that Old Meeting was not the meeting house named in the certificate, and its destruction therefore did not fall within the terms of the Riot Act.[40] Even more notorious was the case of the bellman who had been identified as having had a major role in inciting the mob. He was found not guilty, because 'he was very much in liquor at the time, and it being proved that he was rather addicted to drinking, and an harmless, inoffensive fellow'. The prosecution did not bother to proceed against another because of his youth.[41] Discussing the trials, Priestley told his brother-in-law that:

> every thing has been done by the Court, as well as the country, to screen the rioters. Not one has suffered merely for the riots, but because they were infamous characters in other respects; and those who gave evidence against them are now exposed to insult and danger.[42]

Such was the spirit in which the trials took place that at Warwick one of the counsel for the prosecution felt it necessary to remind the jury of their duty to convict the guilty, for he said 'it was now cried about the streets ... that they were determined to acquit all the rioters'. The judge supported counsel when the remark drew forth an indignant response from the foreman of the jury.[43] As a result of the trials, the reputation of the Warwick jury became so notorious that, according to William Hutton, 'a gentleman, soon after this, hunting with Mr Corbett's fox-hounds, was so sure of killing the fox, that he cried "Nothing but a Birmingham Jury can save him!" '[44]

The same prejudice coloured the trials for compensation. The first claims were tried before a special jury at the Worcester Assizes in March 1792. The judge, Grose, who had sat during the trials for the Gordon Riots in 1780, by all accounts made every attempt to ensure an impartial trial. The members of the jury, however, behaved no better than the jurors who earlier had acquitted most of the rioters. The treatment of the victims by the counsel for the defendants awakened the greatest indignation amongst the Dissenters. John Taylor, in support of his claim, supplied a detailed inventory of every article that had been destroyed, itemizing even the bird-cages and pig-troughs. 'This gave abundance of room for the wit & cavilling ingenuity of the pleaders.' The behaviour of Plomer, the counsel for the defence, who took every opportunity 'to flatter & humour the hostile spirit', aroused particular anger. He 'had the effronterie to charge Mr Taylor with the dreadful crime, of assisting at the *seditious pandemonium*', though he was actually at Cheltenham.[45] Hardly surprisingly, the treatment of Priestley when his case came up for trial at Warwick was even worse. On his appearance in court, 'a man pointing to him, cryed out, "There is DR PRIESTLEY, the man who has been the cause of all these riots, and the death of so many innocent people."' Nonetheless, stories that he had been pelted with stones and dirt by the Warwick crowd were denied, and Priestley himself made light of the insults he had received.[46] During the trials one of the counsel for the defendants, Hardinge, 'the ministerial minion' who was a Welsh Judge, charged Priestley with 'sedition, rebellion & as the author of the infamous handbill, tho' the judge corrected him for the last several times'. Hardinge also read out highly selective passages from Priestley's many publications, to give the impression that his writings were seditious.

The first cause tried at Worcester was John Taylor's claim for £4,000, which the jury reduced by a quarter, awarding a sum of only £3,000. This outcome was unfortunate, as it appeared, according to one observer, to establish:

> a certain mode of calculation or rather estimation, it brought with in a much narrower compass the succeeding tryals. Upon the whole it was agreed to strike more than one third of the demand – & only about £5000 was allowed for above eight that was claimed.[47]

The trials at Warwick followed the pattern established at Worcester. When the compensation for Priestley's losses was assessed, the jury refused to allow him more than half his claim, which, 'when the Land lord is paid for the house will be a very moderate allowance for his furniture. While his MSS, philosophical apparatus & Library pass for nothing.'[48] It seemed to Kenrick:

> So far from the smallest grain of sympathy with the innocent sufferers, or anything like a marked detestation of the promoters of this hellish business – or the most distant wish to bring them to light & condign punishment: one cannot help observing not only a general apathy & indifference on the subject but a smile of triumph & complacency in hearing or rehearsing any part of this disgraceful transaction.[49]

Not only did the victims who successfully pursued their claims receive inadequate compensation, they had to wait two years before such limited compensation as they had been awarded was actually paid. Moreover, interest was only payable from 1 January 1793, though the losses occurred in July 1791. Hutton was convinced that the victims would never have been paid even the inadequate amounts which had been awarded, but 'for the vigilance of Lord Aylesford, and some of the county gentlemen, who seemed determined that the Hundred of Hemlingford should not lie under the stigma of so vile a fraud'.[50]

V

Because the two Unitarian congregations in Birmingham had suffered particularly severely from the mob's fury, it is not surprising that their affairs were in considerable disarray in the months which followed the riots. Both meeting houses had been totally wrecked and could not be used. Moreover, the members of the New Meeting congregation faced an additional complication. Not only was Priestley unable to return, but the second minister, John Edwards, was also absent due to ill-health.[51] Nonetheless, the immediate problem for the two congregations was to find a place in which to worship until the two meeting houses were rebuilt. The search proved difficult, in part perhaps because, having decided to meet together for worship, there were few suitable buildings large enough to accommodate a joint congregation. There was also some reluctance to offer a building to Unitarians at this time, either through fear or prejudice. There were even problems in acquiring an initial place in which to meet until the joint congregation could obtain a building of its own. After an application to use the Wesleyan Methodist Chapel had failed, the two congregations held their first service together at the Carr's Lane Independent chapel on the afternoon of Sunday 24 July. Although it was nearly a week after the riots had ended and peace had been restored, none of the four ministers serving the two congregations had yet returned to Birmingham.[52] The use of the Carr's Lane chapel was intended as only a temporary arrangement, but it was not until three months later that they were able to acquire a three-year lease of the Amphitheatre in Livery Street. The first service in the new premises took place on 13 November, when John Coates, one of the ministers of Old Meeting, preached a sermon from John 4: 23, 24: 'But the hour cometh, and now is, when the true worshippers shall worship the Father in Spirit and in truth.'[53] The problem concerning ministerial supply remained pressing. Although both of the Old Meeting ministers had returned, neither of the New Meeting ministers was able to resume his ministry. The difficulties faced by the New

Meeting were compounded by the uncertainty over whether Priestley would in fact return. It was not until early November that he finally informed the congregation of his resignation.[54] The congregation invited Jones to be his successor, but Jones was not to take up his ministry until the summer of 1792.[55]

The lack of adequate ministerial support together with the uncertainty over Priestley was to prove serious both for the New Meeting and for the recovery of Unitarianism in the town. It was not until nearly three weeks after the riots, on 4 August, that the members of New Meeting again met together as a congregation. They took the opportunity to send an affectionate address to Priestley, and ended by saying that 'although you are not immediately returning to us, yet we look forward with pleasure to those happier times when you may resume your pastoral labours here, with safety and satisfaction'. A few days later the young people of the congregation sent a similarly warm address; nonetheless, they also expressed their fears that Priestley might seek asylum elsewhere. Congregational life gradually resumed. Although progress was slow, services had at least been restarted within a month of the riots. In contrast, at Kingswood, where the meeting house and parsonage had also been destroyed in the riots and the minister, John Hobson, forced to leave, the congregation did not meet together again for worship until early the following year, after a break of some seven months, when through the exertions of Edwards, the minister of the New Meeting, a house was registered and services resumed.[56] Although New Meeting appears to have recovered under Edwards and Jones, there is evidence, for both New and Old Meetings, that the congregations experienced longer-term difficulties as a result of the riots. Despite the original intention to rebuild the two meeting houses as quickly as possible, the rebuilding of Old Meeting was not completed until October 1795, and New Meeting until August 1802. A major cause of the delay appears to have been financial. It was resolved in April 1794 that the work at Old Meeting 'should proceed more slowly than hitherto it has, but in such manner as to keep on some workmen'. But even this proved too much and work had to be suspended two months later. It was also reported that there was 'a considerable deficiency in annual subscriptions due to death & removals'. It is likely that the delays in the rebuilding of New Meeting were caused by similar problems. There are no general meetings of the New Meeting congregation recorded between October 1792 and June 1795, which suggests a falling away of interest. When Jones resigned as minister in 1795, a successor was not appointed; instead Edwards took over as sole pastor.[57]

VI

During the winter of 1792 attacks on Dissenters in Birmingham and elsewhere were overtaken by a more organized and comprehensive government-inspired onslaught against radicals and reformers generally. The violent course taken by political events in France, together with the growth of political radicalism and demands for reform at home, combined to create widespread alarm and, amongst the propertied classes and government, a very real fear of revolution. These fears were to lead to the establishment of local loyalist associations, which were to play a major role, not only in organizing militant conservative opinion, but in intimidating reformers and supporters of France by detecting and suppressing all allegedly seditious activities. Throughout the country Unitarians were among the main victims, because of their unpopular religious opinions and their support for France and reform.[58] Local loyalist associations sought to make it impossible for any individual to avoid having to declare his sympathies in public, and addresses were often drawn up in terms which made it difficult for radicals to demonstrate their loyalty and maintain their principles. In Birmingham, Unitarians overcame this difficulty by holding separate meetings to draw up their own addresses, but they took care to convey their sentiments to the public meeting of loyalists.[59]

The formation of the local loyalist associations was to lead to renewed violence in Birmingham and other towns. In early December 1792 there were serious disturbances in Birmingham and Manchester. The Manchester riots, directed against the houses of the leading reformers in the town, were the worst provincial disturbances since the Priestley Riots. At Birmingham a large party of 'Loyal True Blues' visited the house of William Hutton at eleven at night, 'and violently knocking at the door and window-shutters, they obliged the family to come to the windows, and audibly exclaim "Church and King"'. Another victim of the earlier riots, George Humphreys, had a few windows broken, but was able to bribe the party to depart without further damage after giving them five or six guineas. Another party was said to have visited John Taylor, perhaps the greatest victim of the riots. Both Taylor and Humphreys considered it too dangerous to remain and retired from the town with their families.[60] The activities of the loyalist associations and 'Church and King' clubs were reinforced by government-sponsored intimidation and repression. A series of repressive acts and state trials, together with the suspension of Habeas Corpus, severely restricted civil liberties and brought almost all attempts at reform to a halt. The repressive measures began with the increasing concern of Pitt's government with radicalism and sedition, especially following the publication of the second part of Thomas Paine's *Rights of Man*, and resulted in the proclamation against seditious libels in May 1792. William Belcher, 'bookseller', presumably the son of Priestley's Birmingham publisher, the Unitarian James Belcher, was convicted at the Warwick Assizes for selling *The Jockey Club* and *The Letter addressed to the Addressors on the late Proclamation* and sentenced to three months' imprisonment.[61]

By the mid-1790s the enthusiasm with which Dissenters had welcomed the French Revolution had given way to defeat and a sense of hopelessness as war, repression, and events in France had taken an increasingly disastrous course. Many were to reject their earlier enthusiasm for reform and radicalism, abandoning politics, Dissent and in a few cases even religion itself. They included some of the most promising of the younger ministers, including David Jones, who resigned from New Meeting in 1795, and became a barrister at the Court of Chancery.[62] The long delay in the rebuilding of the Old Meeting, and even more of New Meeting, also points to the loss of enthusiasm and support amongst Birmingham Unitarians. The clearest evidence for this disillusion comes from the numbers who decided to leave the country. The increasingly gloomy political situation led many Dissenters and radicals, of whom Priestley is only the most celebrated example, to emigrate to America. His friend William Russell, the chairman of the New Meeting congregation, retired from Birmingham to Matson House near Gloucester in mid-1793, and in July 1794, four months after Priestley had sailed for America, took passage from Falmouth to follow his friend.[63]

VII

The lasting feature of the Priestley Riots was the level, intensity and persistence of the 'Church and King' spirit and the strength of the disturbances directed against Unitarians both in Birmingham and the rest of the country, which continued long after the riots themselves had ended, and which in turn were to fuel a conservative reaction against radicals in both religion and politics. In Birmingham there is a considerable amount of evidence concerning the widespread expressions of hostility and bigotry towards the victims and Unitarians in general in the weeks and months after the fateful four days in July. Indeed, the victims and their friends were convinced that this hatred, far from dying down, actually increased in the months after the riots. Nonetheless, it is clear that this hostility persisted for a far longer period than the riots themselves could have generated. In part the persistence of such intense hostility is explained by a series of untimely events, in particular the trials of the rioters in August 1791 and the claims for compensation tried in March and April 1792, which helped to reawaken the flames of intolerance. It was unfortunate for the 'Church and King' victims that the main disturbances took place within two different county jurisdictions. On each occasion the Worcestershire trials acted as a rehearsal for the trials which followed at Warwick, thus enabling the 'Church and King' supporters to organize themselves to prevent a verdict favourable to Priestley and the other victims, and to allow for a build-up of prejudice. It is also clear that the outrages at Birmingham encouraged 'Church and King' disturbances in other towns, and that at the time there were very real fears that the riots would spread. During the Priestley Riots the disturbances not only moved outside the town into the surrounding countryside, but Dissenters and reformers were threatened by mobs in Coventry, Bromsgrove, Dudley, Stourbridge, and in places as distant as Bristol, Taunton and Maidstone. At Exeter Sir John Bowring's grandfather was burnt in effigy in the cathedral yard because he was a radical. Priestley's brother-in-law, John Wilkinson, the celebrated ironmaster, thought it prudent to take measures to defend his ironworks near Wrexham with swivels, guns and howitzers.[64]

It is clear that every effort was made to exploit the calamity which had befallen the Unitarians in Birmingham, and to direct and maintain the level of abuse against Priestley, his fellow victims, and Unitarians in general. Ministers who were known for their support of the French Revolution or for their heterodox religious opinions were particularly vulnerable to the increase in 'Church and King' feeling which followed the Priestley Riots. Public celebrations, such as the King's birthday (4 June), provided opportunities for loyalist demonstrations and for attacks on opponents by 'Church and King' supporters. Understandably, the first anniversary of the Priestley Riots in July 1792 proved a worrying time for those Dissenters throughout the country who still supported reform. There were particular fears concerning the rumours that Dissenters in Birmingham intended to hold another dinner on 14 July. To the evident relief of Dissenters elsewhere, this was denied.[65] Individual victims continued to suffer abuse. In April 1792 Samuel Kenrick in Bewdley was outraged to hear someone shout out in public 'Church and King' at the approach of John Taylor's coach. William Hutton, about this time, was the subject of a scurrilous caricature, which attacked in particular his claim for compensation, and the level of abuse directed against Priestley continued unabated.[66] The level of 'Church and King' activity in Birmingham was so strong in the summer of 1792 that Colonel De Lancey, who had been sent by the government to inquire into radical sentiment in the country, was able to report that radicals in the town represented no threat.[67]

VIII

The significance and long-term consequences of the Priestley Riots are not easy to assess. During the 1780s New Meeting had been one of the leading congregations in the country, and under Priestley's leadership its members had been in the vanguard of the campaign for the repeal of the Test and Corporation Acts in 1789–90. After the departure of Priestley, and also of his friend William Russell, the Unitarians in Birmingham were never to take such a prominent part in national politics, and in the aftermath of the riots their involvement in reform movements locally was also significantly reduced until well into the nineteenth century. The ministers who succeeded Priestley were not of his stature. The impact of the Priestley Riots was not, however, restricted to Birmingham. Not only did the disturbances caused by the riots extend far beyond the town, but they influenced the development of 'Church and King' feeling, and indeed indirectly the emergence of modern Unitarianism. Although the difficulties Dissenters experienced as a result of the riots were later to be overshadowed by the loyalist reaction and government-inspired intimidation during the winter of 1792, there is evidence that the Priestley Riots influenced and encouraged the development of 'Church and King' feeling in the country. The riots certainly helped to turn Priestley into a national figure of hate. Priestley not only featured in the satires and caricatures of Gillray and Cruickshank but was burnt in effigy with Tom Paine, identified by contemporaries as the most dangerous of all radicals: 'Damn the Presbyterians' entered the 'Church and King' repertoire.[68] It is also clear that the riots abruptly shattered the confidence that Rational Dissenters and Unitarians felt concerning their position in society and their hopes of removing the remaining civil disabilities against Dissenters. The riots therefore reversed the earlier optimism over the progress of reform. Moreover, the general reaction to the riots, in particular the failure to punish those responsible, the inadequate and tardy payment of compensation, the apparent public condonement of the outrages, and, more significantly, what such behaviour revealed about official and popular attitudes towards Dissent, was as important in undermining Dissenting confidence as the savagery of the riots themselves. There is little doubt of the shock experienced by Rational Dissenters and Unitarians throughout the country on receiving news of the disturbances, nor of the increasing sense of isolation that radicals felt.[69]

The Priestley Riots were not the only serious disturbances against Dissenters in Birmingham or, indeed, in the country as a whole during the eighteenth century. Birmingham had had a history of disorder of varying degrees of seriousness, much of it directed against religious Dissent. In 1715, the meeting houses of both Presbyterian congregations were sacked, and the disturbances were more serious and on a far greater scale nationally than the riots of 1791. Attacks on Dissenters and their meeting houses stretched from Oxfordshire, across the Midlands, to Lancashire and Yorkshire.[70] Old and New Meetings were the main focus for major riots in Birmingham on three occasions in the eighteenth century: in 1714, 1715, and in 1791. In addition, there were also major food riots in 1756 and 1757, 1762 and 1763, and 1766. There were disturbances against Methodists in 1751 and Quakers in 1759, and in 1780 there were very real fears that the Gordon Riots, the anti-Catholic disturbances which set London ablaze in the worst public disturbances in the capital of the modern period, would also lead to disturbances in Birmingham. Although a crowd of about 1500 assembled, the disorder was contained. Compared with other eighteenth-century disturbances, both in terms of loss of life and the depth of religious prejudice, the Priestley Riots were not especially violent. Dr Haydon's study of anti-Catholicism in eighteenth-century England records not only the level of prejudice against Catholics, but also attacks on their persons and property. The early Methodists also suffered severely from the mob. In North America the Episcopalian clergy experienced exile and the loss of their property as a result of the American War of Independence.[71] There was, however, an important distinction between the riots of 1791 and those earlier in the century. In 1714 and 1715 Dissenters had been attacked because of their loyalty to the Hanoverian succession; in 1791 they were attacked for their supposed lack of loyalty. In contrast to the early eighteenth century, the government's response to the victims in 1791 was far less benevolent. Dissenters rapidly realized they could expect little official assistance, and indeed soon became aware of the level of public hostility they faced.

The longer-term impact of the riots upon politics in Birmingham is also difficult to assess. Professor Money has pointed to the complex political response of the town to the outrages. Although the reform movement in the town lost much of its original leadership in the riots, and political radicals in Birmingham were weaker and more moderate than their counterparts in Sheffield, this cannot be attributed to the Priestley Riots alone. Professor Money has also emphasized the underlying conservative outlook of the region and its workforce. Nonetheless, in view of the scale of the outrages and the continuing intimidation of Unitarians as well as radicals in the country as a whole, it is difficult not to believe that the riots had a significant impact on political agitation and radical opinion. Money himself noted that 'far from being consigned to its proper place in the past, the memory of the Priestley riots remained a present obsession which was regarded as providing in itself a sufficient justification for the peculiarities of

Birmingham Jacobitism.'[72] Nevertheless, with the deepening economic depression as a result of war, the concerns of the mob changed:

'Church & King' is now rubb'd off – and a Gallows they trace
Instead of 'No FOXITES', 'No PRIESTLEY', 'No PAINE'
They now write 'No PORTLAND', 'No D——d rogues in GRAIN'[73]

If Unitarians and radicals were no longer subjected to the same degree of overt intimidation as they had suffered earlier, even as late as 1797 Lindsey considered that there was still too much 'Church and King-spirit' in Birmingham for one victim of Pitt's laws against sedition 'to live with comfort or even security in the place'.[74]

Notes

1. The quotation is from a letter written by Dr Thomas Milner, Maidstone, to the Revd William Hazlitt, Wem, on 20 November 1791, expressing horror at the Priestley Riots: see 'The Hazlitt papers', *Christian Reformer* ns 5 (1838), p. 704. Hazlitt, the Unitarian minister at Wem, was the father of the famous essayist. I am very grateful to Dr G. M. Ditchfield for his detailed comments on an earlier draft of this essay.
2. For a discussion of these themes, see G. M. Ditchfield, 'The Priestley Riots in historical perspective', *Transactions of the Unitarian Historical Society* [hereafter *TUHS*], 20 (1991), pp. 3–16.
3. For an attempt to address this omission see D. L. Wykes, 'The Leicester Riots of 1773 and 1787: a study of the victims of popular protest', *Transactions of the Leicestershire Archaeological and Historical Society* 54 (1978–9), pp. 39–50.
4. J. Money, *Experience and Identity. Birmingham and the West Midlands, 1760–1800* (Manchester: 1977); R. B. Rose, 'The Priestley Riots of 1791', *Past and Present* 18 (1960), pp. 68–88.
5. See D. L. Wykes, '"The Spirit of Persecutors exemplified": The Priestley Riots and the victims of the Church and King mobs', *TUHS* 20 (1991), pp. 17–39.
6. This account is based on Rose, 'Priestley Riots', pp. 72–6.
7. Rose, 'Priestley Riots', pp. 76, 84; R. B. Rose, 'The origins of working class radicalism in Birmingham', *Labour History* 4 (1965), pp. 6–14.
8. Ditchfield, 'Priestley Riots', pp. 6–8; Money, *Experience and Identity*, pp. 195–6, 261–3; J. Money, 'Joseph Priestley in cultural context: philosophic spectacle, popular belief and popular politics in eighteenth-century Birmingham', Part One, *Enlightenment and Dissent* 7 (1988), pp. 57–81; Part Two, *Enlightenment and Dissent* 8 (1989), pp. 69–89; C. Haydon, *Anti-Catholicism in Eighteenth-century England, c. 1714–1780: A Political and Social Study* (Manchester: 1991).
9. J. Seed, 'Gentlemen Dissenters: the social and political meanings of Rational Dissent in the 1770s and 1780s', *Historical Journal* 28 (1985),

p. 301; M. Fitzpatrick, 'Heretical religion and radical political ideas in late eighteenth-century England', in E. Hellmuth (ed.), *The Transformation of Political Culture: England and Germany in the Late Eighteenth Century* (Oxford: 1990), pp. 339–72; G. M. Ditchfield, 'Anti-trinitarianism and toleration in late eighteenth-century British politics: the Unitarian Petition of 1792', *Journal of Ecclesiastical History* 42 (1991), pp. 39–40.

10. T. Best, *A true state of the case, or, a vindication of the orthodox Dissenters, from the misrepresentations of the Revd Robert Foley, MA* (Stourbridge: 1795), p. 36; R. Foley, *A Defence of the Church of England, in a series of discourses, preach'd at Oldswinford in Worcestershire* (Stourbridge: 1795), p. 11. The dispute was connected with the Priestley Riots; see Foley, *A letter to Dr Priestley in answer to the appendix ... of his late publication, entitl'd 'An appeal to the public, on the subject of the riots in Birmingham, Part the IId.'* (printed for the author, Stourbridge: 1793).

11. Birmingham Central Libraries, Archives Department [hereafter BCL], MS 510640, 'Letters, copies of letters and other papers chiefly correspondence addressed from Samuel Garbett of Birmingham to the Earl of Shelburne, afterwards Marquis of Lansdowne, 1766–1802' [photostat copies of the originals, now in the William L. Clements Library, Ann Arbor, Michigan, USA], vol. III, 1790–1793, fo. 58, Samuel Garbett, Birmingham, to Dr Jackson, Dean of Christ Church, Oxford, 23 July 1791.

12. *Ibid.*, Garbett to Jackson, 23 July 1791. Cf. [Martha Russell], 'Journal relating to the Birmingham Riots, by a young lady of one of the persecuted families', *Christian Reformer* ns 2 (1835), pp. 296ff.

13. Rose, 'Priestley Riots', p. 74; Thomas Lee Jr., Tamworth, to his friend, J. D. Humphreys, 18 July 1791, in 'The Birmingham Riots of 1791. An original letter', *Birmingham Daily Mail*, 15 July 1891; [Russell], 'Journal', pp. 294ff; BCL, MS 639818, Typescript copy of Joseph Jukes's MS account of the Birmingham Riots, now in the Melbourne Public Library, Australia, pp. 2ff.

14. BCL, MS 510640, Garbett to Lansdowne, 23 July, pp. 56–7; Garbett to Dr Jackson, 23 July 1791, p. 58. See also Garbett to Lansdowne, 31 July 1791, fo. 66; BCL, Records of the Church of the Messiah, MS 238/5/1–2, Thomas Lee, Birmingham, to his daughter Mary, the wife of John Coates, minister of the Old Meeting, 16 July 1791.

15. BCL, MS 639818, Jukes's MS account, pp. 2–3.

16. BCL, MS 297228, 'The Claim of George Humphreys against the Hundred of Hemlingford for damages at Sparkbrook House, during the riots' [1792], p. 10. Cf. Revd W. Jesse to [the Earl of Dartmouth], [17 July 1791], *Historical Manuscripts Commission, 15th Report, App. part 1. The Manuscripts of the Earl of Dartmouth* (London: 1896), III, p. 273.

17. Ditchfield, 'Priestley Riots', pp. 4–5; BCL, MS 510640, fos 56, 66, Garbett to Lansdowne, 23, 31 July 1791.

18. Rose, 'Priestley Riots', pp. 73–4; Catherine Hutton, Birmingham, to Mrs André, 25 August 1791, in C. H. Beale (ed.), *Reminiscences of a Gentlewoman of the Last Century: Letters of Catherine Hutton (Daughter of William Hutton, F. A. S. S., Historian of Birmingham)* (Birmingham: 1891), p. 89;

Priestley, London, to Adam Walker, Lancaster, 30 July 1791, in J. T. Rutt (ed.), *The Theological and Miscellaneous Works of Joseph Priestley*, I, pt 2. *Life and Correspondence* (25 vols, London: 1817–35), p. 127; Sarah Hill, [Kidderminster], to her brother Thomas Wright Hill [Autumn, 1792], in C. Hill (ed.), *An Autobiography of Fifty Years in Times of Reform* (London: 1894), pp. 12–14; *Remains of the late Thomas Wright Hill, Esq., F. R. A. S. Together with Notices of his Life, &c.*, (London, privately printed: 1859), pp. 119–20. Cf. Lt-Col. Oliver De Lancey, Birmingham, to Sir William Fawcett, in A. Aspinall (ed.), *The Later Correspondence of George III: December 1783 to January 1793* (Cambridge: 1962), I, p. 553.

19. BCL, MS 639818, Jukes's MS account, p. 5; Rose, 'Priestley Riots', p. 75.
20. BCL, MS 510640, fo. 57, Garbett to Lansdowne, 23 July 1791. Cf. 'Extract of a letter from Birmingham', 25 July 1791.
21. BCL, MS 639818, Jukes's MS account, pp. 7–8. Cf. De Lancey to Fawcett, in Aspinall (ed.), *Later Correspondence*, 1, p. 553.
22. Hutton, because of his involvement in the Court of Requests, seems to have been a particular object of popular dislike. See R. A. M. Dixon, 'John Ryland, Recollections of Dr Priestley', *TUHS* 4 (1927–30), pp. 417–22; C. Hutton (ed.), *The life of William Hutton, F. A. S. S. including a particular account of the riots at Birmingham in 1791, and the history of his family, written by himself* (London, 2nd edn: 1817), p. 247.
23. BCL, MS 510640, fo. 57, Garbett to Lansdowne, 23 July 1791. Cf. 'Extract of a letter from Birmingham', 25 July 1791; *Leicester Journal*, 29 July 1791.
24. For the part played by the riots in fuelling Church and King feeling generally, see Wykes, 'Spirit of Persecutors', pp. 20–4.
25. The evidence on the state of the town, and the animus directed against Priestley personally, is well documented in the surviving collections of contemporary letters: see Priestley, Dudley, to Lindsey, 15 July 1791, in Rutt (ed.), *Works*, I, pt 2, pp. 123–4; Priestley, London, to the Revd C. Rotheram, Kendal, 21 July 1791, in Rutt (ed.), *Works*, I, pt 2, p. 124; The Royal Society Library, London, General Manuscript series, MS 654, 'Portraits, Drawings, original Letters, Anecdotes and other Memorials of Joseph Priestley, LLD., … collected and arranged by James Yates, MA, FRS &c.', p. 52v, Priestley to Mr Stansfeld of Leeds, 10 August 1791; Dr Williams's Library, London [hereafter DWL], 'Lindsey Correspondence', MS 12.57 (7), Theophilus Lindsey to Samuel Shore, Meersbrook, 26 September 1791; MS 12.57 (3) [copy by Rutt], Lindsey to Shore, 23 July 1791, see postscript; BCL, MS 510640, fos 55, 56–7, 58, copy of an extract of a letter from Dr Priestley in a letter from Garbett to Lansdowne, and another from Garbett to Dr Jackson, Dean of Christ Church, all dated 23 July 1791; Priestley to Russell, 29 July 1791, in Rutt (ed.), *Works*, I, pt 2, pp. 124–6; Royal Soc. MS 654, p. 53r, Lindsey to Tayleur, 4 August 1791; Priestley to Russell, 5 August, 8 August 1791, in Rutt (ed.), *Works*, I, pt 2, p. 137; John Rylands University Library of Manchester [hereafter JRULM], Unitarian College Collection, 'Autograph Letters of Theophilus Lindsey, 1785 to 1800', Lindsey, to Tayleur, 12 September 1791; BCL, MS 510640, fo. 68, Garbett to Lansdowne,

3 August 1791. Priestley had been librarian and literary companion to the Marquis of Lansdowne, then the Earl of Shelburne, from 1772 until he accepted the invitation to become minister of New Meeting in 1780.

26. DWL, MS 12.57 (5), Lindsey, Richmond, to Shore, 16 August 1791. Cf. Matthew Boulton to Charles Dunergue, 18 August 1791, quoted in R. E. Schofield, *The Lunar Society of Birmingham: A Social History of Provincial Science and Industry in Eighteenth-century England* (Oxford: 1963), p. 362.

27. Lindsey, London, to Tayleur, Shrewsbury, 12 September 1791, in H. McLachlan (ed.), *Letters of Theophilus Lindsey* (Manchester: 1920), pp. 116–17, 118–19.

28. JRULM, Lindsey, to Tayleur, 19 October 1791; BCL, MS 621037, 'A Collection of 68 Letters written chiefly by Dr Joseph Priestley to John Wilkinson, 1789–1802' [originals in Warrington Public Library, MS 2, Priestley MS], Joseph Priestley, London, to John Wilkinson, 23 November 1791; *Public Advertiser*, 6 January 1792. C. H. Beale (ed.), *Reminiscences*, p. 99 note*, see letter from Thomas Richards to his daughter, 13 November 1791; DWL, MS 24.157 (170), Wodrow–Kenrick correspondence, c. 1750–1810, Samuel Kenrick, Bewdley, to James Wodrow, Stevenson, 4 January 1792.

29. Royal Soc. MS 654, p. 52v, Priestley to Stansfeld, 10 August 1791; Priestley, Missenden, to Lindsey, 30 August 1791, in Rutt (ed.), *Works*, I, pt 2, p. 150; DWL, MS 12.57 (3), Lindsey to Shore, 23 July 1791; Liverpool Record Office, MS 920NIC/6/3/20, Nicholson Letters, Thomas Nicholson, Manchester, to his mother, 22 August 1791. Cf. Jesse to [Dartmouth], [17 July 1791], p. 273.

30. DWL, MS 12.57 (5), Lindsey to Shore, 16 August 1791; BCL, MS 621037, fos 34–5, Priestley to Wilkinson, 20 August 1791; DWL, MS 12.57 (7), Lindsey to Shore, 26 September 1791. Cf. William Hutton, Birmingham, to his wife, 23 October 1791, in Beale (ed.), *Reminiscences*, pp. 97–8.

31. Draft of a letter dated October 1791, see *Memoirs of the life of Sir Samuel Romilly, written by himself with a selection from his correspondence*, edited by his sons (London, 2nd edn: 1840), I, pp. 447, 448–9.

32. DWL, MS 12.57 (5), Lindsey to Shore, 16 August 1791; University College London Library, Sharpe Papers 11/1(39), Thomas Rogers, Hinckley, to Samuel Rogers, Cornhill, 21 September 1791.

33. Priestley, Missenden, to Lindsey, 30 August 1791, in Rutt (ed.), *Works*, I, pt 2, p. 150; University College Library, Sharpe 11/1(39), Rogers to Rogers, 21 September 1791; BCL, Records of the Church of the Messiah, Birmingham, MS 232/123, 'Minutes of the Vestry Meetings of New Meeting, 1788–1792', s.v. 14 August 1791.

34. J. Priestley, *An appeal to the public, on the subject of the riots in Birmingham* (London: 1791); BCL, MS 621037, Priestley to Wilkinson, 23 November 1791. Cf. JRULM, Lindsey, to Tayleur, 6 November 1791; Josiah Wedgwood, Etruria, to Priestley, 30 November 1791, in K. E. Farrer (ed.), *Correspondence of Josiah Wedgwood, 1781–1794* (1906; Didsbury [1979]),

III, pp. 176–7; Priestley, London, to William Russell, Birmingham, 5 October 1792, in Rutt (ed.), *Works*, I, pt 2, pp. 191–2.

35. J. Priestley, 'An Account of the High-Church Spirit which has long prevailed in Stourbridge', published as an appendix to Priestley's *An appeal to the public, Part II*, in Rutt (ed.), *Works*, XIX, pp. 439, 573–8 (Appendix 20). Cf. Wykes, 'Spirit of Persecutors', p. 21.
36. DWL, 24.157 (173), Kenrick to Wodrow, 10 April 1792.
37. DWL, 24.157 (168), Kenrick to Wodrow, 6 September 1791.
38. DWL, MS 12.57 (5), Lindsey to Shore, 16 August 1791.
39. *Leicester Journal*, 26 August 1791.
40. 1 Geo. I, stat. 2, c. 5, 'An act for preventing tumults and riotous assemblies, and for the more speedy and effectual punishing the rioters', clause iv, see D. Pickering (ed.), *The Statutes at Large, from the Twelfth Year of Queen Anne, to the Fifth Year of King George I* (Cambridge: 1764), XIII, p. 144. The registration certificate stated the location of the meeting house as Philip Street, which as a result of the growth of the town during the eighteenth century was by 1791 some streets away from Old Meeting-house Lane. It was subsequently proved when the claim for compensation was made that the certificate did in fact refer to the Old Meeting. *Leicester Journal*, 2 September 1791; *Nottingham Journal*, 3 September 1791.
41. *Leicester Journal*, 2 September 1791.
42. BCL, MS 621037, fo. 48, Priestley to Wilkinson, 4 October 1791.
43. *Leicester Journal*, 2 September 1791; *Memoirs of ... Sir Samuel Romilly*, I, pp. 446–7.
44. *Life of William Hutton*, p. 277 n*.
45. DWL, 24.157 (171), Kenrick to Wodrow, 21 March 1792.
46. *St James's Chronicle*, 29–31 March, 31 March–3 April 1792 (I owe this reference to Dr G. M. Ditchfield); *Swinney's Birmingham and Stafford Chronicle*, 5 April 1792; BCL, Hutton 130/2–4, Thomas Richards, Birmingham, to his daughter at Miss Stone, Weston House, near Thame, Oxfordshire.
47. DWL, 24.157 (171), Kenrick to Wodrow, 21 March 1792.
48. DWL, 24.157 (173), Kenrick to Wodrow, 10 April 1792.
49. DWL, 24.157 (171), Kenrick to Wodrow, 21 March 1792.
50. *Life of William Hutton*, p. 295; Rutt (ed.), *Works*, I, pt 2, pp. 203, 209, 121; Rutt (ed.), *Works*, XIX, pp. 493–5, 496–7, 499; Rutt (ed.), *Works*, XV, pp. 528, 529; Beale (ed.), *Reminiscences*, p. 99.
51. Edwards was appointed Priestley's assistant following the resignation of Samuel Blyth in April 1791.
52. BCL, MS 232/123, 'Minutes of the Vestry', s.v. 2, 14 August, 18, 29 September, 2 October 1791; BCL, MS 232/85, 'Minutes of the Proceedings of the General Meetings of the Congregation assembling at the New Meeting, Birmingham', 29 July 1771–12 June 1868, pp. 38, 47–51; DWL, MS 12.57 (3), Lindsey to Shore, 23 July 1791; BCL, MS 238/5/2, Thomas Lee, Five Ways, to his daughter Mary Coates, 5 September 1791; Address to Priestley from the New Meeting Congregation, 5 September 1791, in Rutt (ed.), *Works*, I, pt 2, p. 153.

53. C. Hutton Beale, *Memorials of the Old Meeting House and Burial Ground, Birmingham* (Birmingham: 1882), p. 38.
54. BCL, MS 232/123, 'Minutes of the Vestry', s.v. 29 April, 1 May, 7 July, 15 November, 2, 4, 11, 18 December, 1791; BCL, MS 232/85, 'Minutes of ... the General Meetings', pp. 31–6, 61, 64–5.
55. BCL, MS 232/85, 'Minutes of ... the General Meetings', p. 68 (26 February 1792); J. Edwards, *The blessedness of those who are persecuted for righteousness sake; a discourse, delivered at the first meeting of the congregation at Kingswood, subsequent to the riots: in the Union Chapel, in Livery Street, Birmingham, The Sunday before, – and in the Chapel, in High-Street, Warwick, The Sunday after, the Assizes at that Place* (London: 1792), p. iii.
56. BCL, MS 232/123, 'Minutes of the Vestry', s.v. 2, 4, 11, 18 December 1791.
57. Beale, *Old Meeting*, p. 39; BCL, MS 456/1, 'Old Meeting House Minute Book of Subscribers', 1771–1838, reverse of volume, s.v. 2 April, 8 May, 11 June, 24 October 1794; BCL, MS232/85, 'Minutes of ... the General Meetings', pp. 75, 87.
58. Wykes, 'Spirit of Persecutors', pp. 24–9.
59. J. A. Langford, *A century of Birmingham life or a chronicle of local events, from 1741 to 1841* (Birmingham and London: 1868) II, pp. 171–2; Money, *Experience and Identity*, p. 233. The meeting was held on 19 December 1792.
60. *Aris's Birmingham Gazette*, 10, 17 December 1792; *Swinney's Birmingham and Stafford Chronicle*, 6, 13 December 1792; BCL, MS 510640, fos 127–9, 132, Garbett to Lansdowne, 4, 8, 9 December 1792; Rutt (ed.), *Works*, I, pt 2, p. 150 n; T. Walker, *A review of the political events which have occurred in Manchester during the last five years* (London: 1794), pp. 45–66; A. Booth, 'Popular loyalism and public violence in the North-West of England, 1790–1800', *Social History* 8 (1983), pp. 299–300.
61. BCL, MS 329314, 'Brief for defendant in the case against William Belcher of Birmingham bookseller for publishing seditious works, Summer Assizes, 1792' [1793]; for an account of the trial, see *Jackson's Oxford Journal*, 10 August, *York Herald*, 10 August 1793; J. Hill, *The Book Makers of Old Birmingham: Authors, Printers and Book Sellers* (Birmingham: 1907), pp. 93, 103.
62. University College London, Sharpe 180, Maria Kenrick, Exeter, to her husband, Timothy Kenrick, Chester, 15 July [1792]; Timothy Kenrick, Exeter, to Samuel Kenrick, Bewdley, 19 August 1794; Samuel Kenrick, Bewdley, to Timothy Kenrick, 10 December 1794; William Davy, Germantown, to Timothy Kenrick, 22 May 1795; s.v. Counseller White in Mrs W. Byng Kenrick (ed.), *Chronicles of a Nonconformist Family: The Kenricks of Wynne Hall, Exeter and Birmingham* (Birmingham: 1932), pp. 81, 84, 103–4; E. Percival (ed.), *The Works, Literary Moral and Medical, of Thomas Percival, M.D. ... to which are prefixed Memoirs of his Life and Writings, and a selection from his Literary Correspondence* (London: 1807), III, p. ccvi; [T. Percival], *Biographical Memoirs of the late Thomas Butterworth Bayley Esq., F.R.S.* (Manchester: 1802), p. 10; N. Jones, *Life and Death. A Discourse, on occasion of the Lamented Death of Joseph Strutt, Esq.*

(London: 1844) p. 20; Derbyshire Record Office, Matlock, Records of Friargate Unitarian Chapel, Derby, 1312D/A1, 'Account and Minute Book, 1697–1819', Meeting of subscribers, 27 March 1796; JRULM, Lindsey to Rowe, 13 September 1794; Samuel Kenrick, Bewdley, to Timothy Kenrick, 10 December 1794, in Byng Kenrick (ed.), *Chronicles of a Nonconformist Family*, pp. 83–4; Lindsey to Scott, 30 April 1795, in H. J. McLachlan, 'The Scott Collection: Letters of Theophilus Lindsey and Others to Russell Scott', *TUHS* 19 (1988), p. 122; DWL, 24.86 (2), Priestley, Northumberland, to an unknown correspondent, 27 October 1795.

63. Priestley, Clapton, to William Russell, Birmingham, 30 April 1793, in Rutt (ed.), *Works*, I, pt 2, p. 199; S. H. Jeyes, *The Russells of Birmingham in the French Revolution and in America, 1791–1814* (London: 1911), pp. 50–60; *Cambridge Intelligencer*, 15, 22 March 1794; W. W. Currie (ed.), *Memoirs of the Life, Writings and Correspondence of James Currie, M. D., F. R. S., of Liverpool* (London: 1831), I, pp. 189, 210–11, vol. II, pp. 37–42; D. L. Wykes, 'The reluctant businessman: John Coltman of St Nicholas Street, Leicester (1727–1808)', *Transactions of the Leicestershire Archaeological and Historical Society* 69 (1995), forthcoming.

64. Wykes, 'Spirit of Persecutors', pp. 18–19, 22–3; L. B. Bowring (ed.), *Autobiographical Recollections of Sir John Bowring* (London: 1877), p. 32.

65. DWL, MS 12.44 (55), Lindsey to Turner, 14 June 1792; Priestley to Russell, 19 July 1792, in Rutt (ed.), *Works*, I, pt 2, pp. 189–90. For the concern aroused by the rumoured meeting at Birmingham, see [Samuel Parr], *A Letter from Irenopolis to the Inhabitants of Eleutheropolis* (London: 1792); W. Derry, *Dr Parr: A Portrait of the Whig Dr Johnson* (Oxford: 1966), pp. 146–7. Dinners celebrating the 14 July were also discontinued in Liverpool and in other places, see H. Roscoe, *The Life of William Roscoe* (London: 1833), I, pp. 107–8.

66. DWL, MS 24.157 (173), Kenrick to Wodrow, 10 April 1792; B. Walker, 'A Caricature of William Hutton', *Transactions and Proceedings of Birmingham Archaeological Society for the Year 1938* 62 (1943), pp. 41–3.

67. E. C. Black, *The Association: British Extra Parliamentary Political Organisation, 1769–1793* (Cambridge, MA: 1963), pp. 229–30, n. 39.

68. M. Fitzpatrick, 'Priestley Caricatured', in A. T. Schwartz and J. G. McEvoy (eds), *Motion Towards Perfection: The Achievement of Joseph Priestley* (Boston, MA: 1990), pp. 181–210.

69. John Ralph, Halifax, to the Revd William Hazlitt, Wem, 23 July 1791, *Christian Reformer* ns 5 (1838), pp. 702–3; DWL, 12.45, fos 162v–63r, Joshua Toulmin, Wells, to Revd John Sturch, Newport, 25 November 1791; *Life of William Hutton*, p. 281; see also William Hazlitt's letter to the editor of the *Shrewsbury Chronicle* (1791) written at the age of 13, in W. C. Hazlitt, *Memoirs of William Hazlitt: with Portions of his Correspondence* (London: 1867), I, pp. 21–4. A number of ministers published sermons they had delivered in response to the riots; see for example, T. Kenrick, *The Spirit of Persecutors exemplified, and The Conduct to be observed towards their Descendants. A Sermon, Delivered at George's Meeting-House, Exeter, November 5th, 1791. To which are Prefixed, Some Observations*

Upon the Causes of the Late Riots at Birmingham (London: [1792]); [William Christie], *An Essay, on Ecclesiastical Establishments in Religion: Shewing their hurtful tendency; and that they cannot be defended, either on principles of Reason or Scripture. To which are annexed, Two Discourses* (Montrose: 1791), pp. 23–4, 44–5.

70. D. L. Wykes, 'Old Meeting and James II's Religious Indulgence of 1687: The building of the first Nonconformist meeting-house in Birmingham', *Midland History* 16 (1991), pp. 86–102; N. Rogers, 'Riot and Popular Jacobitism in Early Hanoverian England', in E. Cruickshanks (ed.), *Ideology and Conspiracy: Aspects of Jacobitism 1689–1759* (Edinburgh: 1982), p. 70; P. K. Monod, *Jacobitism and the English People, 1688–1788* (Cambridge: 1989).

71. *VCH Warwickshire* VII, pp. 278–9; Haydon, *Anti-catholicism*, p. 216. The early Methodists suffered severely from the mob; see J. Walsh, 'Methodism and the Mob in the Eighteenth Century', in G. J. Cuming and D. Baker (eds), *Studies in Church History: Popular Belief and Practice*, VIII (Cambridge: 1972), pp. 213–27. I owe a number of suggestions in this paragraph to Dr Ditchfield.

72. Money, *Experience and Identity*, pp. 237, 281, 223–8, 234–8. Cf. Rose, 'Priestley Riots', pp. 83–4.

73. BCL, MS 184534, James Bisset, 'Original MSS Songs', 1802–5, p. 51, 'Written on seeing the various Inscriptions on the Walls &c of Birmingham, from the Year 1791 to 1800, faithfully given as they appear'd at the different periods' (5 November 1800).

74. JRULM, Lindsey, London, to John Rowe, Shrewsbury, 27 November 1797. Cf. Bodleian Library, Oxford, MS Montagu d.10, fo. 267r, Letter of the Revd George Walker, Nottingham, to an unknown Birmingham correspondent, 17 May 1797.

CHAPTER 4

Elite and Proletariat in Nineteenth-century Birmingham Nonconformity

John H. Y. Briggs

The chronological limits of this study may be taken to be the Priestley Riots of 1791 on the one hand, and the increased practice of Anglicans and Free Churches working together in the early twentieth century. The Priestley Riots at once signify a Nonconformity committed to the constitutional reform of oligarchic power and privilege in church and state alike, believing that failure to reform the constitution peacefully created a dangerous pre-revolutionary situation. Up to that time, many words had been expended on the Christological debate that separated Unitarians from evangelical Dissent. But the violence of 1791 drew the two parties together in common cause.

Robert Hall, for example, whilst stressing that he believed Priestley's religious tenets to be erroneous, nevertheless supported his genius and his freedom of conscience.[1] The first sermon that Priestley preached after the riots was in the Particular Baptist church in Amersham, on, it has been suggested, the nomination of Hall. Even the Methodists offered Priestley support: Samuel Bradburn, an intimate of Wesley and President of Conference in 1792, preaching in Birmingham the following year, declaimed: 'The curse of God hangs over your town for the infamous treatment Dr Priestley experienced among you.'[2]

I

A radical appreciation of the need for reform was not at this time confined to the Unitarians. Since the story of the contribution of Birmingham Dissent to community life has more often been told in terms of the contribution of Unitarians, Congregationalists and Quakers, this paper will focus particularly on the less well-known contribution of the Baptists, arguing that they made a two-fold input through both those chapels that attracted members of Birmingham's middle-class elite, and those congregations which were much more popularly based.

From the ranks of the Particular Baptists, three figures may stand against any too rapid dismissal of the tradition as wholly pietistic. George Edmonds, button burnisher turned schoolmaster, was the son of the Revd Edward Edmonds, a member of the Cannon Street chapel responsible for planting the second chapel in Bond Street. George Edmonds's name is to be found associated with nearly every radical cause in early nineteenth-century Birmingham. A founder and chairman of the Birmingham Hampden Society for political reform,[3] he chaired a meeting in Newhall Hill in January 1817 which demanded the separate representation of the town. Ten years later he presided at a meeting in a still unenfranchised Birmingham that elected Sir Charles Wolseley as Birmingham's 'Legatorial Attorney and Representative', and for his pains, together with four others, was imprisoned for conspiring to elect an MP.[4] He joined with Thomas Attwood in the 1830s in the forming of the Birmingham Political Union, worked with Angell James in favour of Catholic Emancipation, and was quick to join in the attack upon the Corn Laws.

Edmonds was one of those who secured the incorporation of Birmingham in 1838: in fact, he was appointed first Clerk of the Peace for services rendered, as 'one of the great pioneers of the battle for freedom', and one who 'had suffered imprisonment in the cause of liberty'.[4] He was elected a member of the Chartist National Convention early in 1839, but, like many of the other middle-class members, Edmonds was alienated by its lack of moderation and forthwith resigned from it.[6]

William Morgan, briefly Town Clerk of Birmingham (1852–4), was one of the several talented sons of Thomas Morgan. After retiring early from the pastorate of Cannon Street, the father served as co-pastor to Edward Edmonds at Bond Street from 1820, succeeding to the pastorate after Edmonds's death in 1822, and serving for a further 24 years. William Morgan was the last man in England, it has been suggested, to be challenged to a duel (this for his strong temperance advocacy). He worked with George Edmonds and the Quaker, Joseph Sturge, to secure support in Birmingham for the passing of the 1832 Reform Bill, and continued to be active thereafter in the Complete Suffrage movement.

William Morgan had his goods seized for not paying church rates and gave strong support to the movement to emancipate slaves, William Knibb being a frequent guest in his home. In 1866 he visited Jamaica on behalf of the Anti-Slavery Society at the time of the Governor Eyre affair. He was equally active in opposing the opium trade, and also used his legal skills to secure an ending of the monopoly on Bible printing so that cheaper versions could be provided for the less affluent.

His other concerns included adult school work, relief work in Ireland, and the pioneering of reformatory schools alongside Mary Carpenter and Davenport Hill.[7]

The third example of Baptist Radicalism is to be found in Thomas Morgan's successor at Cannon Street, Isaiah Birt, formerly of Plymouth Dock. His son described him as 'one of those who hailed the commencement of the French Revolution as the day-break of liberty for continental Europe', regarding 'the war that was waged against the infant republic, as a royal crusade against the liberties of mankind'. He especially condemned the way in which the French wars were made an argument for infringing the British constitution, and accordingly came under surveillance from government agents.

By contrast Birt's written work almost exclusively focused on the nature of Christian baptism. In this he proved himself a keen advocate of the Baptist position. After rejecting several other ministerial calls, he moved in 1815 to Cannon Street, where he added to the church's programme daughter Sunday schools, missions, and encouraged one of his more affluent members, John Deakin, a rich benefactor of the Baptist Missionary Society, to establish a very early ragged school. The fellowship prospered under his warm evangelical ministry until ill health caused his retirement to Hackney in 1827. Ivimey called him 'a most animated and almost seraphic preacher'. On resignation from Cannon Street, he was voted an annuity of £100 for life.[8] Even Cannon Street and Bond Street, who clearly made an appeal to the comfortably off, were not frightened of entertaining in their pulpits men highly critical of the established order, whilst immediately spawning a number of specialized agencies concerned with the poor.

II

Early nineteenth-century Baptists were well served by their ministers who developed the work in a way which placed the churches at the centre of the denomination's life. John Clifford once argued that the Particular Baptists came in three forms: 'Strict', 'Spurgeonic' and 'Miscellaneous', arguing that this third group found 'their visible centre in the colleges of Regent's Park, Bristol and Rawdon and the Baptist Missionary Society'.[9]

The passion of Samuel Pearce, minister of Cannon Street for the last decade of the eighteenth century, for the new missionary initiative was clear and infectious. Not only did Cannon Street seal Carey's beginnings with timely financial support, but in Birmingham, Pearce founded the first district auxiliary for the support of the Mission. Moreover, Thomas Potts,[10] one of Cannon Street's wealthy deacons, described as an American merchant, had as early as 1788 agreed to fund the publication of Carey's *An Enquiry into the Obligations of Christians to use Means for the conversion of the Heathen*, and Thomas King, another Cannon Street deacon, a candle manufacturer, became treasurer of the infant missionary society. Although premature death all too swiftly removed Pearce, both laymen served on the committee of the BMS until 1831.[11]

Throughout Baptist life concern for missions overseas also served to reawaken the churches to the demands of mission at home. In 1795 Pearce wrote to William Steadman, a fellow Bristol student and then pastor at Broughton, that the Birmingham church was progressing well with a membership of 295 even after the planting of the Bond Street chapel. Noting that he wanted 'more heart religion', a gentle critique of an over-cerebral Calvinism, he also observed: 'were an acceptable preacher to come here I think with little trouble he might establish another Baptist interest of no small dimensions'.[12] Further afield, Pearce took a house in Shirley for Sunday worship and arranged for the Sunday evening service there to be supported by some thirty members of Cannon Street in turn. In that tradition, the Cannon Street congregation was responsible for planting churches at Alvechurch, King's Norton, Kingswood, Wythall Heath and Yardley Wood. They nurtured the infant cause at Cradley and also managed to instill new life into the historic Bromsgrove church.[13]

Accordingly, Angell James praises the Birmingham Baptists for their commitment to strategic church-planting, rather than new causes being the result as 'is too frequently the case among Dissenters, of a schism in any one of their churches'.[14] There is only one such suggestion of that happening among Birmingham Baptists. The evidence is a footnote in a letter from Andrew Fuller to a Scottish deacon, James Deakin, dated 5 April 1803, where he writes: 'I am told your old friend Mr Edmonds, of Bond Street, is become an Arminian; I mean in the esteem of part of his church; that they have on this account separated and taken the New Jerusalem Chapel. I am going to Birmingham the 18th inst.'[15]

At first sight this looks as if it might be a reference to the founding of the Newhall Street church which certainly took over the former Swedenborgian church in that location. This had indeed been occupied for a while by a sect of Antinomians, but it is not clear that they also held Baptist beliefs: at any rate the sect did not prosper and soon died out. It was not until 1814 and then by deliberate dismission of 52 members from Cannon Street that a new Baptist Church was formed, fulfilling Pearce's earlier hopes. Moreover, Edmonds continued as pastor of the Particular Baptist cause at Bond Street until 1822, so it is difficult to find the fruits of the schism which had been brought to

Fuller's attention. It probably indicates more about the ways in which some Baptist congregations responded to the new stirrings of re-awakened Dissent with its new missionary urgency challenging the older but still influential 'non-invitation' stance of some Particular Baptist churches.[16] Thus the point remains that the extension of the work of the Baptists in Birmingham is remarkably free of schismatic action.

The founding of the Bond Street chapel is itself instructive: Edward Edmonds records how in November 1784 he began preaching in a house at Deritend which soon became too small for the congregation that had been attracted. This led him in the summer of 1785 to preach in the open air. Approaching winter led the little group of seventeen, 'all of whom earned their bread by the sweat of their brow', to collect £50 towards the erection of their own chapel. Shortly, the group had grown to 23, whom Edmonds baptized in the Bromsgrove meeting house in September 1785. Once the chapel at Bond Street was ready, a further 27 were baptized there and, with a further five (of whom Edmonds was one) dismissed from Cannon Street, a missionary-minded church was formed. Their letter to the Association for 1798 reports: 'We send eight of our brethren, two and two, who expound the Word every Lord's Day at Erdington, Yardley, Beech Lanes and Heeley ... In two of these places Sunday Schools have been established.'[17] More formally, churches were planted at Bedworth, Coseley and Harborne. At the peak of its usefulness, Bond Street had a membership of 700 and a Sunday school with an enrolment in excess of 1,000 scholars.[18]

The Baptists developed their work in Birmingham with a firm sense of strategy. The first list of churches is found in the Circular Letter for 1817, where only these three churches are listed:

Cannon Street: Isaiah Birt:	431 members
Bond Street: Edward Edmonds:	278 members
Newhall Street: William Hutchings:	102 members

The listing in the *Baptist Magazine* for 1835 is generally speaking very useful because it often gives hearers and Sunday school scholars as well as members, but unfortunately the Birmingham listing is very incomplete, providing only a list of five churches including the New Connexion church in Lombard Street, the only one, in fact, for which a membership figure is given (228).[19]

The *Baptist Magazine* for that year also provides another clue to Baptist life: a letter from Birmingham dated 1834 on the subject of 'The Duty of Masters towards Servants'. Taking as its authority both Henry Venn's *Complete Duty of Man, or a System of Doctrinal and Practical Christianity* and Scripture, the writer enjoined upon the servant-employing class of church leaders, the need to provide for the old age of those who had given long and faithful service. Neglect of this responsibility, which caused such people to seek parish settlements, constituted a clear injustice and a breach of trust.[20] That such an issue should be raised in this way provides a clear indication of the nature of the Cannon Street and Bond Street congregations.

III

Birmingham Baptists were quite happy to take over other people's buildings if they thought that these buildings could fit into their strategic plans. The early history of Mount Zion chapel in Graham Street most conspicuously put such plans to the test. Built as a private speculation, it was hoped that the rising star of Edward Irving, who offered his patronage, would make this the home of a thriving Scottish Church, but this was not to be; nor did several Independent pastors, one presumably a high Calvinist, since the record designates him an Antinomian, succeed in exploiting the chapel's capacity. The Cannon Street deacons, realizing the chapel's potential, persuaded one of their members, a Mr William Spicer, to purchase the chapel which was by now on the market.

According to Angell James, the property came into Baptist hands in 1827, after the failure of the ministry of a Mr Greig, a Congregationalist whose ordination Angell James for conscientious reasons had declined to attend. The first Baptist minister was a Mr Thongar, formerly an Independent who subsequently became an Irvingite, and thus the first Baptist attempt to establish a church in Graham Street also floundered, though this early initiative, it was noted, 'did not secure denominational recognition'. Notwithstanding Spicer's generosity, there was by now a considerable burden of debt associated with the chapel, and fresh negotiations were needed leading to the establishment in 1829 of a trust for the management of the property and to make it available for evangelical worship (with open communion) according to the rites of the Particular Baptists. It was a difficult process: 'extraordinary trials and difficulties compelled the trustees to entertain thoughts of extricating themselves from responsibility by the sale of the whole property'.[21]

It was at this point that the services of James Hoby were secured by the trustees, since private means enabled him to serve the church without salary. As quickly as possible, efforts were made to bring the new enterprise within the orbit of Baptist church polity. A wholly new church was formed on 23 January when, under the presidency of the Revd T. Waters of Worcester, four persons 'previously baptised ...

gave to each other the right hand of fellowship'. A month later the settlement of Hoby as pastor of the new cause was publicly recognized. The vision was bold: although by April the four had, by 'testimonials and Dismission', become forty, the new pastor had been appointed by a body of trustees to develop a work, where others had failed, to fill a building 'commodiously arranged, elegantly fitted up, and capable of holding a congregation of 2,500'. [22]

All went well under the pastorate of Hoby, who would twice occupy the chair of the Baptist Union: between 1831 and his resignation in 1844 the membership grew to some 235. His successor, the Revd George Dawson, initially seemed to improve on that figure, but within two years he was forced to resign from the pastorate when the Mount Zion deacons became convinced that the liberal views of this too-general Baptist were not in keeping with the chapel's trust. Dawson did not argue the case but removed with a large part of the congregation, many of whom had been won by his preaching from the established Unitarian congregations, to establish the new unsectarian Church of the Saviour. This edifice, 'large and elegant', Angell James grudgingly admits, was 'filled by a respectable congregation, drawn together by his talents as a public instructor': it is as if James cannot bring himself to speak of Dawson as either pastor or minister. [23]

This disruption of chapel life revealed that there was some £4,000 of accumulated debt associated with the mortgage on the Mount Zion property, with the mortgagee more sympathetic to Dawson than the remnant of the orthodox. In these difficult circumstances the deacons took the unusual step of suspending the church's constitution and seeking the help of the other four Particular Baptist ministers in the town, together with leaders from Cannon Street, Bond Street and Heneage Street and four of their own members, who in 1846 formed a committee under the chairmanship of William Middlemore with T. H. Morgan as secretary. The work was secured by donations from Birmingham and from Baptists and others across the country being commended by leading members of the denomination together with Dr Halley of Manchester from the Congregationalists. At a different level, the Bond Street chapel dismissed twenty of its members to Mount Zion to help the church re-establish itself. The next pastor, the Revd Mortlock Daniell, managed to stabilize the situation, but it was only with the pastorate of Charles Vince, 1852–74, that Graham Street fulfilled its true potential. [24]

About the time of the remodelling of the Midland Association in 1841, a more local Birmingham Baptist Union was established in which Baptists of all parts of the family could share, the first fruit of whose labours seems to have been the development of the Heneage Street site. A number of different strands came together in this project: first,

Cannon Street made support of the project its centenary thanksgiving, whilst more generally Birmingham Baptists associated the project with their celebration of the emancipation of Jamaican slaves. Thus the schools, which were the first buildings to be erected, were known for many years as the 'Emancipation Schools'.

There is record of some 5,000 children from Baptist Sunday schools and Lancastrian day schools attending a mammoth rally in the town hall on 1 August 1838, conducted by the Baptist ministers of the towns. Thereafter they sat down to a substantial meal of bread and beef before marching in procession to Heneage Street where the Quaker, Joseph Sturge, laid the foundation stone, and provided a handsome gift to forward the work.[25] The foundation stone for the chapel was laid by William Knibb, who had done so much to help the slaves achieve their freedom.

The chapel was opened for worship in June 1841, with Charles Roe invited by the organizing committee to be the church's first pastor, that is to say pastor of a church not yet formed and which he had to bring into being.[26] Roe was clearly the right man for such a task, having previously served as the indefatigable secretary of the Baptist Home Missionary Society; indeed, Richard Carwardine calls him 'the personi-fication of the revivalist wing of the Baptist denomination'.[27] Under his ministry, the church, which was formally constituted on 27 March 1842, soon grew to a membership of 700 with 1,200 in the Sunday school. For a second time Birmingham Baptists had set their polity on one side, with the wider fellowship, aided by the generosity of particular individuals, taking strategic decisions, whether through trustees or committees, establishing and equipping a mission station with building and pastor ahead of the actual gathering of a church fellowship.

The difficulties at Graham Street did not deter Birmingham Baptists from taking over buildings that others had failed to exploit. In 1847, once more assisted by a wealthy friend of the Cannon Street church, this time named as William Middlemore, they purchased a speculative building, the amphitheatre in Bradford Street.[28] Angell James rightly pays tribute to Birmingham Baptist laymen for their public spirit and liberality in seizing such opportunities for church extension: 'this spirited effort had the sanction and patronage of an influential body of Christian men connected with the congregations assembling in Cannon Street, Bond Street and Graham Street', though those of other de-nominations also provided financial support. Support of a different kind came from Charles Roe, a man of considerable Irish passion, partly because of the worked example of what he had achieved at Heneage Street, partly through his ongoing enthusiasm for home mission.[29]

The chapel was opened for worship in October 1848 with the Congregationalist, Dr Raffles of Liverpool, sharing with the Revd

John Aldis of the historic Maze Pond chapel in London in conducting the opening services. The Revd W. Landels began a notable ministry in January 1850, and interestingly baptized the chapel's benefactor, Mr William Middlemore, aged 48, on 7 July of that year, notwithstanding the fact that he had previously been a member of Cannon Street and had already begun to exercise leadership among Birmingham Baptists.[30]

IV

Devoted and purposeful leadership were certainly of crucial importance in establishing Baptist work in the city of Birmingham. But there were also circumstances beyond human planning. The *Baptist Magazine* for 1846, whilst noting the defection of George Dawson, also bears witness that several Independent ministers, having been baptized, were seeking Baptist pastorates. The most notable of these was the Revd Arthur O'Neill of 'the Christian Chartist congregation at Livery Street', who was baptized by Thomas Swan at Cannon Street on 3 May 1846. O'Neill, speaking from beside the baptismal pool, delivered a most effective address before an overflowing congregation. Most of O'Neill's congregation also chose to become Baptists; he baptized 20 of them at Cannon Street on 4 June, 23 at Bond Street on 17 June, and 17 at Heneage Street on 24 June; on Sunday 28 June, a new church was constituted at Livery Street with 60 members and the Lord's Supper celebrated.[31]

More needs to be said about O'Neill. The son of an Irish Protestant refugee who died three months before his birth, he served for two years as a medical assistant with the 73rd Regiment of Foot. He entered Glasgow University in 1835 as a medical student, but soon his interests were transferred to theology and philosophy, and in 1838 he became caught up with the excitement of the founding of Chartism, being sent as a delegate from Glasgow to Birmingham in 1840 to welcome the Chartist prisoners released from Warwick Gaol.

In Birmingham, he came into contact with a small Independent congregation who invited him to be their pastor and was soon engaged ministering amongst the poorest people in Birmingham, establishing a school which had over 600 scholars. In 1842 his work was interrupted by government persecution; he was arrested at a meeting at Cradley, even though he was entirely a moral-force man, campaigning strenuously against any form of violence. Committed to Stafford Gaol, he was released on bail until his trial in 1843 at which he conducted his own defence in a speech of seven hours' duration. Though he was complimented on his performance by the judge, the jury still found him guilty. His year's imprisonment at Stafford introduced him to Thomas Cooper, who would also become a Baptist later in his life.

In 1844 O'Neill wrote to his people from prison warning them against ambition: 'I believe that in the mysterious ways of God little things are of great importance. I see Jesus washing the disciples' feet; I desire to serve the poor, the sick, the mourning, the ignorant, the aged and the child,' which was not the obscure life the world might take it to be. He accordingly requested no demonstrations on his release, rather asking his people to meet with him for prayer at seven o'clock on the Sunday morning.

In 1847 the Livery Street congregation combined with that in New-hall Street where O'Neill served as pastor for almost fifty years, winning the title 'the apostle of peace and arbitration in the midlands'. His congregation is described as composed of 'small men of the artisan type from which the Birmingham Chartists had been mainly recruited'.[32]

A second foundation from the first half of the century also needs attention and that is the People's Chapel, Great King Street, Hockley, founded in 1848 by 40 members from Newhall Street. Their aim was to establish a new kind of church, democratic in its government, independent of pew-rents in its funding, so that all seats might be free and unappropriated. Finance was to be secured by free-will offerings deposited in boxes in the church so that no collection had to be taken up during the services. They also decided to have no salaried minister, believing that the Holy Spirit could minister to their spiritual needs entirely through committed laymen; the only person on the payroll for the first fifty years was the chapel-keeper, but later, in an attempt to minister to the social need surrounding the chapel, they employed those first called Bible Women and later Deaconesses. Thus they tried to incarnate the title of their chapel thereby giving answer to Thomas Cooper, who remarked: 'The People's Chapel – what a great title! I wonder whether they are worthy of it?'

'This group of obscure Radical artisans', unlike the other Baptist chapels, grew to take a vital interest in matters political, particularly after R. W. Dale had reinterpreted George Dawson's 'civic gospel' in terms acceptable to evangelical Dissenters. At the heart of such involvement was John Skirrow Wright, great-grandson of John Fawcett of Hebden Bridge, a distinguished leader of Yorkshire Baptists. Wright's career started humbly enough, entering the works of George Smith, a button manufacturer, at the age of fourteen. But he worked hard and eventually became a partner in a firm which was doing extremely well, and in this way became one of Birmingham's large employers. After 1868 he was president of the Birmingham Chamber of Commerce of which he was a founder. He also served as chairman of the Birmingham Liberal Association for twelve years. He was elected MP for Nottingham but died before he was able to take up his seat. At the time of his death he was also a director of Lloyd's Bank. A keen temperance reformer, he served on the Birmingham School Board. He was treasurer of the West Midland Baptist Association from 1867 to 1880.[33]

Wright was not simply a businessman and political activist: in 1851 he proposed the dropping of the heading to the Association's Circular Letter which spelt out the Association's Calvinist theology. This was not agreed, but as a compromise the following words were added:

> Also this association embraces those baptist churches who, though they conscientiously object to this, or any other creed of merely human composition, however sound, as a condition of Christian fellowship, yet strenuously maintain the necessity of 'Repentance towards God, and faith in Our Lord Jesus Christ, and cordially unite with the association for the promotion of the important objects it has in view, in the enjoyment of a pure scriptural fellowship.[34]

At once the way was opened up for New Connexion churches to join with Particulars and a conscience clause was offered to those who objected to the neo-credalism of denominational doctrinal standards.

V

The religious census of 1851 provides external evidence for what the Baptists were achieving. For this purpose, it is necessary to take together the three registration districts of Birmingham, Aston and King's Norton,[35] with a combined population of almost 274,000. Using Harold Perkin's simplified method of taking two-thirds of attendances to secure the number of attenders, the following figures emerge:

1851 Religious Census for Birmingham,
Aston and King's Norton Districts

Reg. Dist.	Population	Church Attendances	Attenders	%
393 King's Norton	30,871	9,551	6,367	20.62
394 Birmingham	173,951	66,763	44,509	25.59
395 Aston	66,852	21,519	14,346	21.46

	Anglican			Nonconformist			Other		
[393]	5,913	[3,942]	12.8%	3,638	[2,425]	7.9%	nil		
[394]	30,743	[20,495]	11.8%	30,433	[20,289]	11.7%	5,587	[3,725]	2.1%
[395]	10,854	[7,236]	10.8%	7,565	[50,43]	7.5%	3,100	[2,067]	3.1%

The failure of the churches to secure popular support is obvious and in this respect the more marginal areas fared worse than the urban centre of Birmingham itself, largely because Nonconformity was slower to get itself organized in these areas. By contrast, the Church of England managed to hold its own remarkably well. Many returns indicate the importance of the Peel Act in enabling the established church to establish new parishes legally with relative ease, whilst on the ground they show the established church responding to movements of population by using temporary rooms, prior to the building of more permanent churches.

W. L. Burn's warning not to assume too quickly either the religious commitment of the affluent or the 'irreligiousness' of the lower orders is pertinent here. Burn argued that it was 'unlikely that in a country where middle-class occupations were only gradually coming into existence the bulk of the five million attenders [at church on Census Sunday] were of that or a higher class.' [36]

As has been noted for other districts, the tendency by those making returns is not to falsify the data but rather to explain away disappointing statistics: thus there was widespread reference to it being mid-Lent or Mothering Sunday by Anglican, Unitarian and Wesleyan respondents. The influenza seems to have hit the Cannon Street Baptists, whilst special services filling some churches emptied others. The curate of St James's frankly indicates that the congregations at his church were lower because on this Sunday a quarterly collection was taken for the warden's expenses which always depressed the attendance: nevertheless, 600 adults were present in the morning and 700 in the evening.[37] Significantly, a considerable number of other respondents honestly admit to a larger than usual attendance on Census Sunday.

A distinctive feature of the Birmingham district is the variety of Nonconformity there present: there are twice as many categories of affiliation as in the other two districts which lack the presence of the smaller sects including the Quakers. Other features which stand out are the weakness of the Independents in King's Norton, where other Methodists strikingly outnumber the Wesleyans, and where there was not yet a Roman Catholic presence. The only respondent not able to sign the form, Robert Hawkins, whose mark is recorded, is nevertheless described as a manager. He makes the return for the sixteen-strong afternoon congregation at Water Orton Wesleyan chapel.[38] The Birmingham returns are also eloquent about the impact of railway building on places of worship: four congregations report themselves on the move because their former premises have been requisitioned for railway development.[39]

The returns show quite clearly the importance of the Unitarians,[40] with almost 2,000 people at morning worship in the area and that without the 950 present at the Church of the Saviour, which George Dawson records as 'not connected with any sect; in the marriage registry entered as United Christians, i.e. a free unsectarian church'.[41] A comparison can be made with the Cadbury Census of 1892 by taking the figures for the best-attended services, which yields the following comparison:

1851 [Religious Census, 1851 Districts 393/4/5]

C. of E.	c. 24,650
Nonconformists	c. 21,560
Roman Catholics	c. 4,200

1892 [Cadbury Census]

C. of E.	c. 44,000
Nonconformists	c. 52,250
Roman Catholics	c. 7,250

This clearly identifies the second half of the nineteenth century as the major period of Nonconformist expansion, justifying Asa Briggs in talking of 'the paramount influence of nonconformity' in this period.[42]

VI

There are sixteen returns from Baptist churches which are abstracted in Appendix A. They represent a range of Baptist congregational experience, from the patrician pews of Cannon Street to the pew-hostile People's Chapel.[43] But even Cannon Street had, from its revival at the end of the eighteenth century, sought to penetrate neighbouring working-class areas with schools. Isaiah Birt increased the thrust with additional missions and ragged schools in Fisher Street, Bristol Street and Swallow Street.[44] The returns only partly pick up this kind of work in the returns for the Crescent School and for the Hill Street Preaching Room and the People's Chapel's outreach at Stayney Street.[45] Clearly, such activities were much more difficult to trace and in the King's Norton returns is to be found a copy of a proforma letter from Horace Mann, dated November 1851, to local registrars seeking information 'either from church personnel or from your own knowledge or enquiries' with regard to services in schools, with the instruction that full information was not needed: 'what is most required is the no. of persons frequenting the place for worship/no. of scholars attending schools'. Three registrars are listed and their replies annotated on the letter.[46]

In 1851 the West Midlands Baptist Association set its mind to a strategy for home mission, setting up a committee to investigate opportunities for witness in the mining districts of the Association. In 1852 a new committee was established under the chairmanship of W. Landels of Circus Chapel, which included William Middlemore in its membership, to increase the efficacy of home missions to enable the Association 'to be more equal to the pressing claims of evangelical labour constantly presenting themselves among the teeming population around.'[47] In 1869 a Birmingham and West Midlands Baptist Building Fund was established by the younger G. F. Muntz, son of the MP, and William Middlemore. Birmingham Baptists clearly benefited from the service of dedicated business minds in developing both that vision and those resources which enabled it to respond strategically to population movements.

In appointing Isaac Lord as pastor in 1858, the church at Cannon Street made a deliberate bid to reach a working-class constituency, for Lord came to Birmingham from Ipswich where he had already established a reputation for pioneering popular services in the local theatre, for which initiative he had been arraigned before the magistracy. Lord proved a popular preacher in Birmingham too and soon filled Cannon Street so that in 1859 it boasted a membership of 663. The old Calvinism of the Particular Baptists was moderating: Lord was critical of preaching which focused 'on a few dry dogmas' and 'spent its time working over what were called the six points of the Calvinistic creed', arguing instead for a full proclamation of the whole gospel robustly delivered with true spiritual power. Vince at Graham Street similarly indicated a desire to transcend credal statements which he thought sought a false consistency: 'That is the reason why the creeds of men have not gathered the whole truth of God ... by getting their creed consistent, they [those who argue for credal statements] leave human life undescribed and God's truth not disclosed. To tell the truth of God, I must say things that seem to contradict each other.'[48]

Graham Street, no less than Cannon Street, could claim also to be a chapel for what Clyde Binfield has called 'Baptists ... of the ... opinion-forming sort'.[49] 'Not a few of the most active, energetic and busy men in Birmingham have been strengthened in their moral and religious life by his manly and earnest presentation of the truth', wrote the obituarist of Charles Vince, more than twenty years its pastor.[50] Dale, his contemporary at Carr's Lane, attested the quality of the ministry, though his biographer adds: 'Nonconformist ministers like the Rev Charles Vince who afterwards became one of the most popular and prominent of public men, were almost wholly absorbed by the claims of their ... congregations; and they did not attempt a wider ministry'. Dale himself was also restricted in the years immediately following the death of Angell James in 1859: 'the duties of the pastorate ... for the time engrossed his entire strength'.[51]

More recently Peter Hennock has thrown doubt on whether Vince made a major contribution to the municipal reform movement as such, whilst admitting that only he 'held a position in the public life of the town at all comparable to Dale's'. Vince's contribution was essentially through the School Board, the National Educational League and the Central Nonconformist Committee, an educational pressure group whose chairman and treasurer for many years was William Middlemore. Vince was 'a conventional Radical of the Dissenting sort, keen on Disestablishment and humanitarian causes'. When he spoke in favour of Chamberlain's candidacy in 1872, he indicated that it was the first municipal election in which he had taken part.[52] Nevertheless, under his leadership, the work at Graham Street expanded, with a membership which in 1871 stood at 614 and schools which at their peak enrolled around 1500 scholars.

During this period the Spring Hill church was planted; branch schools, including a ragged school, were commenced; a Bible Woman appointed, and a domestic mission established in the Brookfields area, whilst Mr Vince addressed large untraditional crowds in the town hall on Sunday evenings. Here was a prosperous city-centre church intelligently seeking new ways of extending its usefulness to people of all kinds.[53]

Arthur O'Neill's Chartist background, not to mention the 60 who transferred with him to Newhall Street from the Christian Chartist church in Livery Street, must have given that congregation a different flavour. Bond Street too had its origins in part with the artisans of Deritend, whilst George Cheatle's fifty-year work for the New Connexion at Lombard Street, which was off Bradford Street, was set in the middle of an area of working-class need: his obituary recalls how he also pioneered work at King's Heath, where to start with he encountered violence and 'serious insult from the rude inhabitants' of the area.[54]

The two large preaching centres – Heneage Street and the Circus Chapel, Bradford Street – also needed to establish themselves in popular esteem, and the indications of the census is that by 1851 that was already happening, both showing evening congregations of 850.

The congregations at the People's Chapel were much smaller: 95 in the morning and 175 in the evening, with a further 50 meeting in 'a room in a destitute locality, Stayney Street' on Census Sunday evening, according to an annotation to the form which was not added into the count. This congregation had an influence on Birmingham politics out of all proportion to its size and resources, largely because Skirrow Wright, who has been called 'something of a local boss in the poor district of North Birmingham in which his works and his church were situated',[55] made the People's Chapel the base for his concern to secure municipal reform. A teaching elder of this congregation which rejected a separated ministry, Wright was Superintendent of the Sunday school up to the time of his death and also ran an evening class for about 150 youths as well as teaching in the adult school.

In late 1857 or early 1858, Wright had sought to bring middle class and working class together to promote the interests of reform: with William Radford, a clerk, and William Beddows, a bricklayer, he founded a body called the Reformers' Union which later in 1858 was merged into the Birmingham Reform Association. In 1867 Wright engineered an electoral coup against the existing Board of Guardians: the new Board was little better in the immediate future, though Joseph Beston from the People's Church was for many years to influence its counsels. From the People's Church also came a number of Radical councillors: the first was James Whateley, a pearl-button worker elected as a working men's candidate in 1871, followed by Wright's son, Frank, in 1874, and Samuel Radford in the 1880s. A record of the Whateley election from Samuel Radford sees the conflict as being between the beer interest of the pubs and the prayer interest of the People's Chapel: at an end-of-poll meeting, Radford made his testimony by announcing that he would soon be off to the People's Chapel weekly prayer meeting to give thanks for his friend's success. But Wright was not a thinker: for positive thinking about municipal reform, he and his friends deferred to Dale, who provided a justification for municipal reform that evangelical Dissenters were able easily to embrace.[56]

VII

Robert Gray, first minister of the Moseley church, argued that whilst great respect was paid to the development of Baptist life in the quarter of a century following the religious census, the great period of Graham Street and the other city-centre churches, the growth in membership of that period was less than 400 or only about 15%. By contrast, the last quarter of the century (1877–1902) witnessed much greater growth at a figure of a little under 3,000, in fact approximately a doubling of membership, with some £40,000 applied to church extension in those years. Writing in 1906, J. M. Gwynne Owen noted that whilst the Methodists recycled the resources from the sale of their city-centre churches into the building of the Central Hall, Baptists applied similar resources to the strategic development of suburban witness.[57]

The movement in fact dated back to the 1860s, when two established ministers led church-planting exercises. In 1861 the Revd J. Jenkyn

Brown, who had been pastor of the Circus Chapel since 1857, moved with some of his members to the Wycliffe church on the Bristol Road, a venture largely financed by William Middlemore.[58] The Circus Chapel did not close but continued to exercise a significant ministry for almost thirty years. This is borne out by the experience of Charles Brown, who exercised a distinguished ministry in North London: he recalls visiting Wycliffe in 1870. Outside was a great line of carriages 'owned by the prosperous well-to-do congregation that gathered for the vigorous, robust ministry of John Jenkyn Brown'. But as a poor lad of fifteen, a newcomer to Birmingham, he felt excluded from such grand company and linked up instead with the old Circus Chapel with its more homely atmosphere.[59]

In 1865 the Revd Isaac Lord, with 33 members of Cannon Street, planted what was to become Christ Church, Aston, another new centre for vigorous missionary activity. In the opening celebrations the Congregationalists, R. W. Dale and Alexander Raleigh, shared with Baptist dignitaries.[60]

Ten years later the old chapel in Cannon Street was sold to the corporation for its Central Improvement Scheme, which was to see the building of Corporation Street, though the congregation continued to use the chapel for another five years before migrating, under the leadership of the Revd Arthur Mursell, to Graham Street. That chapel had recently been vacated through a major portion of its congregation moving, with its pastor, the Revd Henry Platten, to the Church of the Redeemer on the Hagley Road in 1881. A smaller portion formed the core of the new Hamstead Road congregation in Handsworth in the following year.

The old Cannon Street congregation continued to worship at Graham Street until 1913, when they dispersed to found or to enrich two other churches. Part went north to establish a new cause, the Cannon Street Memorial Church in Soho Road, Handsworth, whilst those living to the south augmented the cause at Spring Hill in its extension into the City Road area.

Stratford Road, Sparkbrook, provides another example of Baptist pragmatism running ahead of polity. Once more Middlemore purchased the site, and a committee was established, with John Player of the Church of the Redeemer and E. M. Mitton of Moseley as secretaries. It was this committee which, with the aid of funds from the Cannon Street Trust, supervised the building of the new premises and which issued the call to the first pastor. The church was opened in June 1879, the pastor recognized in September but the new church was not formed until November 1880 when several members of a previously existing congregation, who had worshipped in Priestley Road, transferred their membership to the new church. The thinking, no doubt, was that it was better for the best representatives of the district to undertake the strategic planning for the new cause, especially since, through the Middlemore benefaction and the Cannon Street Trust, the resources being deployed were essentially district resources, rather than entrust the task to the leadership of a small struggling cause.[61]

Other churches were more straightforwardly church plants: Spring Hill, where cottage meetings had begun in 1854 though the church was not constituted until 1887; Edward Road, Balsall Heath, 1873; and Erdington 1878. At Bordesley Green, where Mrs Prowse shared the pastoral duties with her husband, leading to some claims being advanced for her being an early female pastor, the church was constituted in July 1873.[62] In 1891, most of the congregation migrated to new premises strategically placed on the Coventry Road, Small Heath, but a rump continued to worship in the old premises, initially as part of one church with two worship centres but soon organizing themselves as an independent church. At the beginning of the new century a new cause, planned in the 1890s, was planted in Acock's Green.

Churches with a New Connexion background were also involved in responding to population movement. The old Lombard Street chapel, which in the 1880s found itself in an area of dereliction, moved to a new site at Highgate Park in 1886. In 1888, the King's Heath church split in two to establish, under the leadership of its existing pastor, a new cause in Oxford Road, Moseley. For almost twenty years the two congregations operated as one church but in 1905 the Moseley congregation graciously sought their independence.

The suburban churches also developed their own missions and branch Sunday schools with their associated diaconal ministries. Christ Church, Aston, for example, sponsored some half a dozen missions, that at Bevington Road during a period of winter distress providing some 4,600 dinners. At the opposite extreme to such a ministry amongst the destitute, Christ Church, Umberslade, 1877, was funded by the generosity of G. F. Muntz, who established a trust for its maintenance and for the support of the ministry. Muntz, the son of the MP of the same initials, a convert from Anglicanism, had been baptized by Charles Vince at Graham Street.

In this pattern of suburban growth, there was scope for both individual initiative and the working out of a corporate strategy. The patrician interest was considerable: in particular, William Middlemore's[63] generosity links these initiatives back to the mid-century. Middlemore's generosity not only gave the Baptists the ability to develop their work strategically, but encouraged other persons of means to follow his example. Corporately, they acted not only through the Birmingham Baptist Union and the Birmingham Baptist Building Fund but more specifically through the trusts created to invest the funds secured from the sale first of the Circus Chapel (which contributed to the establishing of work at Chester Road, Erdington, Handsworth, and Bearwood, and just before the Second World War purchased the site for the new Hall Green Church) and more significantly of Cannon Street. The Cannon Street trustees made major grants to the Church of the Redeemer (£9,000); Hamstead Road, Handsworth (£6,550); Stratford Road, Sparkbrook (£4,000); Smethwick (£3,050); and Oxford Road, Moseley (£3,000), with minor grants to Spring Hill, the People's Chapel, Graham Street, Small Heath, Stratford Road, Lodge Road, and Witton. I am not sure what the theology of such property trusts is, or how they fit into Baptist polity, but for Birmingham Baptists and the development of their witness in a rapidly expanding municipality, they proved to be as important as the Association itself.

One explanation of the success of Baptist growth would lie in both the extraordinary ability of a number of their pastors and their exceptional loyalty to their churches, so that a study of the impact of long pastorates in this process would not be unprofitable. One of the able men who did not come to Birmingham was J. H. Shakespeare, though he clearly thought hard about the possibility as a letter to him from R. W. Dale indicates. The date of the letter is February 1893. The general comment on the city is of considerable interest. In it Dale testifies:

> It was true for many years that the people of Birmingham were less accessible to religious thought and influence than people elsewhere; at least I thought so. Their life was a full life; large numbers of them had increased their resources very rapidly; the old Liberal Party, before the split, had in a lower form many of the qualities of a church, and interest in politics was very keen and almost universal. I have said very often during the last eight or ten years that a great though gradual change seemed to me to have come about in the temper of the city ... But now, I do not know that we are harder or more secular than other people; and there are very many who are living a thoroughly Christian life.

Dale confirmed that the Church of the Redeemer was set amidst a wealthy constituency, and added this note for the attention of future missiologists and sociologists of religion:

> In my judgment, we have cared too little about saving the wealthy, and then have denounced them for their luxury and selfishness. In every part of the country I hear of the mischievous result of an almost exclusive solicitude for the salvation of the working people; and I think it is time to remember that Christ died for the rich and for the cultivated as well as for the ignorant and the poor.

Having made such comment, Dale then reverts to more conventional thinking by advising Shakespeare that the Hagley Road area also contains many families of modest means so that the church could become a 'centre for innumerable evangelistic and philanthropic agencies'.[64] Shakespeare was either not called, or not willing to leave his influential pulpit in Norwich, until five years later he became the secretary of the Baptist Union. After a long interregnum, the Church of the Redeemer secured the services of the Revd J. M. Gwynne Owen of Southampton, who was much involved in the work of the emerging Free Church Council movement. Whatever the problems of the Church of the Redeemer's first minister – and Dale provides very interesting comment on what these were – under Owen, the church soon developed a distinguished position amongst Birmingham's leading Nonconformist congregations.

The new suburban churches looked very much the part. They were churches not meeting houses – even the names were significant: Wycliffe, Christ Church and the Church of the Redeemer. Gone were the tabernacles hidden in back streets from public view. Gone were the austere classic lines of later Dissent. These were buildings for a Dissent which had accumulated wealth and status and influence, and was not a little proud of its own achievement.

The Gothic, replete with spires and towers and lanterns, was belatedly baptized to Baptist usage in a progression of new churches such as those at Wycliffe, Bristol Road (1861, Architect James Cranstoun); Christ Church, Aston (1865, Architect James Cranstoun); Stratford Road, Sparkbrook (1879, Architect William Hale); the Church of the Redeemer (1882, Architect James Cubitt); Hamstead Road, Handsworth (1883, Architect J. P. Osborne); and Oxford Road, Moseley (1888, Architect J. P. Osborne). Indeed, it has been claimed that Wycliffe Chapel was 'the first to bring the beauties of Gothic architecture into common use in Birmingham'.[65]

All of these needed sizeable benefactions, either corporate (from bodies such as the Cannon Street Trust) or individual. Aided by such resources, the new chapels were erected; here now were sanctuaries where respectable Dissent could worship alongside the members of the established church. With them, they entered into better relations in a century where it became increasingly clear that all churches needed to work together to meet the challenges of a secular and pluralistic society. The importance of these new prestigious chapels must not, however, be over-emphasized. Old Cannon Street and Graham Street in their own ways were prestigious enough, and large, active congregations secured prestige within the community quite apart from the architecture of the sanctuary they occupied. Moreover, the 1892 census clearly showed that a significant number of Baptist worshippers were worshipping in mission halls, or in the older chapels, or in more modest suburban church plants. In many ways what was important was not the prestige so much as the strategic development of Baptist life in relation to the changing dynamics of Birmingham life, and the un-traditional instruments for deploying and redeploying resources which made that possible.

Notes

1. See Robert Hall's 'Christianity Consistent with a Love of Freedom' [1791], in O. Gregory (ed.), *The Works of Robert Hall* (London: 1866), IV, pp. 21–4; and *DNB*.
2. *DNB*.
3. W. B. Stephens (ed.), *Victoria County History, Warwickshire* (London: 1964), VII, pp. 286ff.
4. C. Gill, *History of Birmingham* (London: 1952), I, pp. 201–2. See also references to Edmonds in D. Fraser, *Urban Politics in Victorian England* (Leicester: 1976) and *Power and Authority in the Victorian City* (Oxford: 1979).
5. Gill, *Birmingham*, I, pp. 234–6. Edmonds held this office until 1864 when glowing tributes were paid to his long career (pp. 403, 439).
6. Gill, *Birmingham*, I, p. 244.
7. F. W. Butt-Thompson, 'The Morgans of Birmingham', *Baptist Quarterly* (1925), pp. 263–8; William Morgan's brothers were T. H. Morgan (1811–79), a Baptist minister, who was one of the founders of the Birmingham Scholastic Institution at Shireland Hall for the education of the sons of Dissenting clergy; Henry Morgan (1818–94), a strong temperance advocate, who was the secretary of a number of railway companies; and A. F. Morgan (1823–1903), a solicitor, who was very active in the Peace Society for whom he travelled internationally. He was one of the original members of the National Liberal Club.
8. J. Birt, 'Memoir of the Late Rev. Isaiah Birt', *Baptist Magazine* (February 1838), pp. 54ff.; *Baptist Magazine* (February 1827), p. 78. Even his predecessor, the so-called 'Seraphic' Pearce, preached a sermon in February 1790 on *The Oppressive, Unjust, and Profane Nature and Tendency of the Corporation and Test Acts Exposed* which long remained in print; A. S. Langley, *Birmingham Baptists, Past and Present* (London: 1939), p. 245.
9. *General Baptist Magazine* (January 1877), p. 2.
10. Thomas Potts was a close associate of Thomas Attwood in exercising leadership in presenting the needs of Birmingham traders to central government and in campaigning for the separate representation of Birmingham in parliament; *VCH, Warwickshire*, VII, pp. 109, 117, and 290.
11. B. Stanley, *The History of the Baptist Missionary Society* (Edinburgh: 1992), pp. 8-9, 11, 19; J. Angell James, *Protestant Nonconformity ... with an account of the Rise and Present State of its Various Denominations in the Town of Birmingham* (Birmingham: 1849), pp. 162ff.

12. Samuel Pearce to William Steadman in 'Calendar of Letters Collected by Isaac Mann, 1742–1831', *Baptist Quarterly* (1932), p. 181.

13. J. M. Gwynne Owen (ed.), *Records of an Old Association* (1905), pp. 106–7, 136–7.

14. Angell James, *Protestant Nonconformity*, p. 176.

15. 'Andrew Fuller and James Deakin, 1803', *Baptist Quarterly* (1935), p. 328.

16. See my *English Baptists in the Nineteenth Century* (Didcot: 1994), p. 98. The language is familiar: in 1787 the Association Letter coming from the Bromsgrove church, with which Bond Street had close associations, referred to 'fears that the dregs of Arminianism are received by some of the ministers and the churches of the Association'; Gwynne Owen (ed.), *Records of an Old Association*, p. 104.

17. Angell James, *Protestant Nonconformity*, pp. 171–2; Gwynne Owen (ed.), *Records of an Old Association*, p. 106.

18. Langley, *Birmingham Baptists*, pp. 82–3. Langley also records how generous the church was in raising some £13,000 for outside causes between 1815 and 1846. The church also provided the Baptist Union with its first general secretary in the person of Joseph Belcher; Gwynne Owen (ed.), *Records of an Old Association*, p. 107.

19. Gwynne Owen (ed.), *Records of an Old Association*, pp. 109, 112; *Baptist Magazine* (Supplement 1835), p. 564. When the Midland Association was remodelled in 1841 with more confined geographical boundaries, the following figures were produced: Cannon Street: T. Swan: 813 members & 1,000 SS Scholars; Bond Street: T. Morgan: 630 members & 938 SS Scholars; Newhall Street: J. Ham: 127 members & 230 SS Scholars; Mount Zion: J. Hoby: 193 members & 500 SS Scholars. See *Records of an Old Association*, p. 112.

20. *Baptist Magazine* (February 1835), p. 57.

21. Angell James, *Protestant Nonconformity*, pp. 174–5; *Baptist Magazine* (April 1831), p. 156, indicates that the founding of the church had not been without difficulty and included a mortgaging of the property for a sum of half the purchase price, plus other financial considerations, a fact which would be of later significance.

22. Langley, *Birmingham Baptists*, p. 103; Gwynne Owen (ed.), *Records of an Old Association*, pp. 139–40.

23. Angell James, *Protestant Nonconformity*, pp. 178–9; E. P. Hennock, *Fit and Proper Persons: Ideal and Reality in Nineteenth-Century Urban Government* (London: 1973), pp. 63–5.

24. *Baptist Magazine* (March 1846), pp. 173–4, including etching of the building; *Baptist Reporter* (July 1846), pp. 314–15, which also carries an etching.

25. Dr Hoby tells how Sturge's interest in the work of the Jamaica mission was stimulated and how Sturge passed considerable funds through him for educational work amongst the negro population.

26. *Baptist Magazine* (October 1841), p. 511.

27. R. Carwardine, 'The Evangelist System: Charles Roe, Thomas Pulsford and the Baptist Home Missionary Society', *Baptist Quarterly* (1980), p. 212.

28. An etching of the exterior of the chapel is to be found in *The Baptist Reporter* (January 1849), p. 35.

29. Angell James, *Protestant Nonconformity*, pp. 177–8.
30. Langley, *Birmingham Baptists*, p. 95. His wife, Mary, had been baptized at Cannon Street, and his three eldest surviving daughters are recorded as being baptized at the Circus Chapel in November 1850. None of the other children appears to have been baptized in Baptist churches though they were not baptized as infants. W. P. W. Phillimore and W. F. Carter, *The Family of Middlemore* (London: 1901), pp. 222–7. I have to confess some difficulty in handling this information: Langley is clear about the date of Middlemore's baptism, whilst Gwynne Owen (*Records of an old Association*, p. 136), is equally categoric in its description of Middlemore as a member of Cannon Street, and the periodicals clearly indicate his position of leadership among Birmingham Baptists prior to 1850. Angell James refers to the two occasions when in 1745 and 1806 Cannon Street came near to becoming a Union Church with Independents and Baptists sharing membership (*Protestant Nonconformity*, pp. 127–8, 154–6). Writing in 1849, he notes: 'As the church in Cannon Street held, and many of the members still hold, what are called "strict communion" principles, they could not unite with us in the celebration of the Lord's Supper ...' While this opens up the possibility of Cannon Street having opened its table by 1849, it is hardly likely that it had opened its membership. Sir George Goodman of Leeds offers a comparable example of a Baptist worthy not baptized until late in life. See my entry on Goodman in the *Dictionary of Evangelical Biography* (Oxford: 1995), p. 456.
31. *Baptist Magazine* (June 1846), pp. 372, 508; *The Baptist Reporter* (November 1846), p. 472, reports that in fact O'Neill conducted baptismal services for his congregation in all six of the existing Baptist chapels in the district including the New Connexion chapel in Lombard Street. See also *VCH, Warwickshire*, VII, p. 446.
32. *Illustrated London News*, 23 May 1896; *Baptist Handbook* (1897); Langley, *Birmingham Baptists*, pp. 149–53. Curiously, Angell James notes O'Neill as pastor of the Newhall Street congregation but gives nothing of his history. Hennock, *Fit and Proper Persons*, p. 99; *VCH, Warwickshire*, VII, pp. 303–5.
33. Hennock, *Fit and Proper Persons*, pp. 98–103.
34. *Baptist Magazine* (September 1851), pp. 576–7.
35. Working with the three registration districts involves the inclusion of some rural areas, but rural areas very much under the influence of the Birmingham metropolis, as the addresses of Nonconformist signatories on the returns from the several chapels clearly indicates. This does not, however, explain why the Roman Catholic return for Wootton Wawen appears in the Birmingham list, which must be an error of allocation. Errors of calculation were clearly made both by those making returns and those consolidating them, but these do not unduly distort the overall pattern for the area.
36. W. L. Burn, *The Age of Equipoise* (London: 1964), p. 272.
37. HO/129/395/2. Because of the unreliability of the numbering of the returns for HO/129/393 and HO/129/395, I have used the sequential numbering given for these districts. The sub-district system is in good

order for HO/129/394, however, so I have used that for this significantly larger district.

38. HO/129/395/33.

39. Salem Chapel, unfinished, replacing the Cave of Adullam Chapel (HO/129/394/1/9) – this chapel contained a number of Strict Baptists who shortly after this installed a baptistry; St Jude's (HO/129/394/5/3); The Countess of Huntingdon Chapel (HO/129/394/5/9) and Newhall Street Independent Chapel (HO/129/394/5/11).

40. Both the major Unitarian churches (HO 394/4/5 & 394/5/9) refer to having been rebuilt after the riots of 1791. Samuel Bache, one of the two ministers at the New Meeting, writes on his form: 'I have designated the congregation Unitarian because I am myself so and conduct the worship on unitarian principles but our communion is quite unrestricted and we receive all into church membership who choose to become and contribute to the support of religious worship in our meeting rooms.' Their mission chapel in Lawrence Street was erected by the followers of Joanna South-cott. Later used by the Socialists, it subsequently became a dancing salon. The congregation is recorded as being 'made up of the extremely poor of the neighbourhood', but some 250 of these assembled for Sunday evening worship. At the Unitarian Domestic Mission Chapel in Hurst Street (HO/129/394/3/5), there were no pews but rather 'moveable benches with backs to them'; the evening attendance was 85 with a note 'sometimes many more'. Other Unitarian returns are recorded at Kingswood Chapel, also destroyed in the riots of 1791 (HO/129/393/ 15) and The 'Christian Unitarian' church in Newhall Hill (HO/129/394/1/8).

41. HO/129/394/1/5. The other Undefined Churches were Salem Chapel (HO/129/394/1/9), a continuation of the Cave of Adullam congregation which it was claimed had a congregation of 300, and a small congregation of Christian Israelites, the followers of John Wroe, who had met in a house for three years with a congregation of 23 on Census Sunday (HO/129/394/6/4). Salem Chapel was unfinished at the time of the census and therefore there was no service there. By contrast, Rehoboth Chapel (HO/129/394/2/9), which described itself as 'Calvinist Independent', a new congregation of about 40 people meeting in a former warehouse, was allocated to the Independents.

42. A. Briggs, *History of Birmingham, II. Borough and City: 1865–1938* (London: 1952), p. 3. The abstractions made from the religious census in the previous volume are remarkably untrustworthy: Gill, *Birmingham*, I, p. 374.

43. Birmingham Baptists evidently liked this designation for in 1878 a second People's Chapel was constructed in Warwick Street. The was 'a private venture' of the Martin family (Dr S. W. Martin, d. 1897, and S. J. Martin, d. 1921) who were attenders at the Circus Chapel. In the 1892 Census the evening service attracted 213 people. In 1913 the congregation moved to the former St Martin's Chapel in Alcester Street, but closed in 1921 on the death of the younger Martin by which time the area had been depopulated in favour of factories.

44. Langley, *Birmingham Baptists*, p. 36.

45. HO/129/394/1/3; 394/5/10; 394/8/7.
46. Filed as HO/129/393/23.
47. *Baptist Magazine* (October 1852), p. 631.
48. C. Vince, from his sermon 'On Disappointments in Life', in *The Unchanging Saviour and Other Sermons* (London: 1875), p. 205.
49. C. Binfield: 'Congregationalism's Two Sides of the Baptistery', *Baptist Quarterly* (1975), pp. 120, 130.
50. *Baptist Handbook* (1875), pp. 307–10.
51. A. W. W. Dale, *The Life of R. W. Dale of Birmingham* (London: 1902), pp. 139–40.
52. Hennock, *Fit and Proper Persons*, pp. 167–8.
53. Other Graham Street missions included Bethany Chapel, Anderton Street (founded c. 1875), which had an evening congregation of 112 on Census Sunday, 1892, but had closed by 1898; Ellen Street, which was founded in 1866, had an evening congregation of 141 in the 1892 Census; and Slade Lane, Yardley, which had an afternoon congregation of 30.
54. *Baptist Handbook* (1871), p. 208.
55. He also wrote about the changing industries of Birmingham: J. Skirrow Wright, 'An Account of some of the new trades in Birmingham', *T. Nat. Ass. Promotion Soc. Sc.* (1862), reprinted in 3rd Report of the Committee on the Employment of Children, 1864, xxii, p. 151.
56. Hennock, *Fit and Proper Persons*, pp. 98–103, 142–4; Langley, *Birmingham Baptists*, pp. 110–11.
57. Gwynne Owen (ed.), *Records of an Old Association*, pp. 144–5; J. M. G. Owen, 'Birmingham and its Free Churches', *The Free Church Chronicle* (March 1906).
58. *The Church* (August 1861), p. 223. Dr James Hamilton of the Scottish Church in London and R. W. Dale shared with Baptist leaders in the opening celebrations.
59. Langley, *Birmingham Baptists*, p. 224.
60. *The Church* (June 1865), p. 166.
61. Langley, *Birmingham Baptists*, pp. 171ff. Mitton did join the new church and became its first treasurer.
62. Langley, *Birmingham Baptists*, pp. 159–60.
63. Middlemore came of a family which had Roman Catholic associations. The family wealth was made in the leather industry, deriving particular benefit from the development of the bicycle saddle, large-scale military orders and from a healthy export trade. In 1860, with 400 workers, Middlemores were reckoned one of the largest manufacturers of leather items (*VCH, Warwickshire*, VII, p. 146). William Middlemore (1802–87), noted as a radical in politics, served as a Low Bailiff and Councillor for the youthful borough, and was a JP from 1856. As indicated earlier, he is recorded as connected with Cannon Street, even to the point of having membership there, but he was baptized by Landels at Circus Chapel in 1850. A founder member of the Birmingham Liberal Association (1865) and of the Education League (1869), Middlemore in addition to offices in his own company was a director of the Muntz Metal Company, deputy chairman of the Birmingham Joint Stock Bank (subsequently absorbed

by Lloyd's), and chairman of the Birmingham Wagon Company. Of him it was written: 'His munificence was as unstinted as it was catholic: it was bestowed, always under modesty, often under conditions of secrecy' (Phillimore and Carter, *The Family of Middlemore*, pp. 222–7).

64. Dale, *R. W. Dale of Birmingham*, pp. 655–6. In this letter Dale also suggests very pointedly some of the weaknesses of the recently retired founder pastor of the Church of the Redeemer, not named, but in fact the Revd Henry Platten, who served six years at Graham Street and eleven at Hagley Road. He could, Dale suggested, preach divinely, but he only occasionally did so, '... And his best was often remote from the lives of common men. It fascinated thoughtful and mystical women: God bless them.'

65. *VCH, Warwickshire*, VII, p. 436.

Appendix A:
Abstract of Returns from Baptist Churches for Birmingham, King's Norton and Aston [Registration Districts 394/393/395] for the Religious Census of 1851 [HO 129]

394/1/3 Crescent School, Cambridge Street; a new cause only open 6 months
morn.   10 scholars
eve.   12 adults + 25 scholars

394/3/4 Circus Chapel, Bradford Street; amphitheatre rebuilt as church, 1848
morn.   320 adults + 70 scholars
eve.   850 adults

394/5/7 Cannon Street Particular or Calvinist Baptist, 1806
morn.   428 adults + 105 scholars
aft.   110 adults + 158 scholars
eve.   455 adults
Figures noted as the result of an actual count: only half the scholars allowed into chapel at any one service. Figures depressed by influenza.

394/5/10 Hill Street Preaching Room, c. 1837 ('not a branch of any other place but it is managed by the friends from Cannon Street' who appointed the preachers)
morn.   Schools only
aft.   Schools only
eve.   30 adults + 20 scholars

394/6/5 Zion Chapel, Newhall Street; purchased for Baptists 1814
morn.   300 adults + 160 scholars
aft.   150 adults + 160 scholars
eve.   500 adults + 100 scholars
Arthur O'Neill notes that congregations were significantly larger than normal (+ c. 200) because special sermons were preached on behalf of branch schools.

394/8/5 Bond Street Chapel, 1786
morn.   500 adults + 210 scholars

aft.   50 adults
eve.   500 adults

394/8/7 People's Chapel, Great King Street, 1848
morn.   95 adults + 25 scholars
aft.   10 adults + 105 scholars (? scholars/teachers at Sunday School)
eve.   175 adults
Notes that the chapel is used on weekdays 'for free lectures and discussions on moral, social and political subjects'.
'The society has no hired minister or teacher; has no private pews but is supported entirely by voluntary gifts.'
'This society rents a room in a destitute locality, Stayney Street, in which they hold a service on each Sunday evening. Congregation about 50.'
T. Skirrow Wright, Teaching Elder.

394/9/2 Mount Zion Chapel, Graham Street, c. 1824
morn.   460 adults + 120 scholars
eve.   473 adults
Form signed by William Morgan, Elder and Secretary. He amends the printed form to enable him to make the return as secretary 'of the church assembling at the above place of worship'. He claims that an absence of pastor explains a 25% reduction in morning congregation and a 33% reduction in the evening.

393/6 Headley Baptist Strict Baptist, Wythall Heath, 1807
(The designation presumably refers to this church's communion discipline: the chapel was built by Thomas King, deacon of Cannon Street in 1805; 1807 was the date of the first baptisms. Until 1841 it was part of Cannon Street but in that year a separate church was constituted. John Freeman who makes the return for this chapel was a member of Cannon Street, 1848–52.)
morn: 73 adults
aft: 38 adults
Attendances stated as 'near the average'.

393/7 King's Heath Chapel, 1816 (General Baptist New Connexion)
morn.   200 adults
aft.   100 adults
eve.   100 adults

393/12 King's Norton Baptist Chapel, c. 1815 [but chapel built 1847]
aft.   40 adults + 12 scholars
eve.   85 adults

393/26 Union Chapel, Harborne, 1820 [included here but in returns as Undefined]
morn.   45 adults
eve.   100 adults
NB Av. only given for six month because congs have increased consequent upon inc. accomm. funded by voly. subs of friends of this place, and popular style of preaching from Spring Hill College and otherwise.

393/35 Smethwick Particular Baptist Chapel, North Harborne, 1840
morn.   15 scholars

aft.   40 adults + 25 scholars
eve.   30 adults

395/6 Lombard Street Chapel, General Baptist New Connexion, 1786
morn.   220 adults + 240 scholars
eve.   275 adults

395/8 Heneage Street Chapel, 1841
morn.   650 adults + 321 scholars
aft.   30 adults + 376 scholars (? scholars and teachers at Sunday School)
eve.   850 adults

Charles Roe notes nothing special about these numbers which fairly represented the average. Weekday evening services which about 250 people attended held in a separate room, which on Sundays accommodated an Adult Sunday School. In addition to services at chapel on weekdays 20 weekly services in private homes.

395/42 General Baptist, Little Sutton: 'about 100 years' (congregation pre-1770 but admitted to the New Connexion in 1775). Under the superintendence of Revd George Cheatle (Lombard Street) with the assistance of William Snape of Olbery.
morn.   None
aft.   Yes
eve.   Yes

The average was given as 30–40 and the Registrar allowed then 35 for the afternoon service but makes no entry for the evening. The officers of Little Sutton do not miss an opportunity, but write on their form: 'The chapel now under repair: a little pecuniary help would be thankfully rec'd by Charles Ashford or Wm Snape, Collectors for the same.'

Appendix B:
Benefactions of William Middlemore

1847	Purchase of the Circus Chapel	£1,000
1861	Purchase of site and building of Wycliffe	£12,000
1865	Christ Church, Aston amount not known	
1866	Smethwick	£50
1877	Selly Park, Building Fund	£2,600
1877	Stratford Road, Sparkbrook	£1,000
1879–81	Church of the Redeemer	£3,000 [site]
		£500 [building fund]
1884	Small Heath: towards Coventry Road site	£700
1886	Oxford Road, Moseley, site	£800
		£21,650
Baptist Union Annuity Fund		£1,000
Baptist Union Augmentation Fund		£750
		£23,400

Plus many other charitable gifts including the rebuilding of the chancel of Edgbaston Parish Church.

CHAPTER 5

R. W. Dale and the 'Civic Gospel'

David M. Thompson

The association of the Revd R. W. Dale (1829–95), minister of Carr's
Lane Congregational church, Birmingham with the 'civic gospel' in the
later nineteenth century is so well known that it may not seem worthy
of further discussion. It reflected a concern for the possible achievement of good by local government that seems almost symbolic of the
'age of great cities' (to use a phrase of another Congregationalist, Dr
Robert Vaughan).[1] As such, it has been commemorated in secular
history as much as in church or denominational history, for example
by Asa Briggs and Peter Hennock.[2]

The 'civic gospel' is often regarded as a provincial phenomenon. Yet
Dale and Joseph Chamberlain (1836–1914), who as Mayor of Birmingham was perhaps the 'civic gospel's' archetypal exponent and later a
Birmingham MP, were both brought up in London. Their depiction
early in their careers not only as representatives of provincial England,
but also as provincial in their outlook, testifies more to the attitudes of
the press than to the realities of the situation. It deserves re-examination.

Furthermore previous discussion has implied some subtle polar-
izations that merit consideration. Dale's association with Joseph
Chamberlain and his break with Gladstonian Liberalism over Irish
Home Rule left him in something of a political limbo in the last years
of his life. He could not share Chamberlain's readiness to work with
the Conservatives. The latter's membership of Salisbury's cabinet after
1895 has tended to foster the impression that 'gas and water socialism'
(as his Birmingham programme was sometimes called) was significantly
different in emphasis and inspiration from 'state socialism'. Thus Dale
is distinguished from those in the Liberal party who followed a 'new
Liberal' or 'progressive' direction, and in particular he is implicitly set
against John Clifford, the London Baptist minister, who is seen as
Nonconformity's natural Fabian voice. (Two of John Clifford's
addresses were published as Fabian Society Tracts.)

In the light of the shift in national social policy in the 1980s and
1990s associated with Mrs Thatcher's period of office as Prime Minister

(and perhaps indeed in the light of Mr Blair's 'New Labour'), it is opportune to re-examine the direction of social policy in the last hundred years in a way that does not have hidden teleological assumptions behind it. This is the context for this re-examination of R. W. Dale. Dale's view of obligations in local politics cannot be separated from his view of obligations in national politics in the way that has sometimes been implied by selective quotation. It is necessary to reaffirm the significance not only of Dale's doctrine of the church for his understanding of the state (as Peter Hennock does) but also of his understanding of the incarnation for the importance of the social order (like Westcott and Clifford). This is particularly well illustrated by a sermon on 'Christ and the State' preached in 1891 towards the end of his life, which indicates both his political idealism and his political realism. Significantly, this was in John Clifford's presence at his church in London, Westbourne Park, in aid of the Baptist Home Missionary Society. Dale also regarded it as the best sermon he ever preached.[3] 'As a nation becomes increasingly penetrated with the spirit of Christ', wrote Dale, 'its ideal of justice in that temporal order which is under the control of the civil ruler will be gradually elevated.'[4]

My argument is succinctly summarized by Dale's son in his life of his father. The chapter which follows the discussion of 'a Municipal Gospel' begins with these words:

> Political affairs and municipal affairs are often contrasted in a false and mischievous antithesis, as if the interests of the city and the empire were discrepant or even hostile. This was not Dale's belief. He admitted grades in social obligation, but regarded the claims as complementary, not as antagonistic. For himself political and municipal service could not be divorced.[5]

One thing is quite clear about Dale's approach to the civic gospel, and even national politics. It was not a concern which was there from his earliest years. In the 1850s, while he was co-pastor with John Angell James at Carr's Lane, his primary concern was theological. This was the period when he was working out the theological implications of his detachment from the phraseology and thought-world of the old evangelical theology that he criticized so regularly in later years.

A major influence on both his theological and political development was undoubtedly George Dawson, an erstwhile Baptist who became minister of the specially built Church of the Saviour in Edward Street in 1847. This congregation might almost be called the cradle of the civic gospel. Dale attended Dawson's services regularly on Sunday evenings during his first two years at Spring Hill College in 1847–49, and occasionally on Sunday mornings. Even after he began to preach regularly himself, he still continued to attend when he could until his settlement at Carr's Lane in 1853.[6] This was significant for his future, both in that John Angell James did not care for Dawson and that James did not hold Dale's attraction to Dawson against him when persuading him to settle at Carr's Lane.

Dawson's preaching was based on the ideas of James Martineau, minister of the Unitarian church in Liverpool from 1832 to 1857, and then Professor at Manchester New College, London. He emphasized two features in particular: the idea of progressive revelation, discerned by ordinary human beings in a natural way, and the influence of German idealism over against necessitarianism.[7] But the Church of the Saviour was not formally unitarian. Their declaration of church principles stated:

> They unite in the bonds of charity, as Students, with a feeling that each man has much to learn, and perchance much to unlearn: their bond is prospective rather than retrospective – a common spirit rather than a common 'belief' or 'creed'. They unite to do good to others.[8]

Dawson's emphasis was therefore on the practical duties of citizenship – indeed, the practical duties of being human. He criticized the dominant tendency towards individualism in a down-to-earth way. As Dale put it:

> He was not satisfied with insisting on the duty of being unselfish: he attacked the selfishness which would not do municipal work that happened to be unpleasant. He was not satisfied with glorifying patriotism: he glorified the courage of the men who committed themselves to a righteous political cause in its unpopular days, instead of waiting for the hour of its triumph.[9]

This was seen in Dawson's fascination with the Italian nationalism of men such as Mazzini, which was fired not primarily by anti-popery (as with many Protestants) but by the vision of a nation which actually demanded something of its people.

The Nonconformist interest in the movement for Italian unity has not received the attention it deserves.[10] It was linked with the renewed interest in the civic republicanism of the Renaissance in Victorian England, which was not merely echoed in its civic architecture but also provided inspiration for what could be achieved by the city. Dawson looked to municipal corporations to achieve civic renewal, notably in his speech at the opening of the Birmingham Free Reference Library in 1866.[11] The town was the local manifestation of the nation, of the community over against individualism. Many of those in Dawson's congregation were involved in the movement for civic renewal in

Birmingham. Eight of the men who took the first (unsuccessful) initiative for the adoption of the Public Libraries Act in 1852 were from that congregation. Robert Wright, who was largely responsible for the Improvement Act of 1861, was another member and close friend of Dawson.[12] In the end, however, it was not primarily Dawson's men who carried through the changes which have become known as the municipal gospel. These happened towards the end of Dawson's life. (He died in 1876.) They were essentially the responsibility of Joseph Chamberlain.

Chamberlain was first elected to the council in November 1869, fresh from involvement in the agitation for franchise reform and national education. The turning point was his election as Mayor in 1873 on the back of a Liberal landslide in the local elections. His aims were to improve the sanitation, housing and architecture of the town. That needed money – more than could sensibly be achieved from the rates. His solution was to take over local utilities (already municipally owned in some other large cities) to provide a large non-tax revenue. He had two principles: first, that all monopolies which were sustained in any way by the state should be 'in the hands of the representatives of the people, by whom they should be administered, and to whom their profits should go'; and secondly, that the duties and responsibilities of the local authority should be increased so that they should become 'real local parliaments supreme in their special jurisdiction'. [13]

He achieved this first by taking over the local gas companies, which provided street lighting, on terms satisfactory to the companies and the ratepayers. He became chairman of the Gas Committee and made a profit of £25,000 in the first six months. Then he organized the takeover of the water company in 1875. Finally, he embarked on a programme of slum clearance in the city centre using the powers of the Artisans' Dwellings Act of 1875 to buy 40–50 acres of property at £1.5m in 1876. The average death rate in the city centre fell from 53.2 per 1,000 to 21.3 in six years.[14] All these measures involved private Acts of Parliament and therefore committee work in London: they were the springboard for Chamberlain's national political career.

Chamberlain's work was propagated within Birmingham by three leading ministers: R. W. Dale at Carr's Lane Congregational church, H. W. Crosskey at the Unitarian Church of the Messiah (Chamberlain's own church), and Charles Vince of Mount Zion Baptist church, Graham Street. Among these Dale was pre-eminent: Garvin suggested that Dale preached Dawson's gospel of civic regeneration with more commanding power than the originator.[15]

The stages by which this happened must now be examined. The first step was the affirmation of ethical principles as something independent of particular religious commitments. In his account of

Dawson's significance, Dale emphasized that Dawson believed strongly that the laws which govern human life cannot be evaded. 'The facts of the universe are steadfast and not to be changed by human fancies or follies: the laws of the universe are relentless, and will not relax in the presence of human weakness or give way under the pressure of human passion and force.'[16] It is the way Dale explained how Dawson applied this that is particularly interesting:

No matter though you are sincerely convinced that protection to native industry will secure commercial prosperity, you must abolish protective duties or the industry of the nation will be repressed. No matter though you have a most devout and conscientious belief that by mere praying you can save a town from typhoid fever; if the drainage is bad and the water foul, praying will never save that town from typhoid. No matter how deep and strong your faith that you will get on in business by merely reading the Bible and teaching in a Sunday school, and holding a right religious creed; you will soon be in the Bankruptcy Court unless you avoid bad debts, unless you are punctual, unless you are industrious, and unless you know how to keep your shelves clear of dead stock. You cannot make a universe for yourself out of your own head.[17]

The illustrations reflect the characteristic beliefs of the urban mercantile reforming classes.

Dale was also responding to this in the 1860s. In a sermon in Birmingham Town Hall in August 1865 on 'Morality and Religion' he criticized the view held by many Christians that 'goodness and virtue lose their essential character, and cease to be goodness and virtue in men who do not love and fear God'.[18] A similar emphasis is to be found in his 1879 address on 'The Evangelical Revival'. Whilst acknowledging that the revival accomplished a great moral reformation, he argued that it was seriously defective in its moral aims and achievements.[19] The reason was that 'the idea of the obligation resting on the laity to engage in religious work is one of unmeasured potency': what he looked forward to was the recognition of the sacredness of secular business.[20] As yet, he thought, philanthropic work among evangelical Christians was:

little more than a fresh expression of the same spirit that assigned to almsgiving so great a place among the virtues of the medieval Church. But let the idea grow and it will give us a new and Christian conception of the true relation between the rich and the poor, the strong and the weak; or rather it will create a new and Christian theory of the social and political organisation of the State.[21]

The evangelical revival had been very timid. 'It has shrunk from politics. It has regarded literature and art with a certain measure of distrust. In business it has been content with attaching Divine sanction to recognised virtues. We are living in a new world and Evangelicals do not seem to have discovered it.'[22]

Hence Dale argued for a positive view of both politics and secular life. In his first major political speech, 'Churchmen and Dissenters', delivered on 6 March 1862 at a time of controversy over the proposed commemoration of the bicentenary of the Great Ejectment of 1662, he was scathing about the distinction drawn by Anglican evangelicals between conscientious and political Dissenters (the latter being those who campaigned for civil equality for Dissenters, including the dis-establishment of the Church of England). Having said that it was ironical that Anglican evangelicals could co-operate with 'conscientious Dissenters' when they obviously disagreed with them, Dale went on first to deny that political Dissenters were not conscientious, and then to say that 'it is an unhappy sign of our national condition that it should be thought a reproach to speak of any man as political'.[23] Those who studied the laws which affected the welfare and greatness of nations, the history of freedom and the ways in which political institutions could be improved were involved in the next most important study to theology itself:

In a free country like this we cannot cease to be political without forgetting some of our highest privileges and neglecting some of our most urgent responsibilities. If ever the educated and religious classes of the community shall come to regard politics with dislike and contempt, the ancient glory of our country will be near extinction. It has been justly and nobly said that 'the public business of England is the private business of every Englishman'.[24]

The same affirmation of the secular world came in an 1865 sermon preached on behalf of the London Missionary Society in Glasgow.

Men suppose [he said] that we Christian people ought to be altogether indifferent whether the earth is yellow with the ripening corn, or whether it lies undrained, unfenced, and barren; whether the chim-neys of our manufacturing towns are smokeless, and the gigantic machinery motionless and silent, or whether, on every tide, ships, laden with the productions of our industry and skill, sail off to distant parts to return with the wealth of every land; of if, by some strange inconsistency of reasoning, it is supposed that very religious people may be good manufacturers and merchants, it is imagined that if our faith is deep and strong, we must care nothing for great libraries, for galleries of painting and sculpture, for stately buildings, and for noble music.[25]

Such a view entailed the denial of the doctrine of the incarnation.

Christianity, therefore, 'so far from being hostile to the highest and most perfect development of our secular life, is eminently favourable to it', and 'the recovery of the whole world from idolatry, from vice, from atheism, from unbelief, will be accompanied with a condition of material prosperity, of intellectual culture, of social and political freedom, unexampled in human history'.[26] He went on to draw out the political implications of this. In Greek thought the individual existed for the state and the noblest idea of liberty was for each citizen to take part in legislation; apart from that he had no rights and the state claimed absolute control over him. The religion of Christ, however, vindicated the sanctity and dignity of the individual soul; and the nation existed to protect the citizen and to secure his freedom. 'States perish; the individual citizen is immortal.'[27]

This in turn was the basis of the Christian obligation to secure the best possible education for everyone:

> Statesmen may educate to secure the authority of the law against the blind fury of an untaught and brutal population, political economists may educate to augment the material wealth of the country, but the Christian educates because every man was made in the image of God, is the brother of Christ, and because to develop and perfect the faculties of the soul is to do homage to the Creator from whom they came, and to increase the capacity of the creature for knowing God and doing His will.[28]

Dale therefore emphasized the link between practical morality and Christian morality. In another sermon of the same period he regretted that 'the customs and habits of our churches' did not permit him to give up his pulpit now and then 'to some solicitor, banker, or merchant, who would know far more than I do about the morality of our business life'. Such a man 'could correct the follies, point out the perils, warn you against the processes of self-deception, by which thoughtless, careless, feeble men are being constantly betrayed into sin and covered with ruin and shame'[29] It is significant that these sermons, apart from that on the evangelical revival, date from the 1860s; and that the concern for politics and secular life expressed in them is general in scope rather than directed at municipal life in particular.

Dale thus developed a theological response to Dawson's critique of evangelicalism. Peter Hennock rightly noted the importance of Dale's understanding of the church in this process, but missed the significance of his emphasis on the incarnation, or rather on Christology in general.[30] A passing reference to the incarnation in 1865 has already been noted. The implications were more fully developed in two sermons of the 1880s. The Christological emphasis was apparent in a sermon preached at Airedale College, Bradford in June 1880. He noted the decay of traditional theological systems in all churches, and of the Calvinism of the Westminster Confession within Congregationalism. But such systems were but the last stage of medieval scholasticism, and now the appeal was to Christ alone, not to Articles, Confessions or Standards of Faith. This gave Congregationalists a unique freedom and a particular opportunity in the necessary work of reconstruction.[31]

Characteristically he illustrated his point by referring to property and the use of wealth. Absolute ownership of property could be claimed by neither individuals nor communities – 'nothing can be ours, for everything is Christ's', and the possession of wealth entailed an obligation to work for society: 'a wealthy man who declines the work while retaining and enjoying the wages is as dishonest as the carpenter or the plumber who takes money for work he has not done'.[32]

A fuller exposition of the significance of the incarnation came in his sermon of 1884 during the Birmingham meetings of the National Association for the Promotion of Social Science. Having noted that the Christian doctrine of man, by contrast with the doctrine of God, had never been adequately defined in Christian theology, he went on to argue that the doctrine of man was implicated in the Christian doctrine of the Trinity, and that it determined the Christian theory of morals and society. The clue was the incarnation. The alliance between God and humanity in the person of Christ was not transient: 'in Him the eternal Son of God *became* Man, and in Him the eternal Son of God *remains* Man'.[33] Moreover, the incarnation was not an isolated wonder: 'it was God's witness to the true and ideal relation of all men to God'.[34] So in everyone, whatever their state, there existed the possibility of realizing this wonderful relationship to God, and all Christian duties to others – 'in the family, in business, in general society, as members of the same municipality, as citizens of the same commonwealth – are to be modified and controlled by this conception'.[35]

Here there is a Free Church emphasis on the centrality of the incarnation at least as early as that found in Westcott and writers of the *Lux Mundi* school in the Church of England, and it comes from a leading exponent of the doctrine of the atonement. Dale's Congregational Lecture for 1875, published as *The Atonement*, was a major attempt to restate traditional emphases in that doctrine in the light of criticisms of the penal substitutionary theory advanced since the beginning of the century. It is not therefore so easy as has been suggested to equate atonement-centred theology with a negative view of the possibility of significant human improvement on the one hand, and incarnation-centred theology and a more optimistic view of the possibilities of social reform on the other.[36] Rather what was happening was the use of Christological doctrine as a way of overcoming the problems of confessional or even biblical authority when attacked by higher criticism.

Dale's view of the church is set out most comprehensively in an essay of 1871, which itself began with the statement that the supreme fact in the history of the world was that God became man in the person of the Lord Jesus Christ. His main concern, however, was that Congregationalism whilst preserving the apostolic polity did not apprehend 'the Idea from which that polity sprang'. The energy of their protest against secular interference in religious life, the claims of priesthoods or the pretensions of the great churches of Christendom seemed sometimes to imply that the 'whole idea of religion is included in the immediate relations between the soul and God'. That constituted an implicit denial of the necessity for the existence of the church. Yet nothing could be clearer than that 'isolation is not the law of the religious life'.[37] Indeed, the necessity for communion which constituted the church was the spiritual manifestation of a general law of human development – 'a Divine idea which lies at the very foundation of the moral order of the universe'.[38]

Dale therefore regarded the theory of individualism as 'flagrantly inconsistent with the whole organization of human life'. 'We are not isolated individuals, but members of a race', and 'a nation is very much more than a collection of individual men, living in the same country, speaking the same language, and governed by the same laws; there is a national life common to all classes in the State'.[39] The echoes of F. D. Maurice are apparent here, but Dale drew different conclusions. He mentioned several ways of looking at the church which he regarded as inadequate – the idea that a hierarchical church was suited to an aristocratic society, that the church expressed the vigour and unity of national life, that the church civilized people by placing a gentleman in every parish, or that the church provided a learned ministry or an adequate income for every minister. In each case the flaw was that the particular advantages were not central to the 'Idea of the Church'; and in some cases they contradicted it, for example, by confirming national isolation.[40]

The underlying idea of the church was that it consisted of all those who had received the divine life, and this was manifested in a ready acceptance of the mutual obligations of Christians to one another such that the communion of saints would be a visible reality.[41] Dale regarded this as the distinctive mark of Congregationalism, and it is clear that he saw service to the wider community as an integral part of that. Again, the similarity to Maurice is clear.

How did Dale apply this theology in practice? He was aware that he ministered to a wealthy congregation – by the 1870s his annual stipend of £1000 was comparable to that of many cathedral residentiary canons in the Church of England. He was also concerned about the problems of wealth, and this emerged in the discussion of his visits to both America and Australia. In 1877 he visited the United States to give the Lyman Beecher lectures at Yale, and commented on the lack of a continuing sense of political responsibility among Americans. He reckoned that thousands and tens of thousands of the best men in the country thought it possible 'to enjoy the fruits of good government without working for them'.[42] The reason he suggested was that:

> the action of government does not affect the life and interests of the great masses of the people so directly and so powerfully as among ourselves. *The material prosperity of the country has been so great* that there has been no reason for engaging in political agitation in order to resist a policy which was regarded as the cause of national distress.[43]

Similarly, when he visited Australia in 1888, he noted the effect of high wages, and wondered whether they could remain higher than those in Europe for ever.[44] He thought that the economy encouraged the temptation to speculate, which was tantamount to gambling, and that if one could make money more easily by speculation than by work, then the incentive to work would diminish.[45] Moreover, if the churches were seen as essentially philanthropic institutions, what future was there for them if philanthropy became unnecessary? [46]

Dale's comments on America and Australia came late in his career. Nevertheless as early as the 1860s he was emphasizing the responsibilities of wealth, and hence of rich men. Thus, when preaching at the induction of the Revd R. Thomas as minister of Moseley Road Congregational church, Birmingham in November 1863, Dale noted the growth in Birmingham's wealth since 1850 which was most marked in the suburbs. He thought that 'a spirit of luxurious self-indulgence' was spreading silently but surely among the people. Men were shrinking, he believed, 'through sheer indolence and effeminacy, from public secular work, as well as from religious work which requires any moral courage and any laborious painstaking'. They were spending more on their houses, furniture and entertainments and not increasing to the same extent their contributions for the relief of suffering, the instruction of ignorance and religious welfare.[47] This was a special concern of a suburban pastor for, he said, 'it is from your people rather than mine, from those who are prosperous enough to live away from their workshops and their counting houses that the largest measure of support ought to come for hospitals, for schools, for missions to our own poor, for the diffusion of the gospel throughout the world'. These were the people from whom there ought to come those who engaged personally in 'zealous Christian labour among the crowded streets and courts where the working people live, from whom they derive their wealth. *They will be likely to forget this, if you do not remember it.'* [48]

The growth of suburbs symbolized for Dale, as for many of his generation, the widening separation between the poor and the rich, and he worried about its religious implications. In a sermon of 1865 he illustrated the difficulty the wealthy had in appreciating the plight of the poor by a dramatic story of a mother who killed her child. Whenever she tried to get employment, her child was in the way; she went into the workhouse and the child was taken from her. One day she heard it crying, but when she went to comfort it, someone else snatched it from her and the child was beaten for trying to throw itself into its mother's arms. The woman's crime in killing her child was inexcusable, but Dale prayed that God would keep all of his hearers from temptations like hers. [49]

In a sermon on 'The Perils and Uses of Rich Men', published in 1867, he returned to the same theme, but even more specifically. A man of high social rank had a duty to study how the true interests of the poor might be promoted by legislation and to help in conducting the business of the state. Prosperous men belonging to the middle classes had similar public functions:

> They ought to feel 'called of God' to act as 'Guardians of the Poor'. They ought to work on the Committees of Hospitals. They ought to be Aldermen and Town Councillors. They ought to give their time as well as their money to whatever improvements are intended to develop the intelligence of the community. They ought to be reformers of local abuses. They ought to see to it that the towns and parishes in which they live are well drained, well lighted, and well paved; that there are good schools for every class of the population; that there are harmless public amusements; that all parochial and municipal affairs are conducted honourably and equitably. [50]

He was concerned that in nearly every part of the country the prosperous manufacturers and merchants were leaving public duties to men of lower position and culture than themselves, which he thought was ominous for the political greatness and stability of a free nation: 'even the mob prefer a gentleman to a blackguard, in the long run'. [51]

Whilst the tone of this language reflects the anxieties of many of the middle classes at the prospect of the consequences of the 1867 Reform Act, but the emphasis on political action was the basis for what became known as the 'civic gospel'. The same concern for sanitation and education was characteristic of Chamberlain's programme in Birmingham in the 1870s.

To the students at Yale in 1877 he was trenchant about those who said that they were too spiritual to enter the polling booth. Dale even ventured to think it possible that the time would come when people who refused to vote would be subjected to church discipline in the same way as those refused to pay their debts. The choice of such a comparison was significant for someone ministering in a mercantile community. 'The plea that the discharge of political duty is inconsistent with the maintenance of spirituality ought to be denounced as a flagrant piece of hypocrisy.' It was also selfish. 'They consent to accept all the advantages which come from the political institutions of the nation and from the political zeal and fidelity of their fellow citizens.' Such spiritual people ought to decline the services of the police, to use law courts or to accept legacies. 'For men to claim the right to neglect their duties to the State on the ground of their piety, while they insist on the State protecting their persons, protecting their property, and protecting from disturbance even their religious meetings in which this exquisitely delicate and valetudinarian spirituality is developed, is gross unrighteousness.' The fundamental importance which Dale attached to municipal politics, even over against state or national politics, emerged even more clearly. He emphasized that 'honest and effective municipal government lies at the very base of public freedom and public order'. Discharge of municipal duties provided the necessary discipline for the right conduct of public affairs, and a keen interest in local administration formed and strengthened public spirit.[52]

It is significant that in his sermon of 1884 on social science he noted that it had a wider province than political economy because it dealt with questions about man as well as about wealth. Thus, while an improvement in public health might contribute to the increase of wealth in the long run, the true sanitary reformer did not ask 'whether improvements in the water supply of a town, or the increase of its open spaces, or a change for the better in the homes of the people, will add to our exports and imports, increase our turn-out of cotton goods and hardware, make the income-tax more productive'. Likewise education could not be regarded as merely subordinate to economy and trade. Those involved in education did not need 'to consider merely how boys and girls can be made more effective "hands" in a manufactory, but how their whole life – including their life in the manufactory, but also including their life in hours of leisure – can be made more vigorous, more varied, more delightful'.[53]

Here therefore was a justification for a civic gospel; but it also involved a larger view of the state. In an appreciation of John Bright, Dale summed up the shift in the view of the state that he believed had taken place in the later nineteenth century. He described Bright's view that the state should treat citizens like adults rather than children and his support of the extension of the franchise on precisely that ground, that it would teach people self-respect and responsibility. Bright had distrusted the power of legislation to relieve the distress of large masses of people as likely to lessen the penalties of recklessness and wrongdoing, and so to diminish the motives to virtue. Charitable relief should be the work of the churches, voluntary organizations and individuals. However, Dale did not think that the nation had shared this view: 'we are repelled rather than attracted by what I have called the moral austerity which characterized Mr Bright's political faith'.[54]

In a sermon on 'Christ and the State' two years later Dale described the transition differently. In the 1840s, he said, the business of secular government was seen as the repression of force and fraud.

The State was even regarded by many of us as founded on a kind of mutual contract for the purpose of protecting life and property – a Limited Liability Company with its objects and powers strictly defined in the articles of association. To restrict its actions within the narrowest possible area was supposed to be the first duty of a wide and liberal politician.[55]

The change was attributed to John Stuart Mill and Edmund Burke, but above all to Frederick Denison Maurice:

Mr Maurice insisted that the State is a Divine institution – like the Family, like the Church; many of us, I say, probably owe to him more than to any other man the original impulse which started our thought in that direction. But as soon as we began to look seriously into the New Testament we found it there, 'and we were astonished that we had not found it before.[56]

Thus he noted that, according to Paul, government was still a divine institution, even when it was administered by bad men and administered badly; as long as it held society together, it was better than no government at all.[57] He had argued in 1884 that:

the man who holds municipal or political office is a 'minister of God'. One man may therefore have just as real a Divine vocation to become a town councillor or a Member of Parliament, as another to become a missionary to the heathen … The Divine Right of Kings was a base corruption of a most noble truth, so was the fanatical dream about the reign of the saints. We shall never approach to the Christian ideal of civil society, until all who hold municipal, judicial, and political offices, recognise the social and political order of the nation as a Divine institution and discharge their official duties as ministers of God.[58]

Dale explained what he meant when discussing his impressions of Australia. The practical recognition of the spirit and laws of Christian ethics in the actual business of the state was what made the state Christian. Thus he did not accept that the secular nature of the state in Australia made any difference. 'States cease to be secular when the people and their rulers seriously believe that the State is a divine institution – as divine as the Church, though belonging to a wholly different order and instituted for wholly different ends.'[59] This was his alternative to the Anglican view that an established church witnessed to the divine institution of the state, a view which had been strengthened by the tradition of Coleridge and Maurice which in many ways he used. Thus in his *Manual of Congregational Principles*, he emphasized the reciprocal nature of rights and duties and suggested that 'political institutions are at once an expression and a discipline of the character of nations'.[60]

Dale extended the idea of councillors and MPs as ministers of God to the electorate as a whole, and thereby emphasized the importance of the franchise. This is an important context for an oft-quoted section of his 1884 sermon in which he said that he sometimes thought that municipalities could do more for the people than Parliament:

> Their powers will probably be enlarged; but under the powers which they possess already they can greatly diminish the amount of sickness in the community, and can prolong human life. They can prevent – they have prevented – tens of thousands of wives from becoming widows, tens of thousands of children from becoming orphans. They can do very much to improve those miserable homes which are fatal not only to health, but to decency and morality. They can give to the poor the enjoyment of pleasant parks and gardens, and the intellectual cultivation and refinement of public libraries and galleries of art. They can redress in many ways the inequalities of human conditions ...
>
> If, years ago, the Christian people of the metropolis had insisted on having an effective system of municipal government, and had worked its powers vigorously, the 'Bitter Cry of Outcast London' need never have been heard. Now that the cry has come to them the churches will never be able to remedy the evil apart from the action of municipal authorities. Medicine, and not the gospel only, is necessary to cure the sick. Municipal action, and not the gospel only, is necessary to improve the homes of the poor.[61]

The Bitter Cry of Outcast London was, of course, the title of a pamphlet, published in 1883, appealing for funds for Congregational Home Missionaries in London, but it attracted newspaper attention because of its somewhat sensational account of living conditions in the slums. Dale's reference has sometimes been taken as a rather snide comment on the absence of effective local government in London from the perspective of a champion of it in the provinces. But in 1883 the Liberals had had to decide which to put first, the agricultural labourers' franchise or a London government bill: Dale backed the decision to go for the franchise, and this gives point to the reference to it which immediately precedes the passage quoted. In his 1867 speech on the franchise, he had argued that to deprive people of the franchise is to deprive them of the option of peaceful protest, thereby forcing them towards violent resistance.[62]

Peter Hennock asked how Dale's view differed from Dawson's, and suggested that the answer lay in Dale's doctrine of the church.[63] Clearly Dale's understanding of the church was different from Dawson's; but there is a sense in which Dale was translating into his own terms what Dawson had said about municipalities being the successors of the churches. Dale gave the state or municipality a divine role, whilst distinguishing it clearly from the church in a way that Dawson failed to do. The wonder is not so much that he did this, as that it took him so long to do so (as he frankly acknowledged in his 1891 sermon concerning Maurice).

The key point is that it is a mistake to lay too much emphasis on the municipalities over against the state. As a Congregationalist, Dale saw the larger whole encapsulated in the local. But this did not make the local pre-eminent. It is interesting that in his accounts of both the United States and Australia he discussed the relationship between wider and more local legislatures. In Australia (before the Commonwealth of Australia Act of 1901) he noted that state governments had taken on responsibilities otherwise undertaken by municipal authorities – water supply, the construction of roads and bridges, etc.[64] Similarly, he wrote that America was the paradise of Home Rulers, because of the division between federal and state powers. He accepted the necessity for this but said that it divided political interest and that political life lost the depth and force derived from concentration.[65] This was written in 1878, before Dale's disillusionment over Irish Home Rule, and it indicates that he did not see strong municipal government as weakening but rather complementing the state.

It might be suggested that this implies a growing political conservatism in Dale as he grew older. Nevertheless there are strong continuities, which can be illustrated from three sermons at the end of his life. In an undelivered section of an induction sermon in Manchester in 1890, he referred to the threats to the Christian gospel in contemporary thought. The first one he mentioned was the modern doctrine of heredity, which he said was more fatal to a sense of personal responsibility for life and conduct than the old doctrine of original sin. The second was the emphasis on the power of the environment, and especially the social environment, over personal life, which he regarded as 'more fatal to the sense of moral freedom than the Calvinistic doctrine of the Divine decrees'.[66] He described the philosophical theory of necessity as 'Calvinism without a God'. Large numbers of people had just discovered the sins of society and 'in the freshness of their penitence' they were declaring that society, and society alone, was responsible for the wickedness and misery of individuals. 'Create, they say, a new and just and gracious social order, and the wilderness will blossom as the rose; the vices of men will vanish; all men will be virtuous.'[67]

Closely associated with those tendencies was the demand for a social order based on the principles of the Sermon on the Mount. Dale thought that was a confusion, since the Sermon on the Mount was intended for Christians. 'A Christian social order is impossible except to a Christian people ... As long as the great desire of large numbers of our people is for material prosperity, a social order in harmony with the Sermon on the Mount is impossible.'[68] So he did not believe in large schemes for changing the whole order of political or economic life; and he specifically criticized the state socialist solution because the equation contained so many unknown quantities that he could not solve it. He suspected that the evil results of collectivism would outweigh the good. Moreover, 'the *first* object of the Christian faith is not to secure justice and mercy in social institutions, but to make Christian men merciful and just'.[69] Thus employers and employed were required to seek the Kingdom of God and his righteousness, by doing their parts '*as if Christ were the Head of the firm*'.[70] This was not simply a later conservative mood, reacting against the development of socialist ideas in the 1880s. It picked up the themes of an article he had written on Gambetta in 1883, just when the social question was beginning to hit the headlines. It also picked up comments he had made on the gradual effects of legislation in his 1867 lecture on 'The Politics of the Future'.[71]

In his sermon on 'Christ and the State' in 1891 he began by posing the question as to whether Jesus had missed a great chance by not allowing the people to make him king (John 6: 15). In saying no, he suggested that the best social and economic order for a nation was largely determined by its actual material, intellectual and moral condition; thus representative institutions only worked when there were people ready to undertake their duties in public service – a point he had repeatedly made in urging the civic gospel earlier in his ministry. He also noted that laws which were not supported by the moral conviction of the great mass of the people were always ineffective; they might do something to educate the national conscience, but they failed to do even that if they were far in advance of it.[72] It was not Christ's object to give us a social and political order that would certainly secure universal physical happiness for all people. 'Government is a Divine institution but it is through human virtue, human self-sacrifice, human patience, human sagacity, that the material blessings which are possible through the social condition are to be actually won.'[73]

Finally, in his opening address to the International Congregational Council in 1891 on 'The Divine Life in Man', Dale also showed signs of Maurice's influence. The centrality of the doctrine of the incarnation was indicated by his statement that 'as the Incarnation is no afterthought of the Divine mind occasioned by the entrance of sin into the world, neither is the gift of eternal life in Christ a mere expedient for restoring sinful men to holiness'.[74] Similarly his affirmation that 'in Christ is the common root of the life of the race', drawing on Colossians, echoed Maurice as did his description of baptism as that which declared 'that every child is by birth, not only the heir of the infirmities, and sorrows, and perils, and sins of the race, but also the heir of the life, and love, and righteousness, and joy of God'. Thus he said that in our preaching we did not tell people 'that God will become their Father, as a result of their repentance and of their belief in His mercy revealed though Christ; but that because He is already their Father, they should repent and believe'.[75]

Hence the divine life pervaded all aspects of life: 'there is a saintliness of the bank, of the exchange, of the newspaper office, of the court of justice, and of Parliament as well as of the cloister'.[76] For Dale, this was linked naturally with the Congregational idea of the church.

> We believe that a Church is a society of men possessing the life of the eternal Son of God, and having direct access through Him, in the power of the Spirit, to the Father ... of men to whom the truth of the Christian Gospel is authenticated by a most certain experience, the experience, not of an individual life merely, but of a Society.[77]

This shows Dale's theology of the church working through to a responsible challenging of the individual. There was no simple, automatic solution but a reciprocal social and individual responsibility. This was his response to evangelical individualism, and he found simple collectivism no more satisfying. Although John Clifford is sometimes represented as having such a belief in simple collectivism, his social beliefs were also balanced in a similar way.[78]

Four main conclusions emerge from this study. First, Dale's civic gospel is more than civic, but it was rooted in the city just as his

Christianity was rooted in the local church. Secondly, he had an enlarged view of the state that went beyond the scope of political economy and attached high importance to the responsible use of representative institutions. This explained the importance he attached to the franchise. Thirdly, Dale was perceptive enough to see that there would be problems for the church if it was understood primarily as a philanthropic agency, particularly in the context of a general improvement in the standard of living. Finally, Dale's ultimate theological response was Christological as well as ecclesiological. His emphasis on the incarnation and atonement was of a piece with that of contemporary High Church Anglicans, but it was in no way derived from them. Rather, they drew on the same sources in the fathers of the early church and in Coleridge and Maurice more recently. In short, Dale's concern was not so much that the church as such should take a political stance as that Christians should play their proper political role in a state which was itself of divine institution. The civic gospel was a call for political responsibility across the nation as a whole.

Notes

1. Robert Vaughan's book, *The Age of Great Cities* (London: 1843), was a defence of the development of cities but with the caution that only Christianity could save them from peril.
2. A. Briggs, *Victorian Cities* (London: 1963), pp. 185–243; E. P. Hennock, *Fit and Proper Persons* (London: 1973), pp. 61–176. Hennock devotes a whole chapter to the influence of R. W. Dale.
3. A. W. W. Dale, *The Life of R. W. Dale of Birmingham* (London: 1898), p. 602.
4. R. W. Dale, 'Christ and the State', in *Fellowship with Christ* (London: 1891), p. 207.
5. Dale, 'Christ and the State', p. 418.
6. Dale, 'Christ and the State', pp. 50–1. Dale's own estimate of Dawson is to be found in R. W. Dale, 'George Dawson: Politician, Lecturer, and Preacher', *The Nineteenth Century* (August 1877), ii, pp. 44–61, which may be contrasted with John Angell James's somewhat ambivalent remarks in his *Protestant Nonconformity ... in Birmingham* (London: 1849), pp. 178–9.
7. Hennock, *Fit and Proper Persons*, p. 66.
8. Quoted in Hennock, *Fit and Proper Persons*, p. 67.
9. Dale, 'George Dawson', p. 49.
10. D. M. Thompson, 'The Christian Socialist Revival in Britain: A Reappraisal', in J. Garnett and C. Matthew (eds), *Revivals and Religion: Essays presented to John Walsh* (London: 1993), pp. 281–4; cf. Dale, *Life of Dale*, p. 252.
11. Hennock, *Fit and Proper Persons*, pp. 75–6; Briggs, *Victorian Cities*, p. 199.

12. Hennock, *Fit and Proper Persons*, p. 77; Briggs, *Victorian Cities*, pp. 215–16.
13. J. L. Garvin, *The Life of Joseph Chamberlain* (London: 1935), i, p. 188.
14. Garvin, *Chamberlain*, i, pp. 189–99.
15. Garvin, *Chamberlain*, i, p. 182; cf. Dale, *Life of Dale*, pp. 413–15.
16. Dale, 'George Dawson', p. 50.
17. Dale, 'George Dawson', pp. 50–1.
18. R. W. Dale, *Discourses delivered on Special Occasions* (London: 1866), p. 32.
19. R. W. Dale, *The Evangelical Revival and other sermons* (London: 1880), p. 33.
20. Dale, *Evangelical Revival*, p. 37.
21. Dale, *Evangelical Revival*, p. 38.
22. Dale, *Evangelical Revival*, p. 38.
23. R. W. Dale, *Churchmen and Dissenters: their mutual relations as affected by the celebration of the bicentenary of St Bartholomew's Day, 1662* (London: 1862), p. 22.
24. Dale, *Churchmen and Dissenters*, p. 23.
25. R. W. Dale, 'The Influence of Christianity on the Temporal Future of Mankind', in *Discourses on Special Occasions*, p. 220.
26. Dale, 'Influence of Christianity', p. 231.
27. Dale, 'Influence of Christianity', p. 238. This argument was repeated in virtually the same words in Dale's lecture in Birmingham Town Hall of 1867 to those enfranchised by the Second Reform Act; R. W. Dale, *The Politics of the Future* (Birmingham: 1867), p. 18.
28. Dale, *Discourses on Special Occasions*, p. 239.
29. Dale, *Discourses on Special Occasions*, p. 45.
30. Hennock, *Fit and Proper Persons*, p. 163.
31. R. W. Dale, 'The Work of the Christian Ministry in a period of Theological Decay and Reconstruction', in *Evangelical Revival*, pp. 266–7, 270, 272–5.
32. Dale, 'Christian Ministry', pp. 281–3 (quotations from 281 and 282).
33. R. W. Dale, 'Social Science and the Christian Faith', in *Evangelical Revival*, p. 158.
34. Dale, 'Social Science', p. 159.
35. Dale, 'Social Science', pp. 161–2.
36. See Boyd Hilton, *The Age of Atonement: The Influence of Evangelicalism on Social and Economic Thought, 1785–1865* (Oxford: 1988), pp. 255–339.
37. R. W. Dale, 'The Idea of the Church in relation to Modern congregationalism', in *Essays and Addresses* (ed. A. W. W. Dale, London: 1899), p. 92.
38. Dale, 'Idea of the Church', p. 100.
39. Dale, 'Idea of the Church', pp. 100–1, 102, 103.
40. Dale, 'Idea of the Church', pp. 113–16. Dale's discussion may be compared with that of F. D. Maurice in *The Kingdom of Christ* (2nd ed, London: 1842), Part III, ch 2 (Everyman ed, pp. 305–32), where Maurice's emphasis is different.
41. Dale, 'Idea of the Church', pp. 121, 149.
42. R. W. Dale, 'Impressions of America: II', *The Nineteenth Century* 3.14 (April 1878), p. 760.

43. Dale, 'Impressions of America', p. 761 (emphasis added).
44. R. W. Dale, 'Impressions of Australia: IV', *Contemporary Review* 55 (1889), p. 422.
45. R. W. Dale, 'Impressions of Australia: V', *Contemporary Review* 55 (1889), p. 579.
46. Dale, 'Impressions of Australia: V', pp. 562–3.
47. R. W. Dale, 'The Suburban Pastor', in *Discourses on Special Occasions*, pp. 337–8.
48. Dale, 'Suburban Pastor', p. 339.
49. R. W. Dale, 'Morality and Religion', in *Discourses on Special Occasions*, p. 37.
50. R. W. Dale, 'The Perils and Uses of Rich Men', in *Week-day Sermons* (London: 1867), pp. 208–9.
51. Dale, 'Rich Men', p. 210.
52. R. W. Dale, *Nine Lectures on Preaching* (London: 1877), pp. 256–9.
53. Dale, 'Social Science', *Fellowship with Christ*, pp. 151–2.
54. R. W. Dale, 'Mr Bright', *Contemporary Review* 55 (May 1889), pp. 645–8.
55. Dale, 'Christ and the State', p. 200.
56. Dale, 'Christ and the State', pp. 201–2.
57. Dale, 'Christ and the State', p. 207.
58. R. W. Dale, 'Political and Municipal Duty', in *The Laws of Christ for Common Life* (London: 1884), pp. 197–8.
59. Dale, 'Impressions of Australia: V', p. 581.
60. R. W. Dale, *A Manual of Congregational Principles* (London: 1884), p. 3.
61. Dale, *Laws of Christ for Common Life*, pp. 199–200.
62. Dale, *Politics of the Future*, p. 5.
63. Hennock, *Fit and Proper Persons*, pp. 163–4.
64. Dale, 'Impressions of Australia: IV', pp. 415–16.
65. Dale, 'Impressions of America: II', pp. 761–2.
66. R. W. Dale, 'The Ministry required by the Age', in *Fellowship with Christ*, p. 252.
67. Dale, 'Ministry', p. 253.
68. Dale, 'Ministry', p. 256.
69. Dale, 'Ministry', pp. 258–9.
70. Dale, 'Ministry', p. 260.
71. R. W. Dale, 'M. Gambetta: Positivism and Christianity', *Contemporary Review* 43 (1883), pp. 476, 490; *Politics of the Future*, p. 11.
72. Dale, 'Christ and the State', pp. 195–6.
73. Dale, 'Christ and the State', p. 198.
74. Dale, 'The Divine Life in Man', in *Fellowship with Christ*, p. 350.
75. Dale, 'Divine Life', pp. 352, 356.
76. Dale, 'Divine Life', p. 363.
77. Dale, 'Divine Life', p. 366.
78. See D. M. Thompson, 'The Emergence of the Nonconformist Social Gospel in England', in K. Robbins (ed.), *Protestant Evangelicalism: Britain. Ireland, Germany and America, c. 1750–c. 1950, Studies in Church History, Subsidia* 7 (Oxford: 1990), pp. 276–9.

CHAPTER 6

The Contribution of the Welsh Nonconformist Diaspora in the West Midlands of England

W. Eifion Powell

Diaspora, bearing in mind its original meaning, is rather a presumptuous term to use of the Welsh – especially the consciously Welsh Nonconformist – influx into the West Midlands during the nineteenth and twentieth centuries. It has been surmised, on the statistical evidence of Philo, that the numbers of dispersed Jews during the first half of the first century exceeded the numbers of those who lived in Palestine,[1] a fact which is hardly applicable to the Welsh emigration. The term does seem to be more applicable, however, when its figurative meaning is considered, namely that of a people consigned to earthly habitation in an area away from its spiritual homeland; and it becomes more apposite still when we are reminded of the impressive religious statistics of the 1851 census, which described the 976,490 who presented themselves for worship on 30 March 1851 out of a total Welsh population of 1,163,139 as being 80 per cent Nonconformist and 20 per cent Anglican.[2]

Although the Welsh exodus of the nineteenth century can hardly be compared in statistical terms with that of the Irish, or emotively to that of the Scots, it was, nevertheless, a considerable affair considering the size of the population of rural Wales in the mid nineteenth century. The undermining of the position of the highland farmers by the economic situation of the day, compounded by the unwillingness of the landowners to decrease their tenants' rents, led to the marked movement of population from the rural areas to the new industrial centres within Wales and England, as well as to the establishment of a Welsh settlement in Patagonia in the mid-1860s.

It is at this point that I have to express my wish to delimit the parameters of my discourse, both linguistically and geographically. At the time the story begins, during the 1820s, it has been creditably estimated that over 80 per cent of the population of Wales spoke Welsh. The first sound statistical evidence for the number of Welsh-speakers appeared in the 1891 census, when the percentage figure stood at 54.4 of the whole, a figure which was constantly eroded during the sub-sequent century, so that the percentage figure for the Welsh-speaking component in the 1991 census was 18.7. This means that during our period the fraction of Welsh-speaking persons in Wales fell from over four-fifths to less than a fifth. Although one is aware of the presence and contribution of some of the descendants of noted Welsh families to English-speaking Nonconformist congregations in the West Mid-lands, such as for example the Kenricks of Ruabon within Unitarianism and the Lloyds of Dolobran in Montgomeryshire to Quakerism, it would be an impossible task to trace the movement and contribution of Welsh people who worshipped and worked in English-speaking churches within the area. I intend to confine my observations therefore to the development and contribution of the more easily defined Welsh-speaking congregations.

The second consideration is the geographical one, and since I have not as yet met any two Englishpeople who agree on the exact boundaries of the West Midlands, I have decided that any attempt to hold the development of the Welsh churches in Hanley, Crewe and possibly Shrewsbury in juxtaposition to those of Birmingham, Wolverhampton, Coventry and Rugby over the last century and a half would reduce this essay to a series of flurried and confusing statistics. I am reliably informed that a British Rail West Midlands travel pass allows its possessor to journey between Wolverhampton and Coventry, and that is an area which suits my present purpose well, as long as I am allowed a short sortie to Rugby.

Although the names Welsh End, Welsh Cross and Welsh Market testify to an earlier Welsh presence in the Birmingham area it was in 1824 that The Birmingham Saint David's Society was founded, a society which made itself responsible for the maintenance of poor Welsh children at the Blue Coat School.[3] On the afternoon of 16 May in the same year we have reference to the fact that a Welsh sermon was preached at the 'Meeting House' in Bond Street by a certain T. Morris. It was in the following year, however, that the doyen of nineteenth-century Welsh preachers, the Revd John Elias of Anglesey, preached to some hundreds of Welshmen at Carr's Lane chapel on Tuesday evening, 29 March 1825.[4] His appeal to the congregation to establish a Welsh-speaking Christian cause was not answered immediately but some Welsh people did rent a room in the Spread Eagle in the Bull-ring in 1827, where they met on Sundays to read the Bible. Arrangements were soon made to rent an old chapel in Rea Street and they were supported in this venture by the Revd John Jones of Carmarthen, who had come to Birmingham in 1819 as a missionary in the Countess of Huntingdon's Connexion. The fears expressed regarding the character of some of the people associated with the embryonic Welsh cause at the time were well-founded, for although it engendered the support of some local clergy with Welsh connections, and of the Revd Arthur Jones, the later famous Welsh Independent minister at Bangor who was at Birmingham for a period under the auspices of the London Missionary Society, it soon foundered when the treasurer fled to America with the chapel funds.[5]

After that disappointing beginning, matters took a more positive turn with the influx in 1832 of a number of Welsh craftsmen who were imported from Anglesey and Caernarvonshire to work the Anglesey marble used in the construction of the Birmingham Town Hall. It was reported that twenty-eight of these stonemasons and carpenters were Calvinistic Methodists, whilst the other two were Independents.[6] The flourishing Sunday school which they established was in fear of failing when most of these craftsmen and their families returned to Wales between 1835 and 1837. In 1837, however, a pious Welsh blacksmith named Edward Price moved from Oswestry to Birmingham and proved himself a tireless worker on behalf of the Welsh Calvinistic Methodist cause.[7] For the next three years the worshippers met in rented rooms, first in Bromsgrove Street near the Horse Fair, where they were troubled by noisy Irishmen, then in Easy Row and subsequently in Cambridge Street. The direct assistance given them by the Revd John Jones enabled them to purchase a plot of land in Peck Lane, in the middle of Birmingham, on a ninety-nine-year lease. This plot formed part of the property of the King Street church where he ministered, and he himself donated the sum of £5 towards the building of a Welsh chapel there, as did the Revd John Angell James, the minister of Carr's Lane. The chapel in Peck Lane was duly built for the sum of £582 4s., and opened in May 1842.[8]

Before proceeding further with this story we need to turn our attention to a parallel development at Bilston. A cause had been established at Bilston in 1836 in what was described as 'a large dwelling adapted for the purpose, opposite the Wesleyan chapel',[9] for the use of which the members paid an annual rent of £18. In 1841 the membership was fourteen, although according to a report in *Y Drysorfa* there were in 1840 'hundreds of Welshmen in Bilston, most of whom live in complete neglect of the means of grace'.[10] In 1845 the Welsh Calvinistic Methodists built a small chapel at Bilston, which was formally opened on 19 October 1845. In 1843, the congregation had procured the services of the Revd Joseph Thomas, who also ministered at Peck Lane, and he was instrumental in promoting developments at both places before his return to Wales at the end of 1846. The church at Bilston flourished until 1897, when it was closed 'as a result of the departure of many Welsh people from the town'.[11]

The building of the two chapels at Peck Lane and Bilston resulted in a debt of £900 which Edward Price worked assiduously to remove by launching financial appeals and travelling to churches and Presbytery meetings in North and South Wales.[12] But before the debt was completely paid the congregation at Peck Lane was forced to sell the chapel to the London and North Western Railway Company for the sum of £1,000 for the development of New Street station. In their search for a new site some of the church members, of whom there would have been some fifty in all, favoured the Hockley Hill area while others gravitated towards Edgbaston, and it was in Wood Street in the Edgbaston area that the new project, including the building of a chapel and four private houses, was completed in 1849 at a cost of £1,200, the church being officially opened on 20 May of that year.[13] The members of Wood Street chapel who lived in the Handsworth area opened a Sunday school at the corner of Brearly Street, Hockley Hill in 1853. This venture eventually led to the building of a chapel there in 1867, which was formally opened on 12 April 1868 and which by 1869 had its own minister.[14]

Let us now turn our attention to Wolverhampton. A number of Welshmen came to Wolverhampton between 1830 and 1850 seeking work as coalminers and iron workers. It is interesting to note that the religious census of 1851 reveals that there were 150 Welsh worshippers in Wolverhampton at that time compared with the figure of 130 entered for Birmingham. We first hear of Welsh services being held at Wolverhampton in 1853 when a Welsh Independent cause was established there. This cause failed to flourish due to the dissension that prevailed amongst its members and in 1854 the Welsh Calvinistic Methodists inaugurated meetings, first in a room in Bilston Street and two years later in Castle Street and ultimately in James Street in the British School there.[15] Two of the leading lights at that time were Robert Jones and John Parry, both of whom were in the employ of the Great Western Railway, as were a number of the congregation. Most of the Welsh Independents joined with them in these meetings.

The cause at Wolverhampton was actively assisted first by the Revd William Griffiths from the Pwllheli area and then by the Revd David Pierce of Machynlleth, both of whom came to them under the auspices of the Home Mission Society of the North Wales Calvinistic Methodist Association, founded in 1813 for the purpose of 'promoting religious knowledge amongst the inhabitants of the Marches of Wales'.[16] Under their influence and during David Pierce's tenure, a small chapel was built at St George's Parade in 1860. The cost of its construction was £546 8s. 3d. and it is interesting to note that among the preachers at the chapel's opening services on 25 October 1860 was the son of the famous Dr William Carey, who ministered to a Baptist congregation in the town. In 1863 the churches at Wolverhampton and Bilston joined to receive occasional preachers from Wales and in 1867 they called the Revd Hugh Meirug Pugh to be their minister. He remained with them until 1871, when he emigrated to America.[17]

Let us now return to Birmingham and to the founding of the Welsh Independent cause there. Its first recorded meeting was held in a room at the Temperance Hotel at Moor Street on 9 September, 1860. The preacher on that occasion was the Revd John Jones of Newton Smethcott, Shropshire, a man praised for his 'industry in the work of the Gospel along the borders and in Birmingham',[18] and it was partly as a result of that industry that the congregated company formed itself into a Welsh Independent church in November 1860. The church had twelve members, eleven of whose names have come down to us. The preponderance of the surname Pritchard among those names is explained by the fact that John Pritchard, David Pritchard and Richard Pritchard, three of the sons of Vaughan Pritchard, a farmer at Talybont near Aberystwyth, had come to Birmingham to work in the building trade, while their sister, Jane Pritchard, kept house for them. This little company worshipped faithfully and contributed handsomely in order to procure preachers from Wales to conduct their Sunday services, and on 1 January 1861 Gwilym Hiraethog, the Revd William Rees, who has been described as the greatest Welshman of the nineteenth century, delivered a public lecture at Moor Street, for which he was paid the princely sum of £2.[19]

In March 1862 John Cadwaladr of Llan Ffestiniog was called to minister at the young chapel and to the assorted Independents who continued to worship at Wolverhampton. During his short ministry of fifteen months the congregation changed its venue from Moor Street to the Temperance Hall in Ann Street, later renamed Colmore Row, where they continued to worship for the next five years. The year 1866 seems to have been a difficult one as the annual collection fell from £90 1s. 9d. in 1865 to £53 3s. 8d. in that year and a note is added: '15 left, one excluded from membership; six received through letters and one received anew'.[20] Following the three-year ministry of Robert Edwards Williams of Ruthin, the Revd James Camlais Evans, a young Breconshire man, was ordained in October 1867, and during his ministry the congregation bought a plot of land at Wheeler Street, in the Lozells area, where most of the members resided, building a house and schoolroom on it in 1868. Following Evans's departure in December 1869 to take up a pastorate in Anglesey, a call was extended in 1870 to the Revd John Lewis, a native of Coedgruffydd near Aberystwyth. He was inducted in November 1870, and on 8 August 1871 the foundation stone of the chapel at Wheeler Street was laid by Mr J. A. Cooper.

Raising funds to build a chapel was quite an undertaking for the small company who had already expended the sum of £300 on building a schoolroom. But comforted by the fact that they had £200 in hand and were able to call in promises for a further £300 they went to it with a will to collect the necessary sum. The Revd John Lewis, their minister, was co-editor of *Y Llusern*, a small denominational magazine, and in the October 1871 number of that magazine he appealed to every Welsh Independent Sunday School scholar throughout Wales to donate one halfpenny towards the project of building a chapel at Wheeler Street. I quote an extract from the appeal: 'We are all brothers and sisters newly come from among you from the Sunday Schools of Wales. In addition, the development of the town suggests that it is possible that many of you will be here soon to enjoy the Chapel.'[21] The appeal realized a sum of £113 7s. 8½d.; neither must the self-sacrifice of the church members themselves be overlooked, and a respectable Welsh religious historian of the period wrote: 'The church and congregation were notable for their industry in building the chapel with young maids in service contributing £7 and £12 each and workers contributing £8, £12 and £50 each in addition to paying 1/6, 2/– and 2/6 each to the ministerial fund every week.'[22]

The chapel was opened on Saturday, 21 January 1872, with some of Wales's most prominent preachers officiating, as well as the Revds G. B. Johnson and J. Shillito of Birmingham. The cost of building the church came to £1,229 0s. 1d., of which £758 9s. 7d. had already been paid. The church membership at the beginning of 1872 numbered 40, but this had increased to 86 by the end of 1873. One of the reasons for this increase was the development in the building trade following the Franco-Prussian War. According to one contemporary eyewitness, David Lloyd, who had recently left his home in Talybont to work at Birmingham: 'It was a sort of contagion. Where there was a green field the previous month there were now uniform rows of houses; whole portions of countryside were converted into suburbs.'[23]

In his book *Birmingham Baptists Past and Present*, Arthur S. Langley traces the beginnings of the Welsh Baptists' cause in Birmingham back to the year 1870 when six persons met together to worship in a residence in Anne Street. Mr Edward Jones, in whose house the church was formed in 1875, was its honorary pastor until 1883, after which time 'the Church was served by the Reverend R. Richards of Wem and bretheren in the city, until 1887'.[24] In that year Edward Jones resumed his pastoral care of the congregation and 'was set apart to the full work of the ministry'.[25] They met to worship in a building which occupied the site of the present Atlas Buildings in Colmore Row, which housed the offices of the West Midland Baptist Association and the General Superintendent for a period. The congregation was served by the Revd Maurice Morgan between 1890 and 1901 when their increased numbers forced them to move to a larger building which they found at the Masonic Hall in Severn Street. Langley describes Maurice Morgan as 'an earnest preacher, a very attractive Temperance worker, and a Free Churchman, ready to suffer for his principles'.[26]

Having attempted to describe the beginnings of Welsh Nonconformist causes in the area, I now wish to move on to the late twenties and the thirties of the present century, a time which saw the second notable influx of Welsh people into the West Midlands. Before I do so, however, I should briefly mention some of the events which provide a sense of coherence to the developing story. As already mentioned, the Welsh Calvinistic Methodist church at Bilston closed in 1897, its premises being rented to the Salvation Army. Their church at Wood Street (later renamed Granville Street) in Birmingham was sold in that same year and a new site purchased in Suffolk Street, where the new chapel was opened on 1 October, 1898, at the cost of £4,322 18s. 11d.[27] In Wolverhampton the chapel at St George's Parade was sold in 1907 and a new site bought on the corner of Bath Road and Birch Street where the new Bath Road church, together with its adjoining school-room and chapel house, was built for a sum of £2,242 and opened in 1908.[28] This development plunged its membership into substantial debt, which was only gradually removed by the predominantly working-class members of the congregation. A short history of the church refers to the membership of the period in this way:

Most of the members at that time were railway workers, gardeners, maids and nurses. It was said to be a common occurrence to see men attend the Sunday and weeknight meetings in their work clothes. So great was their enthusiasm for the cause that they came directly to the chapel from their work without going home to eat after a long day spent with their different tasks.[29]

In 1928 the churches at Bath Street, Wolverhampton, and at Hockley Hill joined together to form one pastorate, which was referred to incongruously as the most extended pastorate 'in Wales'.[30] Matters proceeded quietly at the Welsh Independent church at Wheeler Street. The chapel debt was cleared in 1894 and reference was made at that time to the joy experienced in accepting the first generation of Welsh youth raised in Birmingham into church membership[31] As a result of the influx of Welsh people to work in the city's factories during the Great War, the church membership reached a peak of 149 during 1916, but the numbers declined at the end of the war and in September 1922 the Jubilee of the chapel's opening was celebrated with a thorough redecoration of the building. During this intervening period the Welsh Baptists moved their meeting place from Severn Street to John Bright Street.

Let me begin a description of this second period, a period of economic depression, with some statistics. In 1921 the population of Wales stood at 2,656,474; by 1925 that number had risen to 2,736,800. By 1939, however, that number had decreased to 2,487,000, a decrease of 249,800 in fourteen years. Yet the actual increase in the number of Welsh people during those years was 140,171, which meant that 389,971 had emigrated from the country during that period.[32] Indeed, the thirties saw a decrease in the population of every single county except Flintshire. As many as 50,000 people left the Rhondda Valleys and 27,000 left Merthyr Tydfil during that same period. Some of the annual reports of the Rhondda chapels in the mid-thirties refer to the exodus of their younger members and its dire social consequences for the life of the local communities, and the Midlands are mentioned as the destination of many of these members.

These statistics are reflected in the rise in membership of the Welsh churches in the Birmingham area. The membership of Suffolk Street Welsh Calvinistic church at the end of 1926 stood at 145 plus 24 children, but by the end of 1939 that number had risen to 252 plus 43 children, with 24 new members being received by letters of transference that year plus two 'o'r byd' (from the world) as well as five of the church's own young people.[33] The church at Hockley Hill experienced a similar expansion. At the end of 1928 its membership was 80, but by the end of 1938 that number had risen to 139.[34] In the short history of the church at Wolverhampton it says: 'During the thirties, a number of Welsh people came to work in the town, some from Anglesey and many from the south because of the depression. The membership rose by between 60 and 70 and there was a flourishing Sunday School.'[35]

The statistics for the Wheeler Street Welsh Independent church were even more revealing. In 1912 the church had 115 members plus 27 children, and the number at the end of 1927 was quite similar, with 117 people on the membership roll plus 16 children. By the end of 1937, however, the figures had risen to 308 members plus 39 children, with 69 new members having been received by letters of transference during that year.[36] In 1934 Wheeler Street church called a young student from the Brecon Memorial College to be their minister, where he remained until 1945. The Revd Idris Hopcyn described how on his arrival at Birmingham he was met by an influx of young people from Wales. 'Not a single Sunday,' he wrote, 'passed without seeing some people in the chapel from back home hoping to find work in the area.'[37] In 1936 the church established a Young Brotherhood which was a fellowship geared to welcome young men, 'assisting them to find work or lodging, and to support them in times of difficulty; to form a connection with them inside the chapel and on the outside'.[38] At one time as many as 240 young people were associated with this Brotherhood.

The late thirties was a flourishing period in the church's history. There existed a strong Sunday school followed by a young people's prayer meeting. These meetings were followed by tea in the vestry prior to the well-attended evening service, which in its turn was followed by a cup of tea and animated discussion. In addition to a church membership in excess of 300, 'hundreds of young men and women' whose church membership remained in their home churches in Wales attended the Sunday evening services 'until the chapel overflowed'.[39] Indeed, the flow of people leaving the chapel at the end of the services was sometimes responsible for halting the progress of the city's trams.

The Welsh Baptist church also had its more modest success at this time. To quote Arthur S. Langley, writing in 1939: 'The church is unable to maintain a pastor as they are specially a Missionary Church, seeking to provide a spiritual home for the Welsh Baptists who come to the city. Their numbers vary according to the fluctuations due to the state of trade. Their last return shows fifty-three members, three teachers and twenty-eight scholars.'[40] But a more intimate picture by one of the church's members in the mid-thirties provides a much deeper awareness of the effects of the exodus from Wales on the Baptist fellowship: 'About that time the influx of Welsh people from South Wales to Birmingham due to the depression in that area was beginning to take place. From then the Church increased in strength and there followed several families from Wales, also a large number of young people.'[41] Indeed, the Sunday services had to be moved from the top floor to a larger room on the first floor of 38 John Bright Street with additional chairs having to be brought in.[42]

The war years were difficult ones for all Birmingham churches and Suffolk Street church was damaged by bombs. In 1942 as a result of the severe bombing of the city and the attendant black-out, the evening services were transferred to the afternoon. In 1943 the government legislated that young women should undertake factory work in order to assist the war effort, and although a number of Welsh girls moved to the Midlands at this time and the Welsh chapels strove to welcome and assist those whose whereabouts came to their knowledge, there were a number of circumstances including the decline in the use of the Welsh language, the decreasing interest in religion in a swiftly changing social environment, and the necessity of working on Sundays, which severely hampered the progress of the Welsh churches during the war years.

We now turn to the third period under discussion, namely the post-war period up until 1970, a period which saw the formation of two new churches at Coventry and Rugby and the building of three modern Welsh Nonconformist chapels in Birmingham. A number of Welsh people found employment in the motor industry in Coventry and a non-denominational cause was established there which soon became a Welsh Calvinistic church. This was formally opened at Ford Street, Coventry, on the 10–11 April 1948. It seemed at first that the expansion experienced by the Birmingham Welsh churches during the thirties would be repeated in Coventry during the fifties. The church membership at the end of 1950 stood at 163, with 25 new members having been received during that year. There were also 66 Sunday school scholars. However, this expansion never occurred, and although the church membership remained at 158 at the end of 1959, the average attendance at the Sunday school had fallen to seven. In 1967 the church found a new home at the Grammar School on Bishop Street, which is reputedly the oldest building in Coventry.[43]

We look next at the interesting development in Rugby. Some Welsh people came to Rugby at the beginning of the century to work on the railway. Their numbers were supplemented at the end of the Great War by others who found employment at British-Thomson-Houston, and in the early 1930s by a number of Welsh farmers who farmed land in the surrounding district, which lay astride the old drovers' routes from Wales to London. In 1925 the Welsh Society at Rugby was reformed and its committee for religious interests began arranging non-denominational meetings in conjunction with the English Congregational church at Albert Street. On 3 November 1951 a non-denominational Welsh church was established in the town, with over a hundred members who met at the Social Club of the Rugby Cement Company in North Street. On 21 October 1967 this church was accepted into the Presbyterian Church of Wales and has since 1990 held its services at the United Reformed church at Rugby. The church at Coventry came under the wing of the Wolverhampton church, while the Rugby church formed a joint pastorate with the Birmingham church.[44]

The population census for 1951 showed that 649,275 persons living in England had been born in Wales, the largest percentage of whom resided in south-eastern England although some of their number had emigrated to the Midlands. John Davies, the Welsh historian, remarks in this context that the Welsh expatriates of the twentieth century were not as determined as their predecessors in creating microcosms of Welsh life in their new localities. Consequently, he remarks: 'neither Coventry nor Dagenham experienced the lively Welsh activity that occurred on the banks of the Mersey'.[45] Nevertheless, a number of young Welsh teachers came to the Birmingham area during the 1950s and their coming benefited the Welsh churches. The end of the war saw the formation of a number of teachers' training colleges which offered an intensive 48-week training course for people returning from the armed services. The Birmingham Education Committee recruited teachers from the colleges at Wrexham and Llandrindod in particular, and Mr Sam Jones, the secretary of Hockley Hill church, became 'the best known Welshman in the Midlands'[46] during this period, due to his valiant efforts to find lodging for between 80 and 100 new Welsh teachers every year for a period of ten years between 1945 and 1955.[47] During the mid-fifties it was estimated that one-eighth of the total number of teachers teaching in the Birmingham area came from Wales. The most successful Welsh church in the area at this period was the Suffolk Street Welsh Calvinistic church, under the dynamic ministry of the Revd John Frederick Smith, which at the end of 1955 achieved a membership of 338, 29 of whom had been accepted by letters of transference during that year.[48] This success was augmented by the fact that a Welsh Young People's Club met at the YWCA nearby.

Despite the fact that the end of 1964 saw the closure of the Hockley Hill church, the period between 1958 and 1970 saw each of the three Welsh Nonconformist churches in Birmingham moving into new premises. The Birmingham City Council had taken possession of Wheeler Street Welsh Congregational chapel as early as 1948, promising to provide the congregation with a new site. It was the Welsh Baptists who were the first to move, however, and they opened their new church at Great Lister Street on 20 September 1958. The money for the cost of the new building was made available by the passing on of a sum paid to a war-damaged Baptist church in Liverpool. At the end of 1958 the church at Great Lister Street had 70 members.[49]

The next church to procure a new building was Suffolk Street. Their site had been requested as early as 1951 as it lay on the route of the proposed Inner Ring Road and the members were promised a new site in Ellis Street by the Birmingham Corporation. It became evident later that the site of the Hockley Hill chapel was also required for the proposed widening of the A41 road, and it was decided that the two congregations should merge to form a new church. This eventually happened when the corporation sold the worshippers a new site at Holloway Head in 1965. The building of the new church began in 1967 and inaugural services were held in Bethel at Holloway Head on 6 and 7 July 1968, during the pastorship of the Revd A. Wynne Edwards.[50] The Welsh Congregationalists continued to worship at Wheeler Street, but their situation became more untenable as the surrounding buildings were demolished, until the chapel stood alone 'like,' in the words of Dafydd Rees, 'a pelican in the wilderness'.[51] Back in 1948, Birmingham Corporation had promised to pay a sum of £14,000 for the site, but as it became more and more unrealistic to build a new chapel with such a sum, a building fund was inaugurated with a special appeal being made to the Congregational churches in Wales, which realized the sum of £2,563.[52] In August 1969 the church at Wheeler Street was seriously vandalized and rendered unusable. Although Bethel and the Welsh Baptist church invited the homeless congregation to use their facilities until its new building should be ready, Welsh Congregationalist services continued in one of the Joseph Lucas Company's welfare halls at Soho Hill.

The complete cost of the new building at Loveday Street, which was opened on 7 and 8 February 1970 during the ministry of the Revd D. J. Wynne Evans, was £40,929. The congregation already had a sum of almost £10,000 in their building fund. Birmingham Corporation was eventually persuaded that a compensatory figure set in 1948 was no longer tenable and its revised compensation figure of almost £35,000 enabled the congregation to begin its life in the new building free of debt.[53]

It was natural that new buildings should enhance the interest of the fellowships who met in them, and so it proved. The Revd Tom Davies, the minister of the Welsh Baptist church at Great Lister Street, traced the working of the Lord's hand on the congregation's movement from its limited accommodation in John Bright Street to its new and more appropriate home,[54] while at the new complexes at Bethel, Holloway Head, and Loveday Street the sanctuaries took up a considerably smaller percentage of the whole building space than in the two previous buildings, leaving more space for halls and useful ante-rooms, which could be used by the fellowships and rented to others.

Both things did in fact happen as week-night meetings of a religious and cultural nature proliferated. The Welsh churches set up active ladies' circles which were responsible not only for providing the Sunday teas but also for organising services of worship. A congregation of the Pentecostal Church of God has met in the Great Lister Street church hall over the last twenty years and this has led in recent years to a monthly united bilingual communion service between the two congregations. The church at Bethel, Holloway Head, has provided a home for the English section of the Young Chinese Christian Society in Birmingham, while the church hall at Loveday Street chapel is being used by a number of societies including the Old Town Hall Christian Society, the Fircone retirement group, the Midlands Male Voice Choir and the 'Argosy' musical drama company. The Welsh churches are also affiliated to the Birmingham Council of Christian Churches and the Birmingham Council of Christian Education.

In summing up the contribution of the Welsh Nonconformist diaspora in the West Midlands, it can safely be said that these churches gave their contribution in maintaining and expressing a continuous Nonconformist witness in the West Midlands over a period of more than a hundred and fifty years. It must be emphasized, however, that we are dealing with a relatively small group of people, hardly reaching a thousand at any one time. I did describe the word 'diaspora' as presumptuous in the context of the Welsh Nonconformists in the West Midlands. The main diaspora occurred in the Liverpool and London areas. Indeed the number of Calvinistic Methodist communicants in the Birmingham area in 1905 numbered 282 compared with 8,094 at Liverpool and 4,398 in London.[55]

It is as well to draw attention at this point to the fact that none of the three main Nonconformist denominations in Wales ever had a recognized association or administrative unit based in the Midlands. So the Calvinistic Methodist churches described in this essay were in association, with other Midlands churches, with the Lower Montgomery Presbytery, while the Congregational churches were affiliated first to the Montgomery Association but later to the Liverpool Association, and the Baptist churches to the Denbighshire, Flintshire and Meirionethshire Association.

While it is notably difficult to convey anything further than an impressionistic account of the contribution made by the members of these Welsh Nonconformist churches to the life of their localities or to the life of the West Midlands in general, one is able to present an illustrative vignette or two. When the new chapel at Suffolk Street was being built in 1898, the two foundation stones were laid by two of the church's elders, Councillor William Jones JP who was also the church's precentor, and Mr Evan Thomas, described as 'a successful builder in the city'.[56] Not only did William Jones contribute a sum of £1,000 to the new chapel but he also contributed similar sums to the Foreign Missionary Society, to Bala Theological College, to Aberystwyth University College and to Birmingham University.[57]

We also come across the name of Mr J. Jenkyn Richards, the precentor at Hockley Hill who is described as being 'very well known in city circles'.[58] Mr Richards was responsible for forming and conducting 'The Birmingham Cymric Costume Choir'. Not only did this choir present a number of concerts at the Central Hall to packed audiences, but they performed with equal success in almost every town in the Midlands, and the writer adds, lest there be any doubt concerning the matter, 'to English audiences of course'. This choir was invited to form part of the 'All Wales Choir' which sang at Wembley Stadium at the time of the Empire Exhibition in 1924 as well as appearing at the Jubilee Celebrations of King George V in 1935. Mr H. Browning Button, a representative of the Great Western Railway Board, arranged for Mr Richards and his choir to accompany him on his visits to Midland towns to attract people to travel on the GWR to holiday in Wales. In the meantime Mr Richards had formed two more choirs, 'The Soho Hill Glee-men' and 'The Birmingham Settlement Choir'. An interesting footnote can be added to this picture. Mr H. O. Wilkes, a Yorkshireman who worked at the drawing office at the Austin plant in Longbridge, married a Welsh girl, learnt the language and became a member of Hockley Hill church. It was he who was responsible for preparing an illuminated address for Mr J. Jenkyn Richards in recognition of his cultural contribution, which was presented to him in 1935, the year prior to his death. It is well to remember that Mr Wilkes was something of an exception; the number of Welshmen who came to seek work in the Midlands, married English women and attended English-speaking churches can hardly be estimated.

Although the Welsh chapels in the West Midlands provided the Welsh Nonconformists with a religious and cultural locus which enabled them to find their bearings in a strange society and adjust themselves better to their new environment, they never formed a different ethnic grouping with its own distinctive social and political affiliations, as did the Irish for instance. This point is very well illustrated by the way in which Mr Delwyn Phillips, organizer of Welsh activities in Birmingham and later secretary of the Welsh Congregational church, was approached by Mr Woodrow Wyatt, the Labour Party candidate for Acton, at the time of the 1945 General Election. Wyatt had been informed by the leader of the Irish Citizens' League that Mr Phillips was 'the controller of the Welsh vote in Birmingham'. Mr Phillips explained to Mr Wyatt that there was no such thing as a specifically Welsh vote, although he was able to assure him that the Welsh working-class background of the majority of Welsh-speaking Nonconformists in the constituency would cause them to tender him their support.[59]

In conclusion then it can be said that the Welsh Nonconformists in the West Midlands assisted with the building of the Birmingham Town Hall, shared their love of music and song with their fellow citizens and provided teachers for the region's children as well as bearing their Christian testimony in the midst of urban life. In the words of the Revd A. Wynne Edwards, written in 1972 in connection with the new chapel in Holloway Head: 'It stands today as one of the most modern buildings in the City, with the cross on its apex facing the new City centre, continuing to provide a spiritual home for exiled Welsh people in whose native language the services are regularly held.'[60]

Notes

1. J. A. Sanders, *Interpreter's Dictionary of the Bible* (New York: 1962), pp. 1854–6.
2. John Davies, *Hanes Cymru* (Llundain: 1990), p. 411.
3. Idris Hopcyn, *Hanes Eglwys yr Annibynwyr Cymraeg Wheeler Street, Birmingham 1860–1960* (n.d.), p. 1.
4. Edward Griffith, *Hanes Methodistiaeth Trefaldwyn Isaf* (Caernarfon: 1914), p. 327.
5. Griffith, *Hanes Methodistiaeth*, p. 330.
6. Griffith, *Hanes Methodistieath*, p. 330.
7. Evan Jones, *Bethel Birmingham Ddoe a Heddiw* (Caernarfon: 1968), p. 8.
8. Jones, *Bethel Birmingham*, p. 9.
9. Griffith, *Hanes Methodistiaeth*, p. 320.
10. Griffith, *Hanes Methodistiaeth*, p. 320.
11. Griffith, *Hanes Methodistiaeth*, p. 323.
12. Griffith, *Hanes Methodistiaeth*, p. 331.
13. Jones, *Bethel Birmingham*, p. 9.
14. Jones, *Bethel Birmingham*, p. 18.
15. Griffith, *Hanes Methodistiaeth*, p. 323.
16. *Royal Commission on the Church of England and other Religious Bodies in Wales and Monmouthshire*, VII, App. XXXII, *Parliamentary Papers*, 1910, XVII (5438), pp. 131–2.
17. Griffith, *Hanes Methodistiaeth*, p. 32.
18. Hopcyn, *Hanes Eglwys*, p. 1.
19. Hopcyn, *Hanes Eglwys*, p. 2.
20. Hopcyn, *Hanes Eglwys*, p. 3.
21. Hopcyn, *Hanes Eglwys*, p. 5.
22. T. Rees and J. Thomas, *Hanes Eglwysi Annibynol Cymru* (Liverpool: 1875), IV, p. 434.
23. Hanes and Thomas, *Hanes Eglwysi*, p. 7.
24. A. S. Langley, *Birmingham Baptists Past and Present* (London: 1939), p. 179.
25. Langley, *Birmingham Baptists*, p. 179.
26. Langley, *Birmingham Baptists*, p. 180.
27. Jones, *Bethel Birmingham*, p. 11.
28. Arthur Davies, *Achos y Methodistiaid Calfinaidd yn Wolverhampton* (Cricieth: 1954), p. 12.
29. Davies, *Achos y Methodistiaid*, p. 12.
30. Davies, *Achos y Methodistiaid*, p. 13.
31. Hopcyn, *Hanes Eglwys*, p. 10.
32. Davies, *Hanes Cymru*, p. 556.
33. *Suffolk Street Annual Church Report*, 1926 and 1939, National Library of Wales, XBX9102 B617.
34. *Hockley Hill Annual Church Report*, 1928 and 1938, NLW *ibid.*
35. Davies, *Achos y Methodistiaid*, p. 13.
36. *Wheeler Street Annual Church Report*, 1912, 1927, 1937, NLW XBX7193.
37. Hopcyn, *Hanes Eglwys*, p. 10.

38. Hopcyn, *Hanes Eglwys*, p. 10.
39. Hopcyn, *Hanes Eglwys*, p. 10.
40. Langley, *Birmingham Baptists*, p. 180.
41. Photostat copy of an eyewitness account passed on to the author by the church's present minister, the Revd Gwendydd Haf Davies Askew.
42. *Ibid.*
43. Information gathered from Ford Street, Coventry, Church Reports, NLW XBX9102 C71.
44. Information gathered from Mr Bryn Williams, secretary of the Rugby Welsh Church.
45. Davies, *Hanes Cymru*, p. 556.
46. Jones, *Bethel Birmingham*, p. 21.
47. Jones, *Bethel Birmingham*, p. 22.
48. *Suffolk Street Annual Church Report*, 1955, NLW XBX9102 B617.
49. *Great Lister Street Annual Church Report*, 1958, NLW XBX6293.
50. Jones, *Bethel Birmingham*, p. 29.
51. Dafydd Rees, *Hanes Eglwys yr Annibynwyr Cymraeg Birmingham oddiar 1960* (Abertawe: n. d.), p. 9.
52. Rees, *Hanes Eglwys*, p. 11.
53. Rees, *Hanes Eglwys*, p. 11.
54. Minister's address in *Great Lister Street Annual Church Report*, 1958.
55. Welsh Calvinistic List of Causes outside Wales, 1905. See *Royal Commission on the Church of England*, 1910.
56. Jones, *Bethel Birmingham*, p. 11.
57. Griffith, *Hanes Methodistiaeth*, p. 336.
58. Jones, *Bethel Birmingham*, p. 20.
59. Information gleaned in conversation with Delwyn Phillips.
60. Norman Tiptaft (ed.), *Religion in Birmingham* (Warley: 1972), p. 195.

CHAPTER 7

Bourne College: A Primitive Methodist Educational Venture

E. Dorothy Graham

Primitive Methodism originated in the borders of Cheshire and Staffordshire around the area of Mow Cop. It arose when Wesleyan Methodism became more established and formalized and certain people began to feel that a return to the evangelical beginnings of Methodism was needed. The principal founders were Hugh Bourne (1772–1852), a moorland carpenter, and William Clowes (1780–1851), a potter. Most probably they would have remained within Wesleyan Methodism if their belief in enthusiastic expressions of faith and the value of outdoor meetings, especially camp meetings, had not met with the disapproval of the Wesleyan authorities. As they were both expelled against their wishes, Primitive Methodism should not be regarded as a secession. After their expulsion Bourne and Clowes with their supporters started the Primitive Methodist Connexion in May 1811. The new denomination appealed particularly to the poorer working people, as it started where the people were, spoke their language and offered salvation on equal terms to all, regardless of class and status.

From the beginning Primitive Methodism was concerned with 'education', albeit not necessarily of the formal type. John Wesley had always encouraged his preachers to read and study and as time went by the Primitive Methodists did the same, largely at the instigation of Hugh Bourne. I think it is a mistake to regard the early itinerants as completely illiterate. Hugh Bourne himself was taught to read and write and do simple arithmetic by his mother. Then he was sent to school in Werrington:

> I well remember writing '1779' in my copy book as the year of Our Lord, so that I was then only seven years of age ... Here I had to tug at arithmetic and at the grammar and dictionary: and learning the explanation of words in the dictionary took my fancy considerably.[1]

Then later he was sent to a school at Bucknall where he learnt reading, English, grammar, arithmetic, easy measurement and the rudiments of Latin. He continued to study after leaving school – tackling more arithmetic, geometry, astronomy, natural philosophy, history, geography and the Bible and religion in particular.[2] In his diary Bourne wrote:

Fri, July 14. Hay-making and studying Greek.
Sat. July 15. Hay-making: to-day I made great progress in Greek.[3]

and:

25th Jan. 1817. I have lately made progress in Hebrew;
24th July 1817. I came home and read in the Greek Testament;
20th August 1817. This week I have committed to memory the first seven chapters of St Paul's Epistle to the Hebrews.[4]

and 'there is evidence that in later years he gained considerable knowledge of Hebrew, Greek, Latin and French'.[5]

Following Hugh Bourne's example and precepts Primitive Methodism was very strong in its advocacy of self-help and self-education. Bourne, in addition to purchasing and passing on tracts, wrote and published many himself and the preachers were urged to purchase suitable literature from the travelling preachers, who were agents for books, pamphlets or tracts produced by the Connexion or for ones duly authorized by it. The travelling preachers were entitled to a 10 per cent discount on the books they sold to encourage them to study and to educate their hearers. A number of the travelling preachers who had the benefit of little formal education *did* educate themselves to very acceptable standards so that they could more effectively minister to their people. No doubt, by some standards, their education was sadly lacking, but the very fact that the preachers were required to keep and present journals to the Quarter Day Meetings ensured that at the very least they had the rudiments of good English. The extracts from their journals, articles and sermons, many of which were published in the *Primitive Methodist Magazine*, read to enquirers or congregations, show a considerable grasp of language, even if a little formal in style, and a practical common-sense view of life and its vicissitudes. It was not regarded as peculiar by the travelling preachers themselves or by their hearers that they were not highly educated. After all, the preachers' mission was chiefly to the poor people who had not had the advantage of much education themselves and who therefore did not see the lack of it – or perhaps even the need for it – in their preachers. Much of the evangelism was carried on in the homes of the people by 'conversation preaching' and a burning evangelistic fervour for the saving of souls rather than erudition was considered important.

In the early days most of the travelling preachers on probation, which lasted for four years, 'learned on the job' and were expected to study, in addition to their preaching and visiting, in order to improve themselves in the fields of education, preaching and pastoral care. There is a series of articles in the *Primitive Methodist Magazine* which gives much practical and common-sense advice.[6] However, eventually the time would come when some preachers were actually expelled from the ranks of the ministry for educational incompetence. So it is obvious that as the century progressed the educational demands of the ministry increased as the education of the congregations improved. As the congregations became more knowledgeable and sophisticated they demanded better-educated ministers[7] and so the need for a more professional approach and a formal programme of ministerial training became evident. The educative role of the preachers had changed and the preachers themselves, therefore, had to be more highly educated and it seemed as if a college education was required.

The main point is that not only had the Primitive Methodist conception of the ministry changed, but the congregations had changed too. Primitive Methodism as it moved from fervid evangelism to consolidation, had started to appeal to and imbibe middle-class ideas and standards. As Geoffrey Milburn points out, social and educational developments during the century were producing better-informed people who were filled with a thirst for knowledge in many different fields.[8] So as Primitive Methodism moved from evangelism to consolidation, it now became necessary not only to cater for converts, but to provide sustenance for its members and their children. Primitive Methodism was having to shift its emphasis in order to cope with the second generation, thus making necessary the setting up and maintenance of church buildings and organizations. Sunday schools proliferated; circuits were reorganized; church architecture became more ambitious; houses were built for the ministers; ministerial salaries were increased; and a new hymn book took over from Hugh Bourne's original collection. Hence, along with these developments, it was obvious that there would be a demand both from the ministers themselves and from the congregations for more specialized training. Therefore, in 1865, a one-year training course for ministers was set up at Elmfield College in York, followed by the establishment of a theological college in Sunderland in 1868.

Primitive Methodism's venture into formal education came through the travelling preachers, who felt that their own children suffered through the itinerant system and that their salaries, especially as many had large families, were insufficient for them to pay even for 'common

schooling'. A writer, using the *nom de plume* 'Aleph', contributed an
article to the *Magazine* on 2 February 1847 'On a School for the
Children of the Itinerant Preachers' in which he advocates the desir-
ability of 'the establishment of a Connexional School, in the central
part of the kingdom, for the children of Primitive Methodist Itinerant
Preachers'. He insists that 'A superior education I do not ask for, but
to a respectable education I think the preachers' children are entitled'
and that the consequent relief to the family would mean that the 'father
[would] know that while he cared for the churches they cared for his
family'. The writer even went so far as to offer to give a generous
donation if others would contribute towards such an enterprise.[9] From
an article in the December issue of the same year it seems that there
had been a Conference resolution on the subject and this was to be
presented to Quarterly Meetings for their opinion. The resolution was
endorsed by the Reading Circuit who 'were thankful that the idea has
been taken up, and pray that benevolent efforts to work it out may be
rendered successful'. They already had an offer of a donation and wished
to know to whom donations should be sent. However, the response
from the Connexion's authorities was not encouraging:

> we beg to say that the Educational Committee has done nothing
> officially ... respecting the Institution ...

Apparently the surplus profits of the Book Room were to be put at
the committee's disposal in attempting to establish the Institution; but
a decrease in missionary money received from the circuits had meant
that the general treasurers had had to borrow the money from the
Book Committee to pay the salaries of the missionaries and hence the
Educational Committee felt it could not ask for aid at the moment,
but would pursue the project as soon as possible. Characteristically, the
reply urges the missionaries, preachers and circuits to work hard to
spread the gospel and become self-supporting so that money for the
institution could be made available.[10]

The 'Consolidated Minutes' of 1849 contained the following:

> We have three kinds of Connexional schools, *and one kind in prospect:*
> namely Sabbath, day and night schools: the one in prospect is de-
> signed for the education of preachers' children.[11]

So it seems that Primitive Methodism recognized the need for an
educational establishment for its preachers' children in particular, but
unfortunately was not in a position to implement the desire. It is
necessary to remember that on the whole the congregations were of
the artisan class, who earned only about the same wages as the

preachers received for their salaries and therefore they had not large incomes from which to fund such an enterprise; indeed many circuits had difficulty in even paying the full salaries of their itinerants, modest though they were. Maximum salaries per quarter in 1824 were £4 10s. for a single man, plus an expense allowance; £2 2s. for females; £9 2s. for married men with allowances for children; by 1850 the married men were receiving around £11 1s.; by 1860 the maximum salary was, 'when [it could] be afforded without involving any station in debt ...', £13 13s. with allowances for children, while the single man received £5 10s. plus £3 10s. in allowances, and by 1892 the *minimum* salary was £21 a quarter with children's allowances.[12] As John Petty says that in 1829 agricultural workers in the Brinkworth Mission only earned six or seven shillings a week, that is between £3 18s. and £4 11s. per quarter, it can be seen that life was a financial struggle for many of the members.[13] So it is easy to understand why the raising of money to found a school was rather low on the list of priorities for many people.

In 1858 it was decided that the Connexion should hold a Jubilee in 1860 to celebrate the formation of the first Class Meeting in 1810 and that 'the chief end of the said jubilee shall be, the spiritual benefit of the Connexion'. The 1859 Conference turned its thought to how 'the approaching jubilee of 1860' should be celebrated and one of the ideas was to have a Jubilee Fund, open initially for two years, but later extended.[14] Its objects were listed the following year and included:

3. A school for preachers' children, and the children of members.[15]

So at the Conference of 1863 'The Establishment of a Connexional Jubilee School' was agreed and twenty regulations were listed. The school was to be at Elmfield, near York, only boys between the ages of nine and fourteen, except in special circumstances, were to be admitted. The fees were to be £20 per annum for boys under twelve and £25 for those over that age. Travelling preachers were only to be charged £15 per son. Donations of £25 per annum would provide one free place which would be offered to a fatherless son of a Primitive Methodist. Subscribers of 10s. were to be given a vote in the choice of the free scholar and those who gave 20s. or more were made life members and given a correspondingly greater say in the choice. In keeping with Primitive Methodism's emphasis on the laity, and its anti-clerical stance, the managing committee of Elmfield College was to consist of two-thirds laymen and one-third ministers. The governor was always to be a Primitive Methodist minister, who would take care of the moral and religious training of the scholars as well as the general oversight of the school. John Petty was appointed as the first Governor, with his wife as the matron. It was decreed that 'The Education shall be Religious, Commercial, and Classical'.[16] The 1864 Conference authorized the purchase of the property for £1,350, approved the building plans and reaffirmed the appointments of Mr and Mrs Petty and appointed Samuel Antliff as secretary.[17] In 1865 it was decided that ministerial students, who were to have John Petty as their tutor, should be admitted. Their fees were set at £30 per annum of which the student contribution was to be at least half.[18]

The Primitive Methodist Society at Summer Hill in Birmingham was meeting in a very unsuitable room and they wished to build a chapel in Brookfields, but the project fell through because of a conditional clause in the original lease from Sir Thomas Gooch, the owner of the land, that no chapels should be built on his land. There was a large house vacant on Summer Hill which had been occupied by St Chad's Grammar School, a Roman Catholic foundation. However, faced with declining numbers and consequent financial problems, it seems that in the autumn of 1873 it was decided to sell the school, valued at £960–£1,000 with adjoining land worth 10s. or 15s. a yard (i.e. £350 or £530). The property passed into the hands of Birmingham Corporation who were prepared to offer it 'on exceptionally favourable terms for philanthropic, educational, or religious objects'. The price was £500, but with a ground rent of £72 per annum, and this was too heavy an undertaking for the Summer Hill Society. The Superintendent Minister, the Revd George Middleton, consulted with his ministerial colleagues and leading local laymen and they formed 'a Trust for the purchase of the property and the establishment of a School for the midlands, with a curriculum and scale of charges similar to those adopted in the York School' at a meeting in West Bromwich in July 1875. Loans were advanced amounting to £693 and £425 borrowed on interest, so the purchase money was found and the cost of important alterations necessary to adapt the premises for use as the college met. Kendall states that the property was bought for £525 on a 78-year lease with a ground rent of £60. Mr J. Nott was elected president and treasurer. The Revd C. Smallman was appointed governor, but resigned after a few months, when the Revd George Middleton who had been appointed secretary also became governor. Mr R. G. Heys, BA was appointed as headmaster, and the college opened its doors to the first students in January 1876, when Dr Dale of Carr's Lane gave the principal address.[19]

The first official notification to the Primitive Methodist Connexion that a school, to be run on similar lines to Elmfield, was planned for Birmingham comes in the *Primitive Methodist Minutes* of 1876 where we read under 'Stations':

In Connexional Offices:– George Middleton, F.G.S., is the Governor and Secretary of Bourne College, Birmingham.[20]

George Middleton was born on 6 March 1830 at Smalldale, near Bradwell, Derbyshire, the youngest of nine children. His father was a farmer and proprietor of a mine. Educated at the village school and in the Sunday school, George became a teacher and a preacher. His brother, Joseph, was already a Primitive Methodist itinerant and George joined him in the Dudley and Brierley Hill District, where he came into contact with John Petty, later governor of Elmfield. George continued to work with his brother when he moved to Ludlow to pursue his studies to become an itinerant, while taking oversight of Gumma, his brother's farm. Here he met James Nott, 'a gentleman of great local influence, who had been converted by Primitive Methodist preaching' and being much of the same age they became fast friends. Later Nott took an active part in the formation of the college, becoming one of the largest shareholders and Chairman of the Board. At 23 George became an itinerant and was stationed in Coventry, Burland, Dawley Green, Wem and then Knighton, where he met his wife, who acted as matron of the college until Middleton's death. From Knighton he went to Hay, a branch of the Presteigne Circuit, then to Welshpool. George Middleton became Superintendent Minister of the Birmingham First Circuit for four years from 1872, but it seems that in 1876 he was moved to take charge of the proposed new school.[21] He seems to have been especially gifted in raising money for, and building, churches and Sunday schools in most of the circuits in which he was stationed, and doubtless this stood him in good stead when he became governor of the proposed new school. Obviously by 1877 the school was in being, as the *Minutes* read:

... and G. Middleton, F.G.S., may attend the Conference of 1878, to give any needful information relative to the Institutions over which they preside.[22]

and indeed the extant 'Bourne College School Entry Book' has as its first entries: 'January 25th 1876'.

The accounts of the Connexional Funds of the same year give the travelling expenses of the 'Committee on Bourne College'. The members of the committee, probably in addition to local members, were:

R. Smith	Birmingham	243 miles at 2*d*.	£2 0*s*. 6*d*.
J. Dickenson	"	264 "	£2 4*s*. 0*d*.
S. Antliff, D.D.	"	264 "	£2 4*s*. 6*d*.
T. Dearlove	"	216 "	£1 16*s*. 0*d*.[23]

Of these John Dickenson was the General Book Steward and secretary of the Book Committee and came from London as did Samuel Antliff who was deputy treasurer and financial secretary of the General Missionary Committee; Robert Smith came from the mission station of Kingston and Thomas Dearlove from Bradford.[24] The following year both Antliff and Smith again visited Birmingham in connection with Bourne College.[25]

The *Primitive Methodist Magazine*'s 'Monthly Chronicle' for May 1877 states that:

> Bourne College, Birmingham, is rapidly taking up a good position, and is likely to develop into a useful and effective middle class educational Institution. It is not a rival to York College, – this latter has indeed removed itself out of the way of any danger from rivalry. There is really room for it as the success of the venture has proved. There is some talk about securing land and erecting more commodious premises in a very eligible situation. We hope friends will move cautiously, and make the ground secure beneath their feet as they proceed. Caution in such an undertaking needs to be closely wedded to enterprise.[26]

In 1878 the *Magazine* gives an account of the prize-giving at the college, starting with the words:

> the friends and supporters of our new and, we may add, efficient – Middle-class School, at Birmingham, met for the annual distribution of prizes ... the governor, Rev. G. Middleton, introduced E. Cross, Esq., of Birmingham, who had been requested to preside and distribute the prizes. R. G. Heys, B.A., the headmaster, gave a report of the year's work ...[27]

The 'Bourne College Entry Books' survive and it is interesting to study and analyse the entries of the first intake on 25 January 1876. Twenty-five pupils, whose ages ranged from two eight-year-olds to one of seventeen years, were registered. The length of stay in the college varied from five to thirty-five months, not always dependent upon the age of entry – that is, an eight-year-old stayed five months and the two fifteen-year-olds for twenty-nine and thirty-five months each. (It is difficult to work out the actual term times from the book, so instead months have been used. In fact, boys were accepted into the school at any time.) Of the entrants 24 per cent were the sons of Primitive Methodist itinerants; 40 per cent (including three itinerants' sons) were from local families. Four of the twenty-five had previously attended 'Grammar Schools', five 'Private Schools', fourteen 'Day Schools' and two 'Board Schools'. The boys were divided into three classes chiefly by age: there were thirteen in Class I – aged thirteen to seventeen; nine in Class II – aged ten to thirteen; and three in Class III – two eight-year-olds and an eleven-year-old. Comments are made about their knowledge, on entry, of Latin, Greek, French, Algebra, Euclid, Arithmetic, Geography, Grammar and History – only one had studied Latin with two others a 'little'; two had a 'little' Greek; one French with three a 'little'; only one had done any Algebra and Euclid with three admitting to a 'little'; the seventeen-year-old and the thirteen-year-old, whose home address was given as Invercayil, New Zealand, were the only ones to have any Geography, Grammar or History, with one of the eight-year-olds having a 'little' Geography. The remarks in the Arithmetic column make the most interesting reading: 'Discount (2); L.C.M.; Proportion; Duodec; V. Fractions (5); Practice; Comp. Rules; Com. Addition; Simple Rules (4); Simple Multiplication; Simple Addition (2); Reduction (2); Simple Division', plus two boys where no comment is made.[28]

From 1878 until the college's close the *Primitive Methodist Minutes* contain its annual report and accounts. In the main they are concerned with the educational attainments of the students, which were very impressive, but occasionally a few other details are included. Thus in the report of the second year's work (1878) it was stated that the accommodation was fully occupied with an average of 50 students, 12 per cent of whom were ministers' sons. The headmaster, Mr R. G. Heys, taught science and it was noted that the boys were much interested in physiology. French, Greek and Latin classes existed and the services of 'a native for the German language, who attends the school weekly' had been recently obtained. The mathematical curriculum included 'algebraic and geometrical classes'. It was reported that the religious work of the college was encouraging and that some boys who had been in the school were now not only members, but also on the preachers' plan.[29]

Following the 1879 report, in which we learn that the college had enrolled with Trinity College, London, because it provided special advantages for musical studies and that the financial position was so good that they had been able to pay a 4 per cent dividend to the original promoters and put £100 into the funds, there is a special report on 'New Scheme, Primitive Methodist Bourne College, Limited'. This report states that in response to the 1878 Conference resolution which had strongly recommended the formation of a 'limited liability company' the trustees had decided that this was the best way forward and 'Memorandum and Articles of Association' were drawn up by C. H. Edwards Esq. and, being agreed, it was registered under the Company's Act with a nominal capital of £25,000 in 5,000 shares at £5 each. It was agreed to purchase land at Quinton from Mr James Nott, one of the trustees,[30] and this was done on 8 October 1879 for £3,210.[31] James Nott was a prominent Primitive Methodist layman, and as we have seen, a close friend of the governor. His address in 1878 was given as Farlands, Lingen, Presteigne, [32] and he was also a trustee of Elmfield College. He seems to have been a considerable benefactor to the Connexion. The initial plans for the building were rejected by the Board as too costly and two further tenders were submitted. Those of D. Smith and Son, of Birmingham were accepted. The firm guaranteed that:

> the entire erection will not cost more than £6,700, including steam engine, heating apparatus, water tanks, gas-fittings, outbuildings, and everything else necessary to make the whole complete.[33]

The *Primitive Methodist Magazine* of 1879 contains an article on the college in which it is said that the purpose of the institution was to provide a middle-class education for:

> the sons of ministers and laymen of the Primitive Methodist Community, or of other Nonconformist or Methodist bodies, with a curriculum of instruction embracing all commercial and classical subjects (including mathematical and languages) for professions, University Examination and matriculation; taking care also to promote their spiritual interests and their instruction in the principles of our Christian faith.[34]

Following the purchase, many improvements were made to the nineteen-acre estate during 1879–80 in preparation for the erection of the college, but unfortunately, although a number of people had given encouragement not many of the shares were taken up and so the building work was postponed.[35] By the next year 400 shares had been taken, but the company wished to have 1,000 subscribed before commencing the building. It seems that many hoped to buy shares as soon as their circumstances permitted.[36] From the 1881 report we learn that 'Mr. T. S. Hooson [the future headmaster of the college] and Mr. E. H. Pritchard (both sons of our own ministers) have passed the London Matriculation Examination, and are now preparing for their first B.A. in the same University'.[37] The new Scheme Report of the same year announced that there had been a pleasing increase in the share subscription and so the trustees had decided to start building part of the scheme, thus providing accommodation for 70 boys at a cost of under £4,000. Therefore the memorial (foundation) stones would be laid on Whit Monday, 6 June, with the contract completed and the building ready for use by the following February.[38] This was obviously a little optimistic as the 1882 report says 'the new college is nearly completed and the work of the school will be transferred to the company shortly'.[39] Immediately after the 1882 midsummer vacation the college moved into its new premises, which met with general approval, in Quinton. The grounds had been developed with much labour and no little expense so that:

> About five acres of land in front of the college have been set apart for the playground, and a portion on the north side of the building has been allotted to the boys for small flower gardens ... nearly two acres have been devoted to the kitchen-gardens, which with an average crop, will produce enough of vegetables for a full complement of students.

The official opening ceremony was held on 24 October 1882 in extremely inclement weather, when the Revd Dr Samuel Antliff gave the address.

Evidence that the trustees were good businessmen is shown by the fact that it is reported that the lease of the old premises had been sold for £650, thus (using Kendall's figure) making a £125 profit over the original purchase price. It is noted that:

> The Institution is making an excellent impression on the district – is regarded as a great educational achievement – as a monument of noble purpose and effort in the interests of the sons of Christian parents, and as a tributary of youthful life and influence to the church with which it stands identified.[40]

A magazine, *Birmingham Places and Faces*, has a very interesting article, which gives an outside, independent assessment of the college:

> In one of the prettiest spots within easy walking distance of Birmingham stands Bourne College. The fine building which bears this name is at Quinton, and from the extensive grounds which surround it one looks across green meadows until, miles away, the eye catches sight of the ranges of hills of which Clent and Walton stand out most prominently. The advantage of the site for a college is that, while surrounded by all that can be wished for in the way of rural picturesqueness, it is within easy reach of Birmingham. Bourne College is connected with the Primitive Methodists, and is chiefly intended for the education of the sons of parents who have identified themselves with that denomination. There is only one other school in the country of like character, this being at York; but it was felt that this school, having accommodation for only 120 boys, did not

meet all the requirements of such a large body as the Primitive
Methodists. It was therefore resolved to establish a school in the
Midlands; but the building of Bourne College, Quinton, was not
commenced immediately. A large building on Summer Hill was called
into requisition for educational purposes, though it was decided that
the occupation of this should only be tentative. The lease of the
premises was secured from the Corporation, on very reasonable
terms, and the probable success of the movement was thus tested.
So gratifying was the support accorded to the College at Summer
Hill that the moving spirits in the matter soon began to look for a
more eligible site with larger and more complete accommodation.
Quinton was selected as the site for the new College. The principal
entrance is by a clock tower about 60 feet high. A school room,
dining room, class room, piano room, a large chemical laboratory,
lavatory, cloakroom, upon the ground floor; the first floor being
devoted to three large dormitories, bathrooms, and lavatories. The
servants' department consists of a large kitchen with serving room
and scullery attached, servants' hall, various store rooms, pantries
and dairy on the ground floor, and bed rooms occupying the first
floor. Adjoining the College is the Governor's house, completely
separated from the servants' portion of the building, and this arrangement gives the Governor control over the two departments.
Apartments are arranged for the sick and for the repairing of clothes.
A spacious kitchen court contains the laundry, wash-house, and
engine-house, and a large drying ground and covered playground
are provided. Water is obtained from a well, the water from which
is pumped into a tank in the roof over the bath room, and the College
is warmed by hot water apparatus. The style of the architecture is
of the Queen Anne period. The walls are faced with pressed bricks
with stone and brick dressings. Mr. E. Walton, Smethwick, was the
builder, and the building was carried out under the superintendence
of the architects, Messrs. D. Smith and Sons, Birmingham, whose
design was selected in limited competition.[41]

The college opened on the Quinton site in 1882, with
T. J. S. Hooson, BA, aged nearly 21, as its one and only headmaster.
Thomas James Stewart Hooson was born on 16 February 1862 in
Rugby. He was the son of Stewart Hooson (1832–1903), a Primitive
Methodist itinerant who married first a Miss Gillett (maybe Matilda)
of Kilkenny, Oxon, and then Miss Humphries of Wootton Bassett,
who survived him. His mother was the first Mrs Hooson and his
grandmother, whose maiden name was Stewart, was one of the 'faithful
workers at Halifax' and is described as 'a saint indeed' by Kendall.[42]
Thus from these few details it can be seen that Hooson was born and

bred in Primitive Methodism. He was educated at Westfield, Hunger-ford, before going first to Elmfield College and then to the newly founded Bourne College. Bourne College Entry Book records:[43]

Name		Age		Last Birthday	Abode		Prev. Sch.	
Hooson, T. J. S.		15		16/2/77	Cirencester		Elmfield	

Lat.	Gr.	Fr.	Alg.	Euc.	Arith.	Gram	His.	Geog.	Class.
yes	yes	yes	yes	yes	disc!	yes	yes	yes	I

Extras	Entered	Left
French	January /78	prom. Sept. /78

Then in the same book in the examination section:

Year	Date	Name		Age	Abode		Exam.	
1879	June	Hooson, T. J. S.		18	Cirencester		Senior Oxford	

Result (passed in)

Prelim	Scrip.	English		Latin	French	Maths	Mech.	Mus.
yes	yes	II Cl.Hon.		yes	yes	yes	—	—

Remarks
Third Div. (II Hons in English)

In December of the same year he passed all the same examinations in the Senior Trinity College with the result that he was awarded '2 Cl. Senior Honours'.[44] A profile of Hooson in *Bourne College Chronicle* in 1899 states:

> Mr Hooson entered its portals early in 1878, as a student ... Ere the close of 1878 he had been elected by the Directors to a junior post on the staff. His work ever since has stamped him as a born teacher.[45]

This statement probably gives the clue to the remark 'prom[oted]/78' in the Entry Book above.

Hooson then studied for the BA degree of the University of London, completing it in 1884 and followed it by taking the Science course, which he studied at Mason College, Birmingham, later to become Birmingham University, and was successful in the Intermediate BSc. So Hooson was well qualified to become headmaster of the college in 1882 as it prepared to move to its new home in Quinton with 21 of the students from Summer Hill and another eighteen who joined the school during that first year in the new premises.[46]

To return to the *Primitive Methodist Minutes* and the official reports of the college to the Conference, we find that the laboratory was improved and a Conference Scholarship, which continued throughout the college's existence, of £25 per annum was established in 1884.[47] Many of the 'Addresses of the Conference to the Churches' commended the college to the Primitive Methodist people as an institution where their boys could get a 'first-class' education at reasonable cost with no worry about 'unsound religious teaching'.[48] The 1886 Conference decreed that names should be submitted from which a vice-governor should be chosen; so far I have not found out who, or indeed if, anyone was appointed.[49] Although the following Conference decreed that the term for the office of governor of the various institutions should be no longer than five years or in special cases seven, this rule was waived in 1888 for Bourne College and in fact George Middleton was governor from 1876 until his death in 1907 – 31 years! It is interesting to note that from 1888 George Middleton actually appears on the Primitive Methodist Stations in the West Midlands District as 'Governor of Bourne College, Quinton, Birmingham'.[50]

The most important events, according to the brief Conference report, during the year 1887–8 were the building and furnishing of a new workshop at a cost of £41 6s. 5d. so that a Department of Technical Instruction could be added to the curriculum, and the unexpected death of James Nott, the Chairman of the Board of Directors.[51] However, in that year the Board of Directors decided to issue a monthly *Chronicle*, later quarterly, and fortunately a number of these have survived, and they provide many interesting details and cast sidelights on the activities and happenings at the college. Thus in the very first volume we have:

In Memoriam, Death of Mr. James Nott, (of Brampton Brian), Chairman of the Board of Directors, aged 59 years.

Nott died suddenly on 'Sunday Night, March 4th', having 'conducted four services … two of which were preaching services', during the day. Returning home, he collapsed and died within 200 yards of his own house. By his death the college lost a good friend and benefactor.[52]

The little Primitive Methodist chapel in Quinton proved to be inadequate when the congregations were swelled by the staff and students from Bourne College and so in 1883 moves were started to sell the old chapel and start a new chapel building fund. The college helped with fund-raising, especially with musical concerts, as did a prominent local family. Edwin Danks of Apsley House, Quinton, was a boiler manufacturer in Netherton and a generous benefactor to both Quinton Primitive Methodism and the college. The foundation stones for the new College Road chapel were laid on 25 June 1888 and the chapel was opened on 18 November of the same year when the governor conducted some of the opening services. Later Mr Danks gave more land to the chapel to be used if any extension should be needed in the future. A pipe organ was added in 1897.[53] It seems that over the years the services of the masters and indeed some of the boys were required to fill local preaching appointments:

> The services of the Governor and Masters are much desired at the Chapel in the neighbourhood, belonging to all denominations, in addition to their regular work. I often find officials of these Places of Worship going to the College a few hours before the service, to get a supply in cases of unexpected disappointment. Some of them seem to think that they can get served as easily as though it were a College for the training of ministers. However, talent is not the first thing that is required in these Chapels. If the youth or young man has the love of God in his heart, he can tell of Jesus and his power to save and his efforts are blessed.[54]

It was reported in 1889 that the financial position was so satisfactory that it was proposed to use the balance to pay off some of the loss sustained in the Summer Hill premises. This preactice continued in the ensuing years, so that the debt was cleared entirely by 1892.[55] In 1889 and 1890 successful and enjoyable concerts were held in the Drill Hall, Halesowen, and the proceeds were used to provide 'two turf tennis courts' and in 'relaying half the cricket pitch; the remainder was spent in the purchase of tennis requisites'.[56]

The 1893 report to Conference, as well as being a very encouraging one, also contains several items of special interest. It states:

> The Institution is now well established, and the position it has taken among the foremost, middle-class schools of the country is an honour to its promoters and the Connexion.

It is perhaps an indication of the popularity and open-minded attitude of the college, in keeping faith with the aims of providing 'first class' education not only for Primitive Methodist boys but also Nonconformists, that the report highlights the fact that the Conference Scholarship this year had been 'awarded to J. H. Banks, son of a prominent Baptist official of Willenhall'. His brother, R. V. Banks, was also the recipient of the Scholarship in 1895. The other rather illuminating comment is in relation to the accounts, where it is recorded that there was a:

> Farm Account Deficiency, arising through
>   death of Milch Cow   £5 12s. 6d.

However, despite this unexpected loss, a 5 per cent dividend was paid and a reserve fund set up with the balance of £155 7s. 3½d.[57]

There had been a number of overseas students at the college from its earliest days, but the first mention of an overseas student in the Conference report comes in 1894 where it is stated that in the examinations of the College of Preceptors:

> Rowland E. Barleycorn of Fernando Po was one of the successful candidates and *passed in every subject* for which he was entered.[58]

Rowland was the son of the Revd William Napoleon Barleycorn, a native of Fernando Po and one of the earliest converts to Primitive Methodism in the island; he was an assiduous, well-respected and beloved missionary to his own people. Mr Barleycorn had visited the college on Thursday 29 September 1887 when he sang to the boys 'in Boobee, his native language'. It was most likely this visit which prompted him to send his sons to Bourne in due course.[59]

Over the years there were many missionary visitors to the college and the *Chronicle* contains several articles from the Revd R. W. Burnett, a missionary in Fernando Po whose sons attended the college. It is also noted that on a visit he and his wife paid to the college he gave an interesting talk to the boys 'on the habits of the natives and their peculiarities' and 'brought with him to the School a couple of African parrots' which 'have just begun to make themselves at home'.[60] No doubt it was these missionary visits which inspired the interest in missionary work, especially in Africa, which was highlighted in the 1897 report along with the information that the college's first missionary meeting had resulted in a collection of £6 for the African fund.

The financial position in 1894 being satisfactory, the Board decided on:

> alterations to the playground £35 1*s*. 6*d*. ... sinking and widening one of the college wells £25, and an extra 5% for depreciation on the furniture, implements etc., £24 6*s*. 8*d*.

This expenditure still left enough to pay the 5 per cent dividend, add to the reserve fund and use £1,000 to reduce the mortgage, so it can be seen that the position of the college seemed to be secure.[61] So much so that the next year it was decided to embark on an extension scheme.

> With the view of providing accommodation for an increased number of students, the Board have taken preliminary steps for increasing the share capital. Six hundred new shares are offered, and our generous friend W. P. Hartley, Esq., J.P., has promised to take one hundred on condition the required number is subscribed within two years.[62]

In 1896 the college was once again congratulating itself on its reputation as being 'among the foremost Middle-Class schools of the country' and the Conference commended the college to Primitive Methodist parents looking for an excellent education for their sons.[63] Beside the usual report of examination successes special congratulations were offered to:

... J. E. Hooson, B.Sc., (the headmaster's brother) on his appointment as Sub-Inspector of Schools under the Science and Art Department; to A. E. Ball, M.A., on his being appointed Vicar of Clee, Shropshire; to H. H. Middleton, A.R.C.M., (the governor's very musical son) on passing the Intermediate Examination for the Degree of Bachelor of Music at Cambridge University; to F. S. Clulow for the position he has taken in the Ministerial Examinations at the Manchester College.

The previous year's proposal to undertake an extension scheme had been accepted. The 600 shares issued had all been subscribed, giving an increased capital of £3,000. Plans having been approved it was hoped to start building towards the end of July.[64] An article in the *Bourne College Chronicle* describes the memorial stone-laying on Monday 8 March 1897. Five stones were laid and all bore Latin names – 'Religio, Humanitas, Vertus, Scientia, and Societas'. The first stone was laid by the vice-president of the Conference, L. L. Morse, JP, and he was presented, by the governor, with 'a golden memento, bearing on one side a miniature engraving of the college, and on the other certain names and date'. The other stones were laid by the Chairman of the Board, the governor, the headmaster and one of the students. The second part of the article gives a detailed description of the new building.[65]

The extension scheme had raised over £4,000 and:

The contract for enlargement is £3,619, without the Lodge and Sanatorium, estimated at nearly £500, the entire outlay therefore, not including the furnishing, will be a little over £4,000. The Memorial Stones were laid in March ... and the work is now rapidly progressing, and is expected to be ready for opening in September. The value of the enlargement can scarcely be estimated. We shall not only have accommodation for 50 more boarders, but greatly improved educational facilities, together with splendid sanitary arrangements.[66]

In addition to all this expenditure, the financial position was healthy enough, with 77 boarders and 20 day pupils, to be able to pay a 5 per cent dividend and put some into the reserve fund, as indeed was done the following year. That year the completion of the extension scheme free of debt was reported. According to an article, 'Our Search Light', by the governor in the *Chronicle* of February 1899 the Board of Directors was not prepared to sit back after the extension was completed, but turned its attention to refurbishing the laundry with:

> ... a vertical Engine, a Washer, Hydro-extractor and an Ironing and Glazing Machine ... A large drying closet also is provided, thoroughly fitted with galvanised iron horses, which are made to run on wheels and so to work with the greatest ease. Spacious earthenware pans, of white glaze and Daulton [sic] manufacture are also provided.[67]

The same article mentions that, chiefly due to pressure from the Board, Birmingham Corporation had been induced to extend its gas main 2½ miles beyond the city boundary to provide gas for the college and after some initial suspicion from local people street lamps had been erected in Quinton.[68]

The next 'Our Search Light' reported that Mr George Davies had suggested that gifts of books should be given to extend the library and more pictures added to beautify the rooms. He had also been the prime mover in getting the grounds landscaped with a tree-planting ceremony being held on a very rainy 26 February.[69] Three items of interest appeared in the following article in this series, namely that a 'new American Organ' had been installed in the college dining room; that both the governor and the headmaster had been elected as 'progressive Candidates' to the Parish Council, with Middleton becoming chairman and Hooson 'the representative on the Technical Instruction Committee for the District', and that the Primitive Methodist Conference at Sheffield had decided that Quinton should become an independent circuit and have its own minister.[70]

It is interesting to note that the 1898 Conference address mentioned that there is no provision for 'the daughters' of Primitive Methodist families. In fact there had been a Ladies' College at The Cedars, Clapham, London, but its existence was short-lived (1875–81). At the Annual Speech Day and Prize-giving at Bourne College in 1892 Mr J. M. Banks, vice-chairman, 'hinted at the possibility of a girls' school being established at The Quinton, or not far from thence, at some future time. (Applause)'.[71] Whether this was just a pious hope or not I do not know, but as far as I am aware nothing came of the idea.

By 1899 the college was happy to report that the increased facilities had meant that the curriculum had been revised and increased 'so as to adapt it to modern ideas and requirements' and therefore the staff had been increased.[72] *Bourne College Calendar* fulfils the purpose of a prospectus, as well as being a calendar of school events and achievements, in that it records the names of the members of staff; describes the school premises and grounds, including the information that 'Cows are kept'; lists the subjects taught; records academic successes; and also sporting prowess. To give some idea of the opportunities offered by the college, it is worthwhile to look at this new modern curriculum as stated in the *Bourne College Calendar* for 1889.

I. – ELEMENTARY STAGE
Boys under 10 years of age.

English –   Reading, Spelling, Writing, Grammar, Geography, English History.

Scripture –   Simple Lessons in Biblical History and Geography with the principles of the Christian Religion.

Arithmetic –   Suitable Instruction in the first stage, Ground Work.

Language –   The Rudiments of Latin.

Hygiene –   Outlines of the Laws of Health.

Drill and Singing –

Drawing –   Freehand.

Elocution –   Simple Rules for Reading and Speaking.

II. – INTERMEDIATE STAGE
Boys between 10 and 13 years of age.

This Division embraces all the subjects in the first stage with higher and more difficult work, together with:–

Music –   Pianoforte or Violin.

Mathematics – Algebra, Geometry.

Science –   Physiography, Geology, Chemistry, Magnetism, Electricity and Hygiene.

Languages –   French and German.

Chemistry –   Theory.

Drawing –   Model.

III. – ADVANCED STAGE
Boys over 13 years of age.

Language –   Greek, (if required) for Degree Examinations.

Drawing –   Geometrical and Perspective.

Chemistry –   Practical Work and Analysis.

Science –   Mechanics, Trigonometry, Mensuration.

Business Training – Mechanical Drawing and the Workshop.

Foreign Correspondence with Shorthand
Book Keeping
Land Surveying
Botany –   Relating to Wild Flowers.

This was clearly a comprehensive list, overseen by six resident general staff, seven specialist staff and two medical attendants. The cost of this education was:

Terms Inclusive.
with Books and Maps, Laundry, Contributions to the Games
Fund, Pew Rent, Collections.

Boarders	under 10 years of age	£12	per Term in Stage I.
"	from 10 to 13	£13. 10s.	" II.
"	over 13	£15	" III.
Day Pupils	under 10	£3	" I.
	from 10 to 13	£4	" II.
	over 13	£5	" III.

There were eight 'Special Rates' listed, of which two are of particular interest:

4.– A limited number of Private Bed Rooms are provided and furnished, and can be had at an extra charge of 35/– per Term.
5.– Boys may be supplied with ham or other Meat for breakfast at a charge of 21/– per Term, and Day Pupils may have dinners at 10d. each or £2 per Term.

The college year was divided into three equal terms, which commenced in the middle of January, near the end of April, and the middle of September. The boys had two weeks' vacation at Easter, seven weeks in the summer and four weeks at Christmas. Reports were sent to parents or guardians three times a year.[73]

We can see that boys who attended the college received a good all-round education which would ensure that they reached a very satisfactory academic standard, although it must be recorded that, as far back as 1888, the headmaster did protest that he felt the Christmas examination of the College of Preceptors was expecting rather a lot when boys of twelve or thirteen were asked to:

give a very full account of *'The Inter-colonial Railway System of the Dominion of Canada'*, or of the various *'Egyptian Dynasties'*, or even of the *'Parliaments of Bats'*.

However, it was not a case of all work and no play, for the College prided itself that:

> in the matter of *Homeliness*, Bourne College does its utmost to make the students happy without weakening its discipline. Believing also that proper physical culture is a great auxiliary to the brain, various popular games are encouraged out of school hours for pleasant recreation.[75]

Hooson was himself a proficient footballer, tennis player, and especially cricketer. In the latter game he was a good right-hand batsman, and a formidable slow left-hand bowler not only in the school matches, but also for the Warwickshire Club and Ground.[76] Another instance of Hooson's 'modern' attitude to education and his belief that it should cater for the whole person is the fact that the *Calendar* for 1909 lists among the members of staff, 'Swedish Drill: Miss A. Ryding' and in 1910 'Miss Smith (from the Anstey Physical Training Centre)'. Miss Rhoda Anstey had opened 'The Hygienic Home and College for Physical Culture' for young ladies at The Leasowes, Halesowen in 1899 where 'she employs Dr. Lang's Swedish gymnastics ... which supplies exercise *for every part of the body* ... Some of them are training for teachers of gymnastics in schools.' It seems that Hooson and the Board of Directors were being faithful to the Primitive Methodist ethos of using the best possible means to hand to fulfil their purpose. Just as the early Primitive Methodists had been willing to have women preachers and not just men, so they were happy to use the 'Anstey young ladies' to instruct their students.[77]

The boys were often taken on visits to places of interest, such as Bingley Hall, Broad Street, Birmingham, to see exhibitions and displays, to recitals in Halesowen, to Clent, to Edwin Danks's Boiler Works and into Birmingham and Quinton to see visiting dignitaries, such as the Prime Minister, Mr Gladstone (5 November 1888) and His Imperial Majesty the Shah of Persia (11 July 1889).[78] Here is further evidence of the broad-based education given to the students.

The college had a number of extra-curricular activities including the popular Social Circle, started in November 1895, which had a variety of speakers and debates on topical subjects. For example, on 12 October 1896 the members debated 'That the present state of Turkey is a disgrace to civilisation, and that England ought to interfere at once.' The following resolution was carried unanimously:

> That the Members of the Bourne College Social Circle having heard of the reported massacres in Armenia, desire to express their sympathy with the present Government in their efforts to secure reform

in the affected districts, and hope that they will be able to find a solution of the eastern difficulty.

A copy of the resolution was sent to Lord Salisbury and the following reply was received:

> FOREIGN OFFICE,
> *October 17th, 1896.*
>
> SIR,—I am directed by the Marquess of Salisbury to acknowledge the receipt of your communication relative to the Armenian question. I am, your most obedient humble servant,
>
> T. H. SANDERSON [79]

It can be seen that the boys, therefore, were given the opportunity to make themselves familiar with life outside the walls of the institution and to practise the art of public speaking which would stand many of them in good stead as they entered the pulpits of Primitive and Wesleyan Methodism and those of other denominations, and the secular professions. A patrol of Boy Scouts, named the 'Wolf Patrol', was started at the college in 1908 and held their first 'tracking' in the snow on 4 March. The patrol leader was given a quarter of an hour's start and the rest of the patrol followed him for about two miles, but as the ground was so trampled 'they lost him at the crossroads near Woodgate'.[80] On the occasion of the General Election in 1910 the college held a mock election on 28 January. The candidates were J. H. C. Morris for the Liberals and N. St John Stembridge for the Conservatives. The sole platform for the election was Free Trade *v.* Tariff Reform. Traditionally the college had been strongly Liberal, but on this occasion the Conservatives made a good showing, losing by only fourteen votes – the results being Morris 39, Stembridge 25.[81]

Another £500 was paid off the mortgage in 1900,[82] but the increase in taxation and the cost of fuel led to a drop in revenue in 1901, so the shareholders only received a dividend of 3 per cent this year. The government's proposals on secondary education and the effect they might have on 'popularly-controlled education' exercised the minds of the Primitive Methodist authorities, and the governors and headmasters of Elmfield and Bourne Colleges were added as members of the Connexional Education Committee to provide practical advice and expertise.[83] This concern continued over the years. It is evident that state schooling had an effect on the college's numbers and therefore its finances, as the 1905 report makes clear:

> ... we regret that our average number of students has not been maintained during the year, and that we have suffered proportionately in our Revenue. The cause we attribute, very largely, to the serious

trade depression of the country and the concessions we have had to make to parents in the fees. The introduction of Secondary Schools by the government, with an advanced curriculum and nominal fees, is also making against Institutions of a private character – with no endowments and depending entirely upon the Students' fees for current expenses. Although we have suffered much from these causes, other similar schools have suffered much more.[84]

This final sentence may reflect inside knowledge of the problems at Elmfield College, where the trustees had to pass the following resolutions on 9 May 1906:

That owing to our inability to meet our expenditure the College be closed on or before December 31st of the present year.
That we apply to Conference for sanction to sell the premises.[85]

In fact, the college technically closed as a Primitive Methodist college, but was 'taken over by a number of the old scholars of Elmfield, and will continue as heretofore to give a sound, high class education to boys'. On 18 December 1906 the property was transferred to them 'on the understanding that it would be continued as a Connexional Institution'.[86]

Bourne College had to report, for the first time in twenty years, a deficit in its accounts in 1906 and again laid the blame at the door of the depression in trade and:

the establishment of High Grade Schools by the Government ... Parents with reduced incomes have been obliged to withdraw their children from private schools, and take advantage of the facilities provided by the nation, and thus private Institutions have suffered, and not a few have collapsed.[87]

Unfortunately, in 1907 the accounts showed another deficit, due to 'exceptional expenditure with our Heating Apparatus and a serious loss in our Farm Stock', and it had to be met by drawing on the reserve fund. However, the good news was that pupil numbers had increased from 56 to 70, so in spite of having to reduce the fees the outlook was felt to be rather better.[88]

The Revd George Middleton, FGS, died on 3 November 1907, aged 77. Middleton had been officially the governor, secretary, chaplain, and unofficially bursar, caretaker-in-chief, handyman and general odd-job man, ready to turn his hand to many things since the foundation of the college. This is shown by his own comment at the 1891 Speech Day when, referring to the long connection he and Mrs Middleton had had with the college, he pointed out that:

the first years of its history were attended with much discouragement, and that at Quinton in their new premises they had often been greatly tried. It had been necessary to work hard and continuously, not simply in organising and managing the College, but in other kinds of labour. Some had suggested that some of his work was hardly in character with his office; but he hesitated not to do any kind of work so that the project might be made a success.[89]

George Middleton had also been active in the local Primitive Methodist Church and Circuit, preaching frequently. The directors filled the vacancy left by his death by appointing the headmaster, T. J. S. Hooson, to the governorship, which was confirmed by the Conference in 1908, while the local Primitive Methodist minister at Quinton, the Revd B. Walton, became the chaplain and took the weekly class meeting. It is interesting to note that T. J. S. Hooson is listed among the Connexional Officers on the Stations and he is the only layman named there. But even more remarkable is that his name actually appears on the Stations in the West Midlands District from 1908–28.[90] This may be the only instance of a layman being listed thus.

Some old boys of the college felt that it would be beneficial to start an Old Boys' Club, although Old Boys' Reunions had been held since 1894, and so an inaugural meeting was held on 8 April 1908 at the Holborn Restaurant, London, attended by sixteen with apologies from another ten. It was hoped to have branches in Birmingham and Manchester and in fact the Birmingham branch met for the first time on 8 December 1908. One of the express aims of the Old Boys' Club was to encourage parents to send their boys to the school and thus ensure its prosperity.[91]

By 1909 there were 80 students and the financial position had improved so that 'the very necessary improvements in our heating system, by the installation of a large locomotive boiler, and also a small vertical boiler, at a cost of £102.9s. were paid for out of the current account'.[92] The same year Sir William Hartley was thanked by the Conference for providing three three-year university scholarships for both Bourne College and Elmfield scholars, as was W. Adams for providing a scholarship to both colleges for boys from the Primitive Methodist Orphans' Home.[93]

An indication of the growth of Birmingham is shown by the following comment:

The incorporation of Quinton with Birmingham, and the decision of the City Council to develop Quinton as a Garden City, will eventually add considerably to the value of the College estate, besides bringing about the erection of villa residences, from which in future many boys ought to be obtained.[94]

This was followed in 1913 by the observation that 'a system of Motor Buses now runs from New Street to Quinton every hour during the day, thus making the College more accessible to parents and friends', and in 1914 it was noted that they had proved a great success and 'the Buses now run three times every hour'.[95] From 1913 the information and articles in the *Chronicle* are chiefly concerned with examination results and sports report and so little can be gleaned about the life of the college from it.

During the war years many old boys served with honour in the forces. J. H. C. Morris, a brilliant student, who died while training with his regiment in Northampton, was the first death recorded. The Tarrant family of Witney suffered the loss of three sons, all old Bourne College boys, in France and Mr and Mrs P. Rowlands of Erdington lost two sons and one wounded. In 1916 the college insurances were increased 'to cover all air-craft risks'.[96] Perhaps because of the war the average age of the students in 1918 was slightly lower than previously.[97] In the first report after the cessation of hostilities in 1919 it was reported that about 300 had taken part in the war and many were killed or wounded and many had gained bravery honours. The old boys of the college resolved to found a scholarship as a memorial to those who had died. It was to be open, especially to sons of old boys, with preference being given to sons of those who had served in the war. The following year it was also decided to 'place in the schoolroom a memorial tablet' to those who 'gave their lives for their country'. The memorial, containing 30 names, was unveiled at the Annual Prize-giving in July 1921.[98] When the college closed in 1928 the memorial was removed to College Road Primitive Methodist chapel, but was apparently destroyed when that chapel was demolished in 1967/8.

In 1920 the college had, for the first time in its history, over 100 boys on the register and the outlook was very promising.[99] Consequently the financial position improved, so in 1922 it was proposed to use the excess income to pay £200 off the mortgage, though subsequently the Annual Meeting of Shareholders decided not to do this, but to put the £524 5s. 11d. aside to purchase further equipment.[100] The mortgage was reduced by the £200 in 1923 when after several years of paying no dividend it was also agreed to pay 2½ per cent as was also done the following year.[101] However, after that matters took a downward turn, as 'owing to the bad state of trade throughout the country, there has been a reduction in our numbers resulting in a deficiency in the accounts of £264 17s. 1d.'.[102] There was a much greater deficiency in 1926 giving a total of £1,252 17s. 10d.; against this the directors set the whole of the reserve fund of £660 15s. 11d., but this still left a deficit of £592 1s. 11d. to be carried forward.[103] The report was a little more optimistic in 1927, as despite the 'industrial disputes and trade depression' numbers had increased, so the deficit this year was considerably less, but with the addition of that carried forward the total was £1,263 6s. 6d. After subtracting the £22 19s. 7d. of unclaimed dividends, the college still had a total deficit of £1,240 6s. 11d.[104] It was obvious that this state of affairs could not be allowed to continue, especially as the deficit by 3 May 1928 had risen to £2,267 7s. 1d. So we find:

> Unfortunately, our financial position is very unsatisfactory and in connection with the Jubilee, we are trying to raise a fund to put matters on a better footing. It is proposed to work with three objects in view:
> (a) To clear off the floating liabilities.
> (b) To provide for necessary renovations and improvements.
> (c) To establish annual Scholarships and prizes.[105]

The college held a Jubilee Celebration on Whit Tuesday 1928 with a cricket match between the old boys and the present boys and staff, which the old boys won by 50 runs. About 250 old boys and friends met to join in the celebrations. The Jubilee Fund was commended by the Chairman of the Board, Dr L. E. Price, but, unfortunately, with little positive effect. There was so little response to the Jubilee Subscription Appeal for £5,000 that only just under £500 was raised.[106]

In spite of the college's precarious financial position, nine boys were still accepted into the school in September 1928 to join the 45 who were already there. Eight of the nine were local and the other one came from Knighton. Of the 54 students, we find that almost 76 per cent were local, so it is quite conceivable that a number, if not all, of these were day boys.[107] It seems that it was at the end of that autumn term of 1928 that the college finally closed its doors, but the *Primitive Methodist Minutes* has no comment to make about its demise. It is interesting to speculate that as the 1928 Primitive Methodist Conference had sanctioned the transference of Elmfield College to the Wesleyan Methodist Secondary School Trust,[108] the prospect of Methodist Union may also have had something to do with the fall in numbers at Bourne College and its consequent financial problems. In other words, outside circumstances contributed to its demise. The contents of the college were auctioned on 13 and 14 March 1929 and its scholarships transferred to Elmfield College. The buildings were sold to the Birmingham Board of Guardians for £9,675 and in 1930, having been refurbished and renamed Quinton Hall, it re-opened as a Poor

Law Convalescent Home for Aged Men.[109] It was closed and demolished in 1979 and a housing estate built on the site.

On 7 March 1930 at Bourne College Old Boys' Dinner at the Imperial Hotel, Birmingham, Mr Hooson was presented with a cheque for £450 to mark his fifty years' association with the college.[110] Mr Hooson died in February 1931 and his funeral took place on 24 February, with a service at College Road Primitive Methodist church, followed by interment at Quinton Old Cemetery.[111] Thomas James Stewart Hooson never married. It would be true to say that Bourne College was not only his life, but also his family.

Many Bourne College boys went on to various universities and university colleges, such as Cambridge, London, Aberystwyth and Mason College, Birmingham. Quite a number studied medicine and qualified as doctors, in some cases becoming university and hospital lecturers, while others became pharmacists, dentists, coroners and medical officers of health. A considerable number entered the teaching profession, with several being heads, lecturers and inspectors. An eminent musician and an artist were also students at the college. There were old boys in the legal world too – barristers, solicitors and JPs. Others became chartered accountants, surveyors, mining engineers, city engineers, inspectors of factories and munitions or entered commerce and industry. The Civil Service, including the Indian Civil Service, had its 'old Bournites', as did the army and navy. Perhaps predictably, quite a percentage of the boys, often after a while teaching, went into the ministry. It is interesting to note that not only were there Primitive Methodist, Wesleyan and Presbyterian ministers, but also several Church of England priests among their ranks. As can be seen, many played a part in public life and were members of their local town and city councils, while C. T. Needham BA became a Member of Parliament for South West Manchester in 1910 and was knighted in 1919. Most of the old boys attributed much of their success to the good education and grounding they had received at the college.[112]

Primitive Methodism had striven hard to educate its people, not only for work in the church but also in the world with considerable success. In its short history of just over fifty years Bourne College provided a very good all-round education for its students, as its academic and musical record shows; but it was not a narrow hothouse cramming academy, for a full range of sports were played and leisure-time activities were encouraged. The fact that students came from all over the world must have added another broad dimension. Contact with the local Primitive Methodist chapel Community in Quinton ensured that the boys were kept in touch with the real world, both religious and secular. The failure of the college can probably be chiefly accounted for by three things – the introduction and growth of free, or relatively cheap state secondary education, the prevailing economic climate, and the imminent prospect of Methodist Union. It had been a brave exciting venture, but had served its purpose by 1928.

Notes

1. Bourne MSS (Auto) C Text, f.4 (MARC).
2. Bourne MSS (Auto) A & C Texts (MARC).
3. Bourne MSS (Journal), 13 September 1809 (MARC).
4. *Ibid.*
5. J. T. Wilkinson, *The Life of Hugh Bourne 1772–1852* (London: 1952), pp. 193–4.
6. *Primitive Methodist Magazine* [hereinafter cited as *PMM*] (1823), pp. 4, 27–8, 55–7, 79–82, 101–2, 121, 124, 146–9, 195–7; (1824), pp. 5–6, 25–7, 49–51, 52–4, 73–4, 97–9, 121–2, 122–3, 145 and fn; cf. H. B. Kendall, *The Origins and History of the Primitive Methodist Church* (2 vols, London: 1904), I, p. 31.
7. *PMM* (1851), pp. 21–30.
8. G. E. Milburn, *School for Prophets: The Origins of Ministerial Education in the Primitive Methodist Churches* (Manchester: 1982), p. 7.
9. *PMM* (1847), pp. 176–7.
10. *PMM* (1847), pp. 748–9.
11. Kendall, *Origins and History*, II, p. 520.
12. *Primitive Methodist Minutes* [hereinafter cited as *PMMins*] (1824), pp. 2–3; (1850), p. 21; *Consolidated Minutes* (1860), p. 51; *Consolidated Minutes* (1892), p. 67.
13. J. Petty, *The History of the Primitive Methodist Connexion* (London: 1880, 3rd edn), p. 265; J. Ritson, *The Romance of Primitive Methodism* (London: 1909), pp. 208–10.
14. *PMMins* (1858), p. 26; (1859), p. 27; (1862), p. 29; (1863), p. 33; (1864), p. 30.
15. *PMMins* (1860), p. 38.
16. *PMMins* (1863), pp. 33–4 (1–20).
17. *PMMins* (1864), pp. 36–7 (1–11).
18. *PMMins* (1865), pp. 35–7 (15–18).
19. *Bourne College Chronicle* [hereinafter cited as *BCC*] 5 (1895–1901), pp. 161ff.; Kendall, *Origins and History*, II, p. 525.
20. *PMMins* (1876), pp. 10, 43.
21. *PMMins* (1875), pp. 25, 101; (1876), pp. 10, 104; *BCC* 5 (1895–1901), pp. 121–6, 160–2; *PMMins* (1908), pp. 21–2.
22. *PMMins* (1877), p. 33.
23. *PMMins* (1877), p. 68.
24. *PMMins* (1877), pp. 16, 106–13.
25. *PMMins* (1878), p. 77.
26. *PMM* (1877), p. 313.
27. *PMM* (1878), p. 5.
28. MSS – Bourne College Entry Book I (1876–92).

29. *PMMins* (1878), pp. 91–4.
30. *PMMins* (1879), pp. 84–9.
31. It seems that the land James Nott owned at Quinton originally belonged to The Right Hon. George William Lyttleton, who sold it to Richard Powell. On Powell's death it was bought by Nott on 9 November 1977. (I am indebted for this information to Mr John Hunt, sometime Administrator of the Birmingham and Midland Institute and local historian.)
32. *PMMins* (1878), p. 5.
33. *PMMins* (1879), p. 87.
34. *PMMins* (1879), pp. 762–3.
35. *PMMins* (1879), pp. 87–8.
36. *PMMins* (1880), p. 92.
37. *PMMins* (1881), p. 96.
38. *PMMins* (1881), p. 97.
39. *PMMins* (1882), p. 89.
40. *PMMins* (1883), pp. 82–4; *BCC* 5 (1895–1901), pp. 163–4.
41. *Birmingham Places and Faces*, 2 November 1891.
42. Kendall, *Origins and History*, I, pp. 491–2.
43. MSS – Bourne College Entry Book I, p. 5 and examination section at the back.
44. *Ibid.*, examination section at the back.
45. *BCC* 5 (1895–1901), pp. 241–3.
46. *BCC* 5 (1895–1901), pp. 241–3; MSS – Bourne College Entry Book I, pp. 9f.
47. *PMMins* (1884), pp. 96–7.
48. *PMMins* (1886), pp. 127 etc.
49. *PMMins* (1886), p. 122.
50. *PMMins* (1887), p. 122; (1888), pp. 127, 130.
51. *PMMins* (1888), pp. 115–16; *BCC* 1 (1887–8), p. 15.
52. *BCC* 1 (1887–8), pp. 121–6.
53. College Road Primitive Methodist Church Trustees Minutes 1882–1927 (13 December 1883); *BCC* 1 (1887–8), pp. 155–6; 5 (1895–1901), p. 34.
54. *BCC* 1 (1887–8), p. 87.
55. *PMMins* (1889), p. 137; (1890), p. 133; (1891), p. 147; (1892), pp. 156–8.
56. *BCC* 2 (1888–9), pp. 156–8, 165; 3 (1889–90), pp. 137–8, 169–70.
57. *PMMins* (1893), pp. 159–61; *BCC* 5 (1895–1901), p. 136.
58. *PMMins* (1894), pp. 154–7; cf. *BCC* 5 (1895–1901), pp. 29, 70.
59. *PMMins* (1926), pp. 255–7; *BCC* 1 (1887–8), p. 28.
60. *BCC* 1 (1887–8), p. 187.
61. *PMMins* (1894), p. 156.
62. *PMMins* (1895), p. 154.
63. *PMMins* (1896), pp. 156, 185–6.
64. *PMMins* (1896), pp. 156–60.
65. *BCC* 5 (1895–1901), pp. 202–7.
66. *PMMins* (1897), pp. 160–4.
67. *BCC* 5 (1895–1901), p. 243.
68. *BCC* 5 (1895–1901), p. 244.
69. *BCC* 5 (1895–1901), p. 262.

70. *BCC* 5 (1895–1901), pp. 282–3.
71. *BCC* 4 (1890–2), p. 165.
72. *PMMins* (1899), pp. 154–7.
73. *Bourne College Calendar for 1899*, pp. 8–10.
74. *BCC* 2 (1899–9), p. 85.
75. *Bourne College Calendar for 1897*, p. 23.
76. *BCC* 5 (1895–1901), p. 242; cf. *The Birmingham Evening Mail*, Friday 7 March 1930.
77. *Bourne College Calendar for 1909*, p. 5; *1910*, p. 6; *BCC* 5 (1895–1901), pp. 227–8.
78. *BCC* 5 (1895–1901), p. 132; *BCC* 7 (1908–13) (1911), pp. 20–2; (1909), pp. 80–4; *BCC* 2 (1888–9), pp. 25, 45, 46, 206.
79. *BCC* 5 (1895–1901), pp. 147, 187.
80. *BCC* 7 (1908–13), p. 60.
81. *BCC* 7 (1908–13), pp. 91–3.
82. *PMMins* (1900), pp. 161–4.
83. *PMMins* (1901), pp. 182–3.
84. *PMMins* (1905), p. 205.
85. *PMMins* (1906), pp. 179–80.
86. *PMMins* (1906), pp. 179–80.
87. *PMMins* (1906), p. 181.
88. *PMMins* (1907), pp. 190–3.
89. *BCC* 4 (1890–2), pp. 84–5; cf. *BCC* 3 (1889–90), p. 11.
90. *PMMins* (1908), pp. 231, 43, 235, 54.
91. *BCC* 7 (1908–13), pp. 1–2, 56–7; cf. *BCC* 4 (1890–2), p. 93.
92. *PMMins* (1908), pp. 181–4.
93. *PMMins* (1909), pp. 197–8.
94. *PMMins* (1911), pp. 213–17; cf. *BCC* 7 (1908–13), p. 75.
95. *PMMins* (1913), p. 230; (1914), p. 224.
96. *PMMins* (1915), p. 227; (1917), p. 189; *BCC* 8 and 9 (1913–21) (1916), p. 1; (1919), pp. 17, 26–32; *PMMins* (1916), p. 178.
97. *PMMins* (1918), p. 184.
98. *PMMins* (1919), p. 196; (1920), p. 191; (1921), p. 191; cf. *BCC* 8 and 9 (1920), pp. 1–2; *BCC* 10 (1922–8) (1921), p. 1; cf. picture facing p. 12; *PMMins* (1922), p. 195.
99. *PMMins* (1920), p. 191.
100. *PMMins* (1922), p. 195.
101. *PMMins* (1923), p. 192; (1924), p. 201.
102. *PMMins* (1925), pp. 209–12.
103. *PMMins* (1926), pp. 215–17.
104. *PMMins* (1927), pp. 215–18.
105. *PMMins* (1928), pp. 213–16.
106. *BCC* 10 (1928), pp. 5–6.
107. MSS – Day Book 2 (1893–1928).
108. *PMMins* (1929), p. 21; *Wesleyan Methodist Minutes* (1929), p. 52.
109. *The Birmingham Post*, Friday 22 March 1929.
110. *The Birmingham Mail*, Friday 7 March 1930; *The Evening Dispatch*, Friday 7 March 1930.

111. *The Birmingham Gazette*, Wednesday 25 February 1931; *The County Express*, Saturday 28 February 1931.
112. *BCC* 5 (1895–1901), p. 165, gives a summary of the successes achieved between 1876 and 1895. For further yearly listings see the different volumes of the *BCC* and the *Bourne College Calendar*. There is also a file of 23 appreciative letters from old boys: of these, nine were doctors or connected with that profession; four ministers; three teachers; one musician; the remaining five were not identified.

Index of Persons

Index of Places and
Place-names of Worship

Note: Unless otherwise stated, street locations refer to Birmingham

Select Index of Subjects

Aberystwyth University College 131, 161

Airedale College 106

American War of Independence 61

Anglicans 26, 29–30, 35, 45, 52, 61, 82, 88, 104, 106, 108, 116, 161

anthropology 106

Antinomians 74, 76

architects 90

Arianism 46

Arminianism 25, 74, 92

Atonement, The 106

Bala Theological College 131

Baptism 73, 93

Baptist Home Missionary Society 78, 100

Baptist Magazine 75, 79

Baptist Missionary Society 13–15, 23, 73–4

Baptists 14–18, 20, 24, 26, 29, 32–3, 36–7, Ch. IV, 100, 102, 123–7, 129–31, 149

Birmingham Council of Christian Churches 130

Birmingham Council of Christian Education 130

Birmingham University 147

Bourne College Ch. VII

Bourne College Calendar 155, 165

Bourne College Chronicle 148, 150–3, 159, 165

Brecon Memorial College 126

Calvinism 22, 25, 45, 74, 81, 94, 106, 114

Calvinistic Methodists 25–6, 121–2, 125–6, 129, 131; *see also* Presbyterian Church of Wales

Cambridge University 151, 161

Chartism 72, 79–80, 85

Christology 46, 71, 100, 105–7, 115–16

Church of Scotland 35

Church Missionary Society 13, 35

Church planting Ch. IV

Civic Gospel 80, Ch. V

Clapham Sect 24, 35

Clarendon Code 2

College of Preceptors 154

Congregationalists Ch. II, 55, 71, 76–9, 93–4, Ch. V, 121–3, 125, 128–32

Countess of Huntingdon's Connexion 29, 121

discipline 4–6, 10

ecclesiology 100, 107, 113, 115–16

education 105, 110, Ch. VII

Elmfield College 137, 139–40, 145, 147, 156–8, 160

Evangelical Magazine 20, 22, 24–33

Evangelical Revival 104

Fabian Society 99

Franco-Prussian War 124

French Revolution 44, 46–7, 58–9, 73

Gordon Riots 45, 61

Gosport academy 25, 34

Great Awakening 13

Great Ejectment 104

incarnation *see* Christology

Independents *see* Congregationalists

individualism 107

Irish Home Rule 113

Irvingites 76

Labour Party 100, 132

Ladies' College, Clapham 152